MARKETING THEORY:
EVOLUTION AND EVALUATION

MARKETING THEORY:
EVOLUTION AND EVALUATION

Jagdish N. Sheth
University of Southern California

David M. Gardner
University of Illinois

Dennis E. Garrett
University of Oklahoma

WILEY

JOHN WILEY & SONS

New York   Chichester   Brisbane   Toronto   Singapore

Library of Congress Cataloging in Publication Data:

Sheth, Jagdish N.
    Marketing Theory : evolution and evaluation / Jagdish N. Sheth.
David M. Gardner, Dennis E. Garrett.
       p.   cm.
    Bibliography: p.
    ISBN 0-471-63527-8
    1. Marketing.   I. Gardner, David Morgan, 1936-   . II. Garrett,
    Dennis E.   III. Title
  HF5415.S4414   1988
  658.8'001--dc19
                                          88-10162
                                           CIP

Printed in the United States of America

10 9 8 7 6 5 4 3 2 1

PREFACE

This book is both a chronicle of the evolution of marketing thought and its metatheory evaluation as a discipline. The evolution of marketing taught over the past 75 years is both fascinating and impressive. Indeed, exploring the writings of early marketing scholars and wondering about the rationale behind their thinking has been as exciting and nerve-racking as exploring the wonders of nature!

The book was written more to satisfy our curiosity about the roots of marketing than to serve a market. We were curious about the origin of marketing, its early thinkers, the socioeconomic context in which marketing was practiced, and its maturity as a discipline. As we began to research and write about the evolution of marketing, we experienced all kinds of emotions: innocence of the child, mischief of the adolescent, rebellion of the young, and the déjà vu of the experienced.

Indeed, we found that the modern marketing concept is as old as the marketing discipline; that the recent value chain analysis is the foundation of the functional school of thought; and the current vacillation between macro and micro perspectives or between economic and behavioral perspectives was equally true in the earlier histroy of marketing.

Above all, our journey through the marketing evoulution has given us a sense of pride and respect for the discipline. We hope the readers of this book will experience some of the same emotions we did, and that they will find our narrative and comments interesting and useful.

This book is likely to accomplish one or more of the following objectives:

- Preserving the rich heritage of marketing as a discipline which may otherwise be lost in the accelerating pace of the marketing discipline, especially among some recent marketing scholars whose training has been based in such other disciplines as social psychology, sociology, and economics.

- Developing a typology of different shcools of marketing thought which will discover the underlying shifts in the substantive and methodological perspectives in marketing. For example, although marketing's origins were in economics and from the viewpoint of the seller, marketing has evolved more and more toward non-economic explanations for marketing practice and has increasingly adopted the viewpoint of the buyer.

- Providing a metatheory framework which is both comprehensive and useful. For example, we have reduced numerous metatheory criteria to these six: structure, specification, testability, empirical support, richness, and simplicity.

- Evaluating each of the twelve schools of marketing thought with the use of the six metatheory criteria to assess their relative contributions to the discipline. Not surprisingly, the buyer behavior school of thought has had a significant impact on marketing. However, more unexpectedly, the managerial school also had an equally powerful impact on the development of marketing thought.

- Developing a list of concepts and axioms which will be useful in developing a general theory of marketing. For example, we assert that such widely accepted concepts as exchange, market transaction, and customer orientation may not be sufficient to develop a general theory of marketing.

Although the book was not written with a predefined reader in mind, we believe it will be useful to serious students, young scholars, and history buffs. We also believe some marketing professionals will find the book interesting. One of the major strengths of the book is its comprehensive bibliography, especially the early references.

This book itself has been an evolution over the last 10 years. Originally, it was planned to be a single-author book but over the years it has benefitted enormously by the addition of two more authors. Similarly, it was originally planned to be a review of the behavioral theroies of marketing, but it evolved to include both behavioral and economic perspectives.

A number of colleagues, reviewers, and students provided significant insights and comments to our thinking and writing. The early drafts of the book were used in the doctoral seminars at the University of Illinois, the University of Southern California, and the University of Oklahoma. Our thanks and gratitude to all for the encouragement we received in carrying out this project.

We would like to express our special thanks to Barbara Gross, a doctroal student at the University of Southern California, and Paul Trapp, a doctoral student at the University of Illinois, who provided superb assistance in collecting and verifying all the references, in ensuring that the quotes are accurate, and in assisting in the final draft of this book.

Of course, we are all curious and apprehensive about how the marketing scholars will evaluate this book on our own metatheory criteria!

Jagdish N. Sheth
David M. Gardner
Dennis E. Garrett

CONTENTS

PREFACE v

CHAPTER 1 INTRODUCTION 1

Resurgence of Interest in Marketing Theory 2

The Era of Turbulent Transition 3

What Is, Or Should Be, the Dominant Perspective in Marketing? 3
What Is, Or Should Be, the Relationship Between Marketing
  and Society? 5
What Is, Or Should Be, the Proper Domain of Marketing Theory? 8
Is Marketing a Science or, at Best, a Standardized Art? 13
Is It Really Possible to Create a General Theory of Marketing? 15

Framework for the Book 19

Chapter 2: Noninteractive–Economic Schools of Marketing 23
Chapter 3: Interactive–Economic Schools of Marketing 24
Chapter 4: Noninteractive–Noneconomic Schools of Marketing 25
Chapter 5: Interactive–Noneconomic Schools of Marketing 27

Metatheory Criteria for the Evaluation of Theories 29

Summary 33

CHAPTER 2 NONINTERACTIVE–ECONOMIC SCHOOLS OF MARKETING 35

The Commodity School of Thought 35

Evlauation of the Commodity School 48

The Functional School of Thought 52

Evaluation of the Functional School 57

The Regional School of Thought 60

Evaluation of the Regional School 67

Summary 70

CHAPTER 3 INTERACTIVE–ECONOMIC SCHOOLS OF MARKETING 73

The Institutional School of Thought 73

Evaluation of the Institutional School 83

The Functionalist School of Thought 86

Evaluation of the Functionalist School 94

The Managerial School of Thought 96

Evaluation of the Managerial School 105

Summary 107

CHAPTER 4 NONINTERACTIVE–NONECONOMIC SCHOOLS OF MARKETING 109

The Buyer Behavior School of Thought 110

Evaluation of the Buyer Behavior School 124

The Activest School of Thought 127

Evaluation of the Activist School 135

The Macromarketing School of Thought 138

Evaluation of the Macromarketing School 144

Summary 147

CHAPTER 5 INTERACTIVE–NONECONOMIC SCHOOLS OF MARKETING 149

The Organizational Dynamics School of Thought 150

Evaluation of the Organizational Dynamics Schools   158

The Systems School of Thought   162
Evaluation of the Systems School   171

The Social Exchange School of Thought   173
Evaluation of the Social Exchange School   179

Summary   181

CHAPTER 6   WHAT WE HAVE LEARNED   183

Is Marketing a Science or, at Best, a Standardized Art?   184

What Is, Or Should Be, the Proper Domain of
  Marketing Theory?   191

What Is, Or Should Be, the Dominant Perspective
  in Marketing?   195

What Is, Or Should Be, the Relationship Between
  Marketing and Society?   197

It It Really Possible to Create a General Theory
  of Marketing?   199

REFERENCES   203

1

INTRODUCTION

This book discusses and evaluates various schools of marketing thought that have evolved since the inception of the discipline in the early 1900s. In addition to the more traditional schools of thought such as the commodity school, the functional school, and the institutional school, the book describes and evaluates the more contemporary schools of thought that have emerged since the early 1960s. These include the macromarketing school, the buyer behavior school, the managerial marketing school, and the systems school of marketing.

There are two reasons for writing this book. First, after an extended period of distraction and neglect, there is a resurgence of interest in theorizing about the discipline. We believe that a contemporary assessment of existing schools of thought will enable scholars to incorporate the existent knowledge in their efforts to generate newer theories and schools of thought in marketing.

Second, the discipline of marketing is entering turbulent times as indicated by five major controversies:

1. What is, or should be, the dominant perspective in marketing?
2. What is, or should be, the relationship between marketing and society?
3. What is, or should be, the proper domain of marketing theory?
4. Is marketing a science or at best a standardized art?
5. Is it really possible to create a general theory of marketing?

These questions are, on one hand, creating an identity crisis for the discipline and, on the other hand, presenting exciting opportunities to generate more innovative ideas. We hope an appreciation of marketing's rich tradition will provide a sense of security and at the same time enable scholars to improve on our knowledge.

In this chapter, we will examine each of these issues in detail, provide a classification of various schools of thought, and suggest metatheory criteria with which to evaluate each school of thought.

RESURGENCE OF INTEREST IN MARKETING THEORY

The strongest signal of the renewed interest in marketing theory was the publication of the Fall 1983 issue of *Journal of Marketing,* which focused exclusively on theoretical issues. In addition, several new books have been recently published on theory construction and marketing theory (Zaltman et al. 1982, Hunt 1976a, Hunt 1983b, Brown and Fisk 1984, Sheth and Garrett 1986b). Finally, the American Marketing Association (AMA) has organized annual winter educators' conferences that focus exclusively on marketing theory.

While this trend is laudable and long overdue, our contention is that we must understand our roots and foundations of knowledge as we go forward toward generating new and innovative theories in marketing. Therefore, this book will attempt to provide in one single volume a summary of the development and evolution of marketing thought, as well as evaluate it utilizing metatheory criteria.

Some extant review papers summarize the history of marketing thought. The classic, although dated, volume is Bartels' excellent review of the development of marketing thought up to the late 1950s (Bartels 1962). His chronicling of marketing history is also summarized in Bartels (1965). Another valuable resource, which is not widely acknowledged, is P. D. Converse's paper that discusses the beginnings of marketing thought in the United States (Converse 1959). Updates of the history of marketing thought are provided by Sheth and Gardner (1982) and by Sheth and Gross (1988), chronicling the more recent schools of marketing developed since the early 1960s.

Although these are very useful reviews, they do not provide a sense of history because of space limitations. In this book, we hope to provide a much more in-depth summary and discussion of the various schools of thought. Furthermore, we hope to provide a more comparative perspective by bringing together all the major schools of thought in one volume. In addition to identifying and discussing various schools of marketing thought, it is equally important to evaluate the contribution of each school to the development of marketing theory. This evaluation may be useful to future theorists of marketing in terms of capitalizing on the strengths and avoiding the weaknesses of past theories. We plan to utilize a metatheory approach for this evaluation process. Metatheory has a rich tradition in marketing, starting with Halbert (1964) and Bartels (1970), and more recently Zaltman et al. (1982) and Hunt (1983b).*

THE ERA OF TURBULENT TRANSITION

A second reason for writing this book is to provide a sense of security and heritage during the turbulent stage of transition that marketing is currently experiencing. We have identified five areas or major controversies that have impact on the discipline and are likely to become critical issues for further research on marketing theory.

What Is, or Should Be, the Dominant Perspective of Marketing?

Throughout its history as a separate discipline, marketing thought has been generally dominated at any one point in time by one prevailing perspective. Most recently during the 1960s and 1970s, consumer behavior had been the dominant perspective. Beginning with early scholars such as Katona (1953) and Howard (1963a), the marketing discipline moved rapidly to push consumer behavior to the forefront of academic discussion and research.

During its reign, the consumer behavior perspective generated several notable concepts on such diverse topics as perceived risk (Bauer 1960), information processing (Bettman 1979), reference group influence (Bourne 1965), social class (Martineau 1958), involvement (Krugman 1965), psychographics (Wells 1975), attitudes (Hansen 1972), and situational influences (Belk 1974). However, to borrow terminology from the product life cycle framework, the consumer behavior perspective has begun to move from the maturity stage to the saturation stage during the late 1970s. Scholars have become increasingly frustrated with consumer behavior's inability to fulfill quickly its once promising potential. Jacoby (1978) caustically wrote that:

> . . . judging from papers which continue to be published in our most prestigious journals and from research reports which often form the basis for important marketing management and public policy decisions, it is all too apparent that too large a proportion of the consumer (including marketing) research literature is not worth the paper it is printed on or the time it takes to read. (p. 87)

---

*Metatheory perspectives have been also provided by Sheth (1967), Howard and Sheth (1969), and Zaltman et al. (1973) in consumer behavior.

Likewise, Sheth (1979b) emphasized consumer behavior's shortcomings by noting:

> It would be simply exhilarating if we can evolve some agreed upon and properly validated laws of consumer behavior. So far, it seems that we have discovered only two obvious laws of consumer behavior: those who don't need the product, consume it and secondly those who need it, do not consume it! (p. 426)

While the marketing discipline still regards consumer behavior as a worthy perspective, a movement is in progress to elevate strategic marketing to the position of dominance once held by consumer behavior. As an indication of the growing importance of, and interest in, strategic marketing, the Spring 1983 issue of *Journal of Marketing* was devoted entirely to papers analyzing strategic issues. Fundamentally, strategic marketing has emerged in response to criticisms that marketing has failed to consider adequately the development of long-term competitive advantage (Wind and Robertson 1983). Thus, we witness in the following definitions that strategy involves the judicious matching of a firm's resources with environmental opportunities and constraints so as to achieve a long-run competitive advantage:

> Strategy is the match between an organization's resources and skills and the environmental opportunities and risks it faces and the purposes it wishes to accomplish. (Hofer and Schendel 1978, p. 11)

> ... strategic management is a manner of thinking that integrates broadly defined strategic and operating viewpoints and decisions for the purpose of directing resources toward opportunities consistent with enterprise capabilities to achieve a sustainable differential advantage. (Kerin and Peterson 1983, p. 4)

Although the strategic marketing perspective is relatively new, some scholars are already advocating that the optimal basis for future marketing theory development is the combination of both the strategic marketing perspective and the consumer behavior perspective. This dual focus on competitive and consumer analysis is particularly evident in Anderson's (1982) constituency-based perspective:

> Thus, from a constituency-based perspective, marketing's role in strategic planning reduces to three major activities. First, at both the corporate and divisional levels it must identify the optimal long-term position or positions that will assure customer satisfaction and support ... marketing's second major strategic planning activity involves the development of strategies designed to capture its preferred positions. This will necessarily involve attempts to gain a competitive advantage over firms pursuing similar positioning strategies ... Finally, marketing must negotiate with top management and the other functional areas to implement its strategies. (p. 24)

Similarly, Day and Wensley (1983) reflected this duality of the strategic and consumer behavior perspectives when they asserted:

> . . . we foresee a growing consensus around the notion that the marketing function initiates, negotiates, and manages acceptable exchange relationships with key interest groups, or constituencies, in the pursuit of sustainable competitive advantages, within specific markets, on the basis of long run consumer and channel franchises. (p. 83)

Thus, in the midst of this transition from domination by the consumer behavior perspective to an emphasis on the strategic marketing perspective, we can detect the emergence of a viewpoint that posits that marketing should be founded on two pillars—a thorough understanding of the consumer's needs and behavior and a critical analysis of opportunities for competitive advantage (Day 1984, Bagozzi 1986). The challenge for future marketing theorists is to develop theories that adequately incorporate both of these equally important foundations.

What Is, or Should Be, the Relationship Between Marketing and Society?

Because it is a tremendous responsibility to gather resources from the environment, transform these resources into need-satisfying products and services, and then distribute these products and services to consumers in a society, it is probably inevitable that not everyone in society will agree with the manner in which marketing performs these functions (e.g., Goble and Shaw 1975, Sethi 1979). Indeed, particularly during the second half of this century, marketing has come under sharp criticism for its presumed poor utilization of scarce environmental resources and its alleged disregard for the public welfare.

As the population of the world increased dramatically and marketing struggled to continually advance the general standard of living for this growing populace, many members of society began to realize that some critical resources in the environment were being placed in jeopardy (Kangun 1974). This concern for marketing's impact on the environment focused on three issues. First, in the process of extracting resources from the environment to use in the creation of products, marketing placed a heavy burden on certain nonrenewable resources such as petroleum. In addition, the extensive use of forestry resources caused many critics to wonder about the loss of recreation utility from the forests. Second, marketing faced rebuke because the actual use of many products by consumers had a direct impact on environmental quality. Perhaps the most publicized example in this area is the concern about the noxious fumes emitted by automobiles and the subsequent lowering of the air purity levels. Finally, the disposal of many products placed a strain on the environment (Zikmund and Stanton

1971). Social analysts were concerned that marketing may be using excessive packaging, which makes waste collection more difficult and costly. Further, the use of nonreturnable cans and bottles was criticized because this marketing practice supposedly encouraged consumers to litter the highways with refuse (Crosby and Taylor 1982). But perhaps the major concern regarding the disposal of products was the adverse impact on water resources, with the waterways becoming increasingly polluted and even the underground water resources becoming tainted due to the runoff from garbage disposal sites.

Fortunately, the marketing discipline has responded to society's call for greater analysis of marketing's impact on the environment. Within the academic community a number of outstanding volumes pertaining to the marketing and environment interface were published, including Kangun (1972), Fisk (1974), and Fisk et al. (1978).

In addition to environmental issues, social critics have also taken marketing to task for its treatment of the consumer. One specific focus of concern has been the potentially harmful effects of product consumption, which received early scrutiny with Upton Sinclair's (1906) exposé of the deplorable sanitary conditions in the meat packing industry. However, it was not until the 1960s that the issue of product safety truly became a paramount issue. During that decade two major events occurred that riveted the consumers' attention on the questions of product effects. First, in 1962 it was revealed that thalidomide, a new tranquilizing drug often used by pregnant women, caused birth defects. Second, in 1965, Ralph Nader published his best-selling book, *Unsafe at Any Speed*, which alleged that the General Motors' Corvair was inherently dangerous to drive.

Beyond the grave issue of the negative effects of product consumption, the marketing discipline has refined its focus to concentrate on marketing's overall treatment of specific groups of consumers. Included in this analysis are:

The elderly consumer: Numerous articles have considered the effects of aging on the consumer and how marketing should respond positively to these changes (e.g., Phillips and Sternthal 1977, Schewe 1985, French et al. 1983).

The young consumer: Marketings' relationship with children as consumers has generated much interest, particularly regarding the persuasive effects of television advertising (McNeal 1987, *FTC Staff Report on Television Advertising to Children* 1978, Popper and Ward 1980).

Ethnic minorities: Many critics have questioned marketing's treatment of prominent minority groups, such as blacks and hispanics, who spend large amounts in consumer goods markets (Andreasen 1982, Sexton 1971, Sturdivant 1968).

Foreign consumers: As marketing becomes more global in perspective, critics have attacked marketers for supposedly taking advantage of consumers in less developed countries. A notable example of this type of controversy has been the criticism of Nestlé's promotion of infant formula (Post 1985).

Unquestionably, consumer activists have exhorted consumers to adopt a more aggressive stance regarding businesses' marketing tactics (Day and Aaker 1970). As a result there is increasing interest in consumer complaining behavior (Czepiel, Rosenberg, and Suprenant 1980; Day and Landon 1977). Recently articles have investigated negative word-of-mouth by dissatisfied consumers (Richins 1983) and appropriate managerial responses to consumer complaints (Resnik and Harmon 1983).

In addition to analyzing more assertive consumer responses to marketing activities, marketing discipline is beginning to concentrate more seriously on how governmental regulation attempts to monitor and control social impacts of the marketing function. Although pricing policies have long been open to governmental scrutiny, greater emphasis is now placed on restrictions on distribution (Cady 1982), product liability issues (Morgan 1982), and advertising regulation (Dunn 1981).

The most significant recent development in the area of the marketing and society relationship has been the emergence of a separate sector of marketing thought called *macromarketing*. Although there is some disagreement regarding the precise definition and boundaries of macromarketing (Hunt and Burnett 1982), macromarketing basically analyzes the impacts and consequences of interactions between marketing systems and social systems. The vitality of this relatively new field is reflected in the excellent series of macromarketing seminars (Slater 1977, White and Slater 1978, Fisk and Nason 1979, Fisk et al. 1980) and in the launching of the *Journal of Macromarketing*.

For the marketing theorist, the challenge is to create theories that adequately incorporate volatile issues of the relationship between marketing and society. Should we conclude, as Levitt (1958) did in his classic article, that marketing should definitely *not* be responsible to society for any of its activities? Or should we probe for new theoretical foundations that help marketing cope with the social consequences of its functions? In our view, we clearly must accept the fact that marketers must join forces with consumer advocates and public policymakers in government to forge new visions of marketing's responsibility to society and society's responsibility to marketing. To accomplish this admittedly difficulty task, we urgently need stronger theories rather than the haphazard, ad hoc regulatory reaction that has dominated the marketing and society relationship in recent years.

What Is, or Should Be, the Proper Domain of Marketing Theory?

Although it is somewhat embarrassing to admit, marketing discipline must acknowledge that we honestly do not know precisely what the proper domain or boundaries of marketing should be. This indecision and debate is concentrated on two distinct fronts. First, we are unsure as to the correct external boundaries of marketing. Specifically, should marketing be applied to social, nonprofit, and general exchange situations? Second, we are just now beginning to rekindle an old controversy regarding the homogeneity of the internal subdivisions within marketing. This raises a series of questions: "Are domestic marketing and international marketing similar or dissimilar?" and "What, if any, are the differences among consumer marketing, industrial marketing, and services marketing?"

In one of the classic articles, Kotler and Levy (1969) proposed that marketing is a pervasive societal activity that is applicable beyond the traditional business arena. In fact, they argued that every organization is involved in marketing whether or not these activities are recognized as such. To advance this perspective even further, Kotler (1972a, p. 49) presented a generic concept of marketing: "Marketing is specifically concerned with how transactions are created, stimulated, facilitated, and valued. This is the generic concept of marketing."

In an attempt to clarify the broadened boundaries of marketing, Kotler (1972a) focused on the importance of transaction:

> The core concept of marketing is the transaction. A transaction is the exchange of values between two parties. The things of value need not be limited to goods, services, and money; they include other resources such as time, energy, and feelings. Transactions occur not only between buyers and sellers, and organizations and clients, but also between any two parties. (p. 48)

Not everyone agrees with this generic concept of marketing. Luck (1969, p. 53) took vigorous exception to this new perspective and derisively noted that "if a task is performed, anywhere by anybody, that has some resemblance to a task performed in marketing, that would be marketing." Instead, he counterargued that "a manageable, intelligent and logical definition of marketing can be fashioned when its scope is bounded within those processes or activities whose ultimate result is a market transaction" (p. 54). Although numerous scholars added their viewpoints to the debate (Arndt 1978, Carman 1973, Dawson 1979, Nickels 1974, Robin 1978, Tucker 1974), Bartels (1974) presented one of the more insightful and succinct statements of the nature of the unresolved problem when he wrote:

> The crux of the issue is this: is the identity of marketing determined by the *subject* matter dealt with or by the *technology* with which the subject is handled? Specifically, is marketing the application of certain functions, activi-

ties, or techniques to the dissemination of *economic goods* and *services,* including the satisfactions they provide? Or is it the application of those functions and techniques to the dissemination of *any* ideas, programs, or causes — noneconomic as well as business? (pp. 74-75)

In an effort to make sense of the myriad of conflicting opinions concerning marketing's proper boundaries, Hunt (1976b) suggested that the scope of marketing may be delimited in terms of three dimensions — nonprofit/profit, micro/macro, and positive/normative. Although this framework certainly represents an important step forward, the controversy is still far from settled.

Most marketing scholars are familiar with this debate about the proper boundaries of marketing. In fact, the American Marketing Association (AMA) has established separate divisions, special conferences, and tracks to accommodate the debate. However, we are not as cognizant of the controversy regarding the homogeneity of the internal subdivisions in the marketing discipline. Specifically, three separate questions, with obvious theoretical implications, must be answered.

The first question focuses on "Is services marketing different from products marketing?" Although discussion of the marketing of services appeared in the marketing literature in the 1960s (Judd 1964), within the last few years we have witnessed a more vigorous analysis of the nature and potential uniqueness of services marketing. In an excellent review of this area, Uhl and Upah (1983) concluded that there are four major differences between products and services. These differences relate to (1) tangibility, (2) ability to be stored, (3) ability to be transported, and (4) ability to be mass-marketed. Based on these four points, they offered a definition of a service:

> A service is any task (work) performed by another or the provision of any facility, product, or activity for another's use and not ownership, which arises from an exchange transaction. It is intangible and incapable of being stored or transported. There may be an accompanying sale of a product. (p. 236)

In an attempt to also advance our knowledge of the nature of services marketing, Lovelock (1983) presented an extensive classification system for services. Drawing from the precedent established in the commodity school of thought (Copeland 1923), Lovelock developed five classification schemes that aim to answer the following five questions:

1. What is the nature of the service act?
2. What type of relationship does the service organization have with its customers?
3. How much room is there for customization and judgment on the part of the service provider?
4. What is the nature of demand and supply for the service?
5. How is the service delivered?

While Lovelock (1983) and Uhl and Upah (1983) focused on the reasons why services marketing should be considered as a distinct area, Levitt (1981) argued strongly against this view:

Distinguishing between companies according to whether they market services or goods has only limited utility. A more useful way to make the same distinction is to change the words we use. Instead of speaking of services and goods, we should speak of intangibles and tangibles. Everybody sells intangibles in the marketplace, no matter what is produced in the factory. (p.94)

Enis (1979) and Enis and Roering (1981) have also argued that goods and services share many common characteristics, and that marketing of goods and marketing of services may appropriately call for similar strategies. More recently, Zeithaml, Parasuraman, and Berry (1985) developed a conceptual framework suggesting some unique characteristics of services (intangibility, inseparability of production and consumption, heterogeneity, and perishability), and some unique marketing problems and strategic responses that stem from these characteristics. However, they also point out that important differences exist *among* services as well as *between* services and goods.

Future marketing theorists must grapple with the issue of the differences and similarities between goods and services. Further, they must decide whether their theories are applicable to services marketing and/or products marketing, if indeed they conclude there is a clear distinction between the two classes.

The second question takes the form of "Is there a difference between consumer goods marketing and industrial goods marketing?" Generally, marketing scholars have tended to accept the notion that there are substantial differences between these two marketing activities. As a reflection of this belief, we have separate books devoted specifically to industrial marketing (Hill, Alexander, and Cross 1975, Haas 1986) and entire academic courses that concentrate solely on the marketing of industrial products and services. In 1954, an Industrial Marketing Committee Review Board published in the *Journal of Marketing* a classic article entitled "Fundamental Differences Between Industrial and Consumer Marketing." They cited such factors as:

Rational buying motives appear to predominate in the industrial field (as against emotional motives in the consumer field) but their influence declines with the increase in product similarity. (p. 153)

Multiple-buying responsibility is commonplace in the industrial field in the purchase of major items of equipment and in the establishment of formulas for purchases of raw materials and component parts. (p. 154)

The channels of distribution for industrial goods are likely to be shorter than channels for consumer goods. There are fewer middlemen in the industrial chain and a much larger percentage of industrial goods is sold direct to the buyer in industrial marketing than the percentage sold direct to the consumer in consumer marketing. (p. 155)

As a further reflection of the basic belief in differences between industrial and consumer marketing, the marketing discipline generated a separate research area to explore industrial buying behavior (Webster and Wind 1972, Sheth 1973, Wind and Thomas 1980).

However, it would be premature to conclude at this juncture that there are, in fact, fundamental differences between industrial and consumer marketing (Fern and Brown 1984). Sheth (1979a) has argued that there is really greater variation in marketing methods *within* industrial marketing and consumer marketing than there is *between* these two types of marketing. Thus, for example, he notes that certain consumer goods, such as houses, may require direct marketing techniques, while some industrial goods, like solvents and lubricants, may be mass-marketed.

Therefore, the marketing theorist is presented with yet another intellectual challenge. Does the proposed theory relate to both consumer goods marketing and industrial goods marketing? If not, how does the theorist defend making a distinction between these two categories of marketing?

The third and final question regarding the internal subdivisions within marketing is arguably the most important for the future development of marketing theory. With the increased emphasis on global markets and international trade, we must ask, "Are domestic marketing and international marketing similar or dissimilar?" Numerous anecdotes relate the follies of companies that failed miserably, and often humorously, when their marketing managers attempted to employ their successful domestic marketing strategies in foreign markets (Ricks, Arpan, and Fu 1974). Because of these costly mistakes, the marketing profession has questioned whether a company should standardize its international marketing program (Bartels 1968a, Britt 1974, Buzzell 1968, Sorenson and Wiechmann 1975).

There have been numerous advocates of standardization. Fatt in 1967 asserted that some consumer needs are universal:

> The desire to be beautiful is universal...In a sense, the young women in Tokyo and the young women in Berlin are sisters not only "under the skin," but on their skin and on their lips and fingernails, and even in their hair styles. If they could, the girls of Moscow would follow suit; and some of them do. (p. 61)

In a less dramatic endorsement of the prostandardization view, Buzzell (1968) wrote:

> My thesis is that although there are many obstacles to the application of common marketing policies in different countries, there are also some very tangible benefits. The relative importance of the pros and cons will, of course, vary from industry to industry and from company to company. But the

benefits are sufficiently universal and sufficiently important to merit careful analysis by management in virtually any multinational company. Management should not automatically dismiss the idea of standardizing some parts of the marketing strategy, at least within major regions of the world. (p. 103)

If anything, it appears that the movement toward increased use of standardization has gathered strength in recent years. Levitt (1983) asserted:

A powerful force drives the world toward a converging commonality, and that force is technology. It has proletarianized communication, transport, and travel. It has made isolated places and impoverished people eager for modernity's allurements. Almost everyone everywhere wants all the things they have heard about, seen or experienced via the new technologies. The result is a new commercial reality—the emergence of global markets for standardized consumer products on a previously unimagined scale of magnitude. (p. 92)

But, once again, we witness a lack of unanimity among marketing scholars regarding this issue. For example, both Kotler (1986a) and Wind (1986) are diametrically opposed to Levitt's hypothesis, and Sheth (1986) suggests a contingency framework that identifies situations where standardization will be successful and other situations where customization is necessary.

Beyond debating the wisdom of standardizing marketing programs in the international markets, some critics have even suggested that theory development in marketing is restricted because of the predominance of the American viewpoint. Dholakia, Firat, and Bagozzi (1980) presented five intriguing points for discussion when they asserted that:

1. Marketing concepts are a product of, and contextually bound to, the American industrial system.
2. This fact limits the spatial and temporal validity of marketing concepts.
3. The context boundedness inhibits the emergence of a universal conception of the nature and scope of marketing.
4. Specific biases and barriers are created in terms of theoretical development in the field.
5. Efforts are needed to deconceptualize, reconceptualize and thereby universalize the analytical categories of marketing. (p. 25)

Therefore, the marketing theorist must inquire, "Is this theory applicable only to marketing in country X or is it relevant to marketing in any country?" Clearly, this is a perplexing issue that remains to be resolved.

The question of defining the proper domain of marketing is a monumental problem that is likely to cause marketing theorists many sleepless nights. Our basic point is that, when a scholar proposes a new theory, he or she must explicitly explain the domain to which this theory is relevant. Is it applicable to for-profit marketing, nonprofit marketing, social marketing, industrial goods marketing, or international marketing? If not, why not? Can the marketing theorist convince the marketing community that the theory should have only limited applicability? In many ways, the discipline of psychology has faced a similar dilemma. For example, to what extent does social psychology differ from consumer, clinical, community, or cross-cultural psychology? The American Psychological Association (APA) has been forced to create more than 40 divisions to accommodate diverse applications-based perspectives and has begun to address the more fundamental question: Is this really necessary or desirable for the discipline? Indeed, the APA is in the midst of consolidating divisions into assemblies but is experiencing significant opposition.

Is Marketing a Science or, at Best, a Standardized Art?

The disagreement over marketing's possible status as a science has been continuing relatively unabated for almost forty years (O'Shaughnessy and Ryan 1979). Some marketing scholars firmly believe that marketing can never be a science. For example, Hutchinson (1952) argued:

> There is a real reason, however, why the field of marketing has been slow to develop a unique body of theory. It is a simple one: marketing is not a science. It is rather an art or a practice, and as such much more closely resembles engineering, medicine, and architecture than it does physics, chemistry, or biology. (p. 289)

However, most of the discussion has concentrated around the definition of a science and how well marketing meets these scientific requirements. Bartels (1951), Buzzell (1963), and Hunt (1976b) have all presented views regarding appropriate scientific criteria:

> If marketing is to be so regarded as a science then study of it both in form and content must correspond to the standards of science in the social realm. First, the objective of observation and investigation must be the establishment of general laws or broad principles, not merely settled rules of action or operating procedures. Second, prediction made possible through the development of laws should be of social import and not merely institutional application. Third, theory and hypotheses employed in prediction and in the drawing of further inferences should be useful for the extension of knowledge as well as for guiding administrative means toward profitable ends. Fourth, abstractions as well as concrete facts should be used in the explanation of marketing phenomena. (Bartels 1951, pp. 322-323)
>
> ... it is generally agreed that a science is (1) a classified and systemized body of knowledge, (2) organized around one or more central theories and a number of general principles, (3) usually expressed in quantitative terms, (4)

knowledge which permits the prediction and, under some circumstances, the control of future events. (Buzzell 1963, p. 33)

... sciences (1) have a distinct subject matter drawn from the real world which is described and classified, (2) presume underlying uniformities and regularities interrelating the subject matter, and (3) adopt intersubjectively certifiable procedures for studying the subject matter. This perspective can be appropriately described as a consensus composite of philosophy of science views on science. (Hunt 1976b, p. 27)

The reason why this topic of marketing and science is particularly relevant now is that several scholars writing in the 1983 *Journal of Marketing* special issue on marketing theory attacked marketing's perception of science. In particular, concerns were raised about marketing's reliance on the logical positivism/empiricism perspective. Anderson (1983) maintained:

... it is clear that positivism's reliance on empirical testing as the sole means of theory justification cannot be maintained as a viable description of the scientific process or as a normative prescription for the conduct of scientific activities. This point is essentially noncontroversial in contemporary philosophy and sociology of science. Despite its prevalence in marketing, positivism has been abandoned by these disciplines over the last two decades in the face of the overwhelming historical and logical arguments that have been raised against it. (p. 25)

Along a similar vein, Peter and Olson (1983) argued:

While we recognize that no defensible criterion for distinguishing science from nonscience has been found, we believe that the main task of science is to create useful knowledge. To the degree that marketing has done so, then it can be labelled a science. As marketing scientists we should be concerned to make our discipline more effective in creating useful knowledge about our subject matter. We believe that such improvements are best achieved by adopting the relativistic/constructionist approach to science, the context specificity of scientific knowledge, and other features of the R/C program that can give marketing scholars the freedom and confidence to create new conceptual schemes and perspectives. This is in contrast to following the outdated rules of the Postivistic/Empiricist approach that focuses only on testing theories we already have. (pp. 123-124)

Thus, this controversy regarding the scientific status of marketing creates a major dilemma for marketing theorists: If the logical empiricism perspective is no longer relevant, how then should theories be created and evaluated? Indeed, how does a scholar, who was trained to be objective and to master numerous empirically based methodologies, go about developing and testing theories given the apparent shift in perspectives within the marketing discipline?

The marketing literature has recently given considerable attention to these important questions. In a very influential article, Bagozzi (1984) focused on the structural aspects of theory construction, summarizing the logical empiricist model of theory structure (the Received View), then presenting an alternative, more operationally oriented, approach (the Holistic Construal) whose philosophical roots lie in the realist theory of science. Other scientific orientations recently explored in the marketing literature include criticism and constructivism (Arndt 1985); relativism (Anderson 1983, 1986, Peter and Olson 1983, Cooper 1987, Muncy and Fisk 1987); and humanism (Hirschman 1986). Further, Sternthal, Tybout, and Calder (1987) have advocated that comparative approaches, as opposed to more traditional confirmatory approaches, be used in judging the rigor of theory tests.

Is It Really Possible to Create a General Theory of Marketing?

The topic of a general theory of marketing has not received sufficient attention by marketing theorists. Unfortunately, in the past, marketing scholars have tended to address only a very limited area of marketing's domain when they sought to develop "new and improved" theories. As a result, the discipline has become almost cluttered with a dizzying array of theories that have considerable depth but also an appalling lack of breadth. El-Ansary (1979) spotlighted this issue by urging the field to seek a general theory of marketing:

> Marketing theory began as a single, rather broad theory. As time passed, marketing practice and viewpoints have changed, and marketing concepts and approaches proliferated. All these changes have altered both the content and the form of marketing thought providing greater diversity of theories. The proliferation of facts, concepts, and theories is forcing integration of knowledge on higher planes of unification and abstraction. A general theory of marketing is needed to unify the diverse theories of marketing. (p. 399)

Does this mean that the marketing discipline has never before proposed a general theory of marketing? Of course not. Several attempts have been made to create a general theory of marketing. Bartels (1968b) proposed a general theory that was composed of several component subtheories:

1. Theory of social initiative: "Society, not the business entrepreneur, is the basic undertaker of all activity. Marketing is that activity undertaken by society at large to meet its consumption needs—the producing, distributing and consuming of products needed for human existence." (p. 32)

2. Theory of economic (market) separations: "The reasons that the people

of a society need some form of marketing is that producers and consumers are separated . . . The separation of producers and consumers, however, are of many types: spatial (physical distances), temporal (time difference between production and consumption), financial (buyers not possessing purchasing power at the time they have willingness or need to buy)." (p. 32)

3. Theory of market roles, expectations, interactions: "Pursuing its economic objectives in removing market separations, society acts in numerous roles, each of which is responsible for part of the process of marketing." (p. 32)

4. Theory of flows and systems: "Flows are the movements of elements which resolve market separations. Marketing does not occur as a single movement, but rather as a number of movements, in series, parallel, reciprocal, or duplicatory." (p. 33)

5. Theory of behavior constraints: "Action in the marketing system is not determined wholly by any one individual or set of participants. It is governed by many determinants and occurs within constraints defined by society." (p. 33)

6. Theory of social change and marketing evolution: "No systems of marketing remain static; all are in stages of adaptation to continuing change, both in the external environment and within the marketing organization itself." (p. 33)

7. Theory of social control of marketing: "As society sanctions the emergence of a marketing mechanism, it also evaluates and regulates its appraisal." (p. 33)

However, Hunt (1971) critically examined Bartels' proposed general theory of marketing and concluded that the seven subtheories did not meet the theory-building criteria to qualify as theories. Instead, Hunt claimed that "they represent an assemblage of classification schemata, some intriguing definitions, and exhortations to fellow marketing students to adopt a particular perspective in attempting to generate marketing theory" (p. 68).

Although Wroe Alderson never formally presented a general theory of marketing, Hunt, Muncy, and Ray (1981) reviewed his extensive writings and compiled their interpretation of an Aldersonian general theory of marketing. They highlighted six major elements in this general theory:

1. "Marketing is the exchange which takes place between consuming groups and supplying groups (Alderson 1957, p. 15)." (p. 268)

2. "The household is one of the two principal organized systems in marketing (Alderson 1965, p. 37)." (p. 268)

3. "The firm is the second primary organized behavior system in marketing (Alderson 1965, p. 38)." (pp. 268-269)

4. "Given heterogeneity of demand and heterogeneity of supply, the fundamental purpose of marketing is to effect exchanges by matching segments of demand with segments of supply (Alderson 1957, pp. 195-199)." (p. 269)

5. "A third organized behavior system in marketing is the channel of distribution." (p. 270)

6. "Given heterogeneity of demand, heterogeneity of supply, and the requisite institutions to effect the sorts and transformations necessary to match segments of demand with segments of supply, the marketing process will take conglomerate resources in the natural state and bring about meaningful assortments of goods in the hands of consumers (Alderson 1965, p. 26)." (p. 271)

A third major general theory of marketing was proposed by El-Ansary (1979). Although the details of this theory are somewhat sketchy, El-Ansary emphasized that the vertical marketing system, composed of consumers and commercial organizations, formed the foundation for his general theory. In addition, El-Ansary indicated the need for supporting theories of consumer behavior, channel institutions, micromarketing, macromarketing, and strategic marketing.

Obviously, we do not currently have a well-defined and universally accepted general theory of marketing. Recently, Hunt (1983a) has redirected attention toward the attainment of this goal. In his article, Hunt provides the distinguishing characteristics of general theories and the fundamental explanada of marketing. As to the nature of general theories, he wrote:

> We may conclude that general theories explain a large number of phenomena and serve to unify the lawlike generalizations of less general theories. Theorists concerned with developing general theories should be alert to the problems involved in empirically testing their theoretical constructions. When key constructs in the theory become highly abstract, in the sense of being too far removed from observable reality or in the sense that relationships among key constructs become too loosely specified, then empirical testability suffers, predictive power declines, and explanatory impotence sets in. Despite these limitations, such theories or models might still serve the useful purpose of "road maps" for guiding the theoretical efforts of others. (p. 12)

Regarding the fundamental explanada of marketing, Hunt (1983a) has suggested four areas for theory development:

1. The behavior of buyers directed at consummating exchanges.

2. The behavior of sellers directed at consummating exchanges.

3. The institutional frameworks directed at consummating and/or facilitating exchanges.

4. The consequences on society of the behavior of buyers, the behavior of sellers, and the institutional framework directed at consummating and/or facilitating exchanges.

Finally, Hunt has noted that a general theory *of* marketing would explain all phenomena within all four of these areas, while a general theory *in* marketing would explain all phenomena within just one of these four areas.

Why should marketing scholars even endeavor to develop a general theory of marketing? We can present at least three reasons why the development of a general theory of marketing should be given high priority. First, the marketing discipline, as it gains more breadth and sophistication, is becoming increasingly fragmented. Indeed, some scholars become such "experts" in certain narrow topical areas in marketing that they completely lose sight of the entire scope of the marketing discipline. In fact, some members of the marketing community openly admit, for example, that as consumer behaviorists, they know nothing about distribution channels and, furthermore, they do not care to fill this knowledge deficiency. With a general theory as a reference point or "home base," theorists pursuing a limited theory in any particular area would be encouraged to relate their specific theory back to the general theory. By doing so, these theorists could draw upon the richness of the propositions suggested by the general theory and they could also demonstrate how their theory supports or even modifies the general theory.

Second, marketing is undergoing an identity crisis. Consider how difficult it is to answer, in a brief and comprehensive fashion, the simple question: "What is marketing?" The fact is that we currently are not very sure just exactly what marketing is and what it should be. A general theory of marketing could help remedy this identity crisis by delineating the nature of the discipline of marketing.

Third, in addition to an identity crisis, we are also experiencing a credibility crisis. Marketing practitioners are becoming increasingly disillusioned with the advice offered by their academic counterparts and often regard the knowledge generated by academic researchers as irrelevant to their concerns (Myers, Massy, and Greyser 1980). There are far too many instances in which marketing scholars abandon the pursuit of developing a theory about subject X because (1) they simply lose interest in the task, (2) the debate over the appropriateness of the proposed theory degenerates into a clash of powerful egos, or (3) they have developed a theory that is so convoluted that nobody in the applied or academic community can possibly understand it. A general theory of marketing, if properly designed and clearly communicated, could help convince marketing practitioners, and even scholars in other disciplines, that marketing theorists are pursuing worthwhile objectives in a logical and orderly manner.

It is our hope that the description and evaluation of past schools of marketing thought will provide a sense of security as well as a guide for future scholars during these turbulent times.

FRAMEWORK FOR THE BOOK

This book will describe and evaluate all the major schools of marketing thought that have surfaced since marketing's emergence as an independent discipline in the early 1900s. Before we discuss each school of marketing thought, it is important to clarify what we mean by a school of thought and why we have chosen the twelve schools of marketing as the comprehensive body of knowledge.

A school of marketing thought must possess the following criteria: First, it must have a distinct focus relevant to marketing goals and objectives, specifying *who* will or should benefit from marketing activities and practices. Second, it must also have a perspective on *why* marketing activities are carried out or should be carried out by the stakeholders. Finally, in addition to a pioneer thinker, a school of thought should be associated with a significant number of other scholars who have contributed toward the thought process. In other words, there must be group consensus that the viewpoint espoused by the pioneer scholar is interesting and worth pursuing in marketing.

The twelve schools of thought discussed in this book meet these three criteria. However, we recognize that what we consider to be a "school of thought" may be considered by some of our collegues to be a "theory" and by others to be a "marketing thought process." Indeed, we have ourselves struggled with this issue. Rather than letting a definitional problem paralyze our research on the evolution of marketing thought, however, we have followed in the tradition of Bartels (1962, 1965) in referring to the various approaches to the study of marketing as schools of thought.

To denote the similarities between certain schools of thought and to enhance the organization of the book's contents for the readers' benefit, a 2-by-2 matrix will be used to classify the various theories. The foundations for this classificatory framework are the two dimensions of interactive versus noninteractive perspective, and economic versus noneconomic perspective (see Table 1.1).

The interactive versus noninteractive dimension captures basic assumptions about the role of marketing and its objectives. First, schools of thought based on interactive processes incorporate the concept of balance of power between sellers and buyers in the marketplace. In contrast, this is assumed away in schools of thought based on the noninteractive perspective. The earliest schools of marketing thought typically adopted a noninteractive perspective in which one party in the marketing process, usually the producer, was portrayed as an action agent who has impact on the behavior of buyers in the marketplace. This noninteractive viewpoint was also predominant among certain marketing theorists in the 1960s and 1970s who reversed the earlier positions and focused on the consumer as the primary party of importance and action in the marketing process.

Table 1.1 Classification of Marketing Schools

	Noninteractive Perspective	Interactive Perspective
Economic Perspective	Commodity Functional Regional	Institutional Functionalist Managerial
Noneconomic Perspective	Buyer Behavior Activist Macromarketing	Organizational Dynamics Systems Social Exchange

However, other schools of thought have rejected this noninteractive perspective and have instead adopted the position that marketing is best understood as an interactive process involving relations and effects among producers, channel members, and consumers. This interactive viewpoint has advanced two separate, but related, propositions. First, it is generally acknowledged that basic marketing activities are not necessarily role-bound. Schools of thought predicated on the interactive perspective generally allow for the performance of marketing functions by either the buyer or the seller. For example, the transportation function may be performed by the producer, a channel member, or even the consumer. One of the earliest supporters of changing roles in the interactive perspective was McInnes (1964) who wrote:

> This conceptual approach also opens the door to considering the consumer as a marketing agent capable of assuming market functions herself and, there-fore, capable by her impact of altering marketing institutions. The functions would still exist; it is only the agent performing them that changes. There still has to be transportation, storage, financing, merchandising, assembly, etc. But these may, and have been, shifted to parties other than producers, wholesal-ers, or retailers. (p. 65)

Second, proponents of the interactive view have also maintained that a marketing actor does not perform in a vacuum. In contrast to the noninteractive perspective, the interactive perspective forces the theorist to think of reactions to a marketing activity by one party and counterreactions by the other party. Each actor in the marketing process has an effect on, and in turn is affected by, the other actors with whom contact is made. Bonoma, Bagozzi, and Zaltman (1978) summarized the distinction between the interactive (dyadic) and noninteractive (unit) perspective:

> ... the behavior of *single* buyers or organizations is considered a direct and usually linear function of the imposition of certain stimuli from the environ-

ment. We term this perspective in marketing, in which an "organism" (e.g., industrial buyer, consumer) is presented with a stimulus from without (e.g., advertisement) and the effect of this stimulus on his behavior the "unit paradigm." (p. 51)

... (1) behavior of whatever kind, cannot be analyzed or explained independently of the context in which it occurs; (2) to "reduce" explanations into constructs (however simple) which violate the structure of the interaction under consideration, is to guarantee confusion, and most importantly, (3) since marketing is a *social* activity, marketers should adopt a social perspective for marketing analysis. This perspective assumes that the basic unit of social activity is the dyad. (p. 53)

Expounding on this interactive (dyadic) perspective, Bonoma, Bagozzi, and Zaltman suggested that four main variables should be analyzed when employing this viewpoint:

1. Relational variables: "Relational variables are concepts specifying the nature of the connections binding actors in a dyad. They are characteristics of the interaction rather than attributes of the actors or properties of outside forces. Typical relational variables include dependence, power, influence, conflict, reciprocity, exchange, intensity, and competition." (p. 59)

2. Social structural variables: "They may be defined as (1) the conditions of the situation within which the dyadic relation occurs and (2) the social positions that actors in the dyad occupy." (p. 60)

3. Social actor variables: "Social actor variables refer to the characteristics of individuals that contribute to or hinder the resolution of dyadic relations." (p. 62)

4. Normative variables: "Normative variables are concerned with how people, or categories of people, ought to behave." (pp. 62-63)

Therefore, it is evident that the schools of marketing thought that emphasize the interactive perspective are more concerned with the interdependent relationship between marketing actors. Conversely, the noninteractive marketing theories focus on the influence activities of one actor on other marketing actors. In short, persuasion or selling (buying) becomes the primary focus for the noninteractive schools whereas exchange or relationship becomes the focus for interactive schools of thought.

The second dimension of the matrix framework focuses on the economic versus noneconomic orientation of theories, and was selected to emphasize the different approaches to achieving marketing's objectives, either from a seller's viewpoint or from a buyer's viewpoint. Some schools of marketing thought (many of the early writings in marketing's history) adopted a strong economic perspective in which the actions of marketing actors were considered to be driven by economic values. From this vantage point, the goal of the marketing system was the fulfillment of basic consumer needs with producers, channel members, and consumers endeavoring to perform their respective functions in the most efficient manner possible in order to maximize their profits. In these economic theories the focus is clearly on critical economic variables such as production and distribution efficiency, prices of inputs and outputs, and consumer income levels.

At the other end of this dimension are those schools that heavily reflect a noneconomic influence. Scholars working in these areas perceived that the actions of producers, channel members, and consumers could not be adequately explained based on economic analysis alone (Cyert and March 1963, Dichter 1964, Howard 1963a, Katona 1960, Mallen 1963). Instead, they advocated increased investigation of the social and psychological factors that may influence the behavior of marketing actors. Therefore, we perceive a decided shift in which (1) producers were hypothesized to strive for survival and long-term stability rather than maximum short-run performance; (2) distribution channel structure was seen to be the result of the interplay of power, conflict, and channel norms instead of economic efficiency forces; and (3) consumer behavior was perceived to be the result of complex psychological motivations and pervasive social pressures rather than the simple use of finite incomes to satisfy unlimited needs and wants.

In our opinion, the dichotomy of economic versus noneconomic perspective is extremely important in classifying various schools of marketing for the following reasons: First, as compared with noneconomic perspectives (such as psychological, sociological, and anthropological), the economic perspective provides a highly focused but probably a narrow perspective about why sellers and buyers behave the way they do in the marketplace. Second, the economic perspective enables the theorist to relate back to the origins of marketing as a subdiscipline of economics, providing a distinct identity for marketing by associating it with a distinct domain of human behavior. This is not true if one takes a psychological, sociological, or anthropological perspective, primarily because those disciplines have not recognized marketing as a subfield of their domains of interest. Finally, the economic perspective tends to be normative whereas the noneconomic perspectives tend to be descriptive.

Taken together, the two dimensions of interactive versus noninteractive and economic versus noneconomic allow us to fully comprehend the differences among the various schools of thought in terms of their values, orientation, and basic philosophies of human motivation and human behavior. Each of the next four chapters of this book will concentrate on one of the four cells in our classification framework. For the readers' benefit, we will briefly overview the nature of the theories that will be presented and evaluated in the remainder of the book.

Chapter 2: Noninteractive-Economic Schools of Marketing

In this quadrant are the classic perspectives in marketing that emerged when marketing was first cast as a discipline divorced from the founding field of economics. What is particularly fascinating is that, although many reform movements have swept through the marketing theory arena, these early schools still possess incredible relevance to modern marketing practice and analysis.

The *commodity school* concentrated on the physical characteristics of products and the related consumer buying habits for different categories of products. Although Charles Parlin was the initial proponent of the commodity perspective (Gardner 1945), Melvin Copeland (1923) is generally cited as the most influential early writer in this area because he presented the now famous tripartite classification of convenience goods, shopping goods, and specialty goods. This classification system has demonstrated remarkable durability as evidenced by the fact that these terms are still in the vocabulary of present-day marketing practitioners, consumers, and scholars. Our extended analysis of the commodity school will also reveal how several scholars have attempted to challenge and refine Copeland's system and how other scholars, particularly Aspinwall (1958), have launched alternative commodity classification systems.

Whereas the commodity school concentrated on the characteristics of products, the *functional school* pursued a different tack by focusing on the activities that must be performed during the marketing process. Arch Shaw (1912) is generally acknowledged as the founding father of the functional perspective, although it is intriguing to note as an historical oddity that Shaw's original 1912 article of sixty pages devoted only ten pages to the functional concept. However, this spark was sufficient to ignite widespread interest in this approach. As we will discuss later, one of the major problems with the functional perspective has been the inability of scholars to agree on a standard set of marketing functions. Perhaps because of this unresolved flaw, the functional school has not received much attention recently from marketing theorists. Ironically, however, we may note that many marketing departments in corporations are organized along functional lines with separate groups devoted to functions such as product management, sales, advertising, market research, and distribution. Also, the academic curricula in many universities' marketing departments reflect the functional influence with separate courses offered in product management, promotion, market research, sales force management, pricing, and distribution. Thus, we might ask, "Should marketing theorists reconsider the possible contributions of the functional school?"

While the commodity and functional schools are both well known and supported by copious bodies of literature, the *regional school* is often overlooked in discussions of major schools of marketing thought. This regional perspective can be traced back to the writings in the 1930s and 1940s by Reilly (1931) and Converse (1943, 1949), who analyzed, by way of formulas or "laws of gravitation," where consumers were most likely to do their shopping. Obviously, this concern for shopping patterns is still reflected today in the great care that retailers take in choosing their store locations. The regional school is also founded on the writings of E. T. Grether (1950, 1983), whose influential contributions to the marketing discipline have spanned approximately a half century. In many respects, Grether's interpretation of regionalism is much richer than the Reilly-Converse view because he focused on the flows of materials and goods among regions of the country that are varied in terms of their resource abundance. As a reflection of the practical importance of the regional perspective, we may point to the current interest in and, in some cases, alarm over the movement of masses of consumers and businesses from the "Snowbelt" to the "Sunbelt," as well as the increasing import and export trade between the United States and the rest of the world. Further, the regional approach is relevant to issues of geographic market segmentation (Kahle 1986).

Chapter 3: Interactive-Economic Schools of Marketing

The interactive-economic schools of thought generally emerged in the marketing discipline at least a decade later than the noninteractive-economic schools discussed in Chapter 2. Therefore, these three schools, with their interactive components, demonstrate a somewhat more advanced and sophisticated view of the marketing task.

The *institutional school* is generally considered, along with the commodity and functional schools, to be one of the "grand old foundations" of marketing thought. While the commodity school dealt with the characteristics of the product and the functional school concentrated on marketing activities, the institutional school was concerned with analyzing the organizations involved in the marketing process. The early stimulus for this school of thought was the belief, often voiced by consumers in a derisive manner, that the "middlemen" between the producer and the consumer added more cost than value to the products. Therefore, marketers were placed on the defensive and forced to evaluate these institutions to determine their contributions to marketing. From this beginning, the institutional school moved forward to investigate the structure and evolution of channel systems. The important point to raise, however, is that scholars in the institutional school consistently sought to explain these structural and evolutionary phenomena by means of *economic efficiency* criteria. As we shall see, the organizational dynamics school, a direct descendant of the institutional school, pursues marketing institutions analysis from a behavioral rather than economic perspective.

Although the commodity, functional, regional, and institutional schools of thought were all supported and advanced by the writings of numerous marketing scholars, the *functionalist school* is an exception in that this perspective was largely founded on the work of one person, Wroe Alderson. Based primarily on his two landmark textbooks in 1957 and 1965, Alderson introduced a new and intriguing approach to the marketing intellectual community. The heart of Alderson's conceptualization was the fundamental importance of the exchange process and the heterogeneity of demand and supply. Beyond providing other marketing scholars with a fresh orientation, Alderson also differed from others with his creative vocabulary, including such terms as transvections, assortments, collections, conglomerates, sorting, and transformations. Although some critics argue that Alderson's work is flawed by his rather undisciplined writing style and his failure to evaluate and integrate prior literature, it is undeniable that his thoughts are still generating considerable interest in marketing theory. Indeed, there have been two excellent reviews of Alderson's contributions published recently (Hunt, Muncy, and Ray 1981, Blair and Uhl 1977) and several other articles presented at the marketing theory conferences sponsored by the American Marketing Association.

The third school in the interactive-economic quadrant is the *managerial school* of thought. While many of Alderson's terms are still ambiguous to even experienced marketing scholars, the terminology of the managerial school is familiar to probably any student who has progressed past the introductory marketing course. The strength and popularity of the managerial school can be traced to its uncomplicated, elegant focus on such concepts as the marketing concept, marketing mix, product life cycle, and market segmentation. These concepts were developed and nurtured by such eminent marketing pioneers as Joel Dean, John Howard, Wendell Smith, Neil Borden, William Lazer, Theodore Levitt, and Philip Kotler. Unfortunately, a major problem with the emergence and growth of the managerial school of thought with its emphasis on marketing practice was the simultaneous and perhaps inevitable loss of interest in marketing theory. We believe it is imperative that we examine critically the managerial perspective and integrate its more worthy elements into the theoretical realm.

Chapter 4: Noninteractive-Noneconomic Schools of Marketing

The noninteractive-noneconomic schools are comparatively new perspectives with origins in the 1960s and 1970s. These schools represent a dramatic shift in orientation because of the emergence of interest in behavioral, or social and psychological, influences in marketing.

The one school that has undoubtedly received more attention than any other school ever in the history of marketing is the *buyer behavior school*.

Whereas the six schools already mentioned focused almost exclusively on the producer or seller of market goods, the buyer behavior school performed a sharp about-face and concentrated on the buyer of these goods. The leading scholars in this school, including Ernest Dichter, John Howard, George Katona, James Engel, and Francisco Nicosia among others, concluded that it was unsatisfactory to accept that the buyer was simply an "economic person" seeking to allocate his/her finite income wisely to satisfy his/her numerous needs. Rather, they suggested that marketing theorists should dig deeper into the consumer's actions and seek to discover more complex, but also more realistic, reasons for the consumer's behavior. Thus, these scholars began to borrow concepts developed in other disciplines, especially psychology and sociology, and apply them in marketing. It is well known that the general response to the behavioral school was enthusiastic and optimistic with support finally reaching such proportions that a separate academic organization called *Association for Consumer Research* was formed to focus on research and theory on consumer behavior. Unfortunately, as with other schools of thought that have generated too much interest, the buyer behavior school soon began to lose contact with the broader marketing discipline. This separation between marketing and buyer behavior is currently the subject of heated debate that shows no clear signs of resolution.

The *macromarketing school* represented another clear shift in perspective when some scholars, notably Robert Holloway and George Fisk, asserted that more consideration should be given to environmental and societal forces. Included among these forces are technology, political regulation, societal trends, and competition. The most significant contribution of this school of thought was the emphasis on analyzing those largely uncontrollable environmental factors that have a tremendous effect on marketing practitioners' activities. Thus, marketing theorists were forced to acknowledge that the marketing process was not conducted in a vacuum devoid of outside influences that may indeed be uncontrollable, bothersome, and detrimental to the pursuit of maximum efficiency. The environmental school has prospered in recent years to the point that we have now coined a new term, macromarketing, for this school of thought. In addition, the interest in macromarketing is verified by the emergence in 1981 of the *Journal of Macromarketing* and by the annual macromarketing conferences.

Although the macromarketing school was based primarily on impartial and rational analysis of the impact of environmental variables on marketing, the *activist school* was oriented toward critiquing, often in a highly partisan and emotional manner, the effects that marketing has on the environment. It is fascinating to note that the activist school is perhaps the only major school of marketing thought that was initially spawned outside the traditional confines of the marketing discipline. Only after social and environmental "watchdogs," such as Ralph Nader, riveted society's attention on marketing failures did marketing scholars begin to pay attention to the dark side of marketing practice. However, once marketing scholars such as Norman Kangun, Lee Preston, Fred Sturdivant, Alan Andreasen, Keith Hunt, and others turned their attention to these issues, rapid progress was made. We now have sizable bodies of literature pertaining to topics like product safety, consumer satisfaction/dissatisfaction, disadvantaged consumers, product disposal effects on the environment, and social responsibility of businesses. The paramount question that we must now ask ourselves is "Was our concern for the social and environmental effects of marketing only a passing fancy?" Indeed, with the recession of the early 1980s and the return to more conservative values and political leadership, some skeptics suggest that the activist school may be relegated to the annals of marketing history.

Chapter 5: Interactive-Noneconomic Schools of Marketing

In the last of the four cells we have three schools of thought that utilize the noneconomic and interactive orientations. As might be expected with the dual complexity of both the noneconomic and interactive facets, these schools have emerged in the marketing discipline only within the past two decades.

The *organizational dynamics school* has generated a rather impressive amount of interest by arguing that interorganizational behavior is the key focal point for understanding the marketing process. Clearly, this school is a direct descendant of the institutional school, but scholars in the organizational dynamics field have opted to dissect the interplay among marketing institutions by means of social and psychological concepts rather than economic concepts. Therefore, such early writers as Mallen (1963) and Stern (1969) asserted that the concepts of power, conflict, control, and roles would have great relevance for marketing theorists. To bolster their contentions, scholars in the organizational dynamics school have borrowed heavily from works in organizational behavior, social psychology, and sociology by authors like French and Raven (1959), Emerson (1962), Aldrich (1979), and Pfeffer and Salancik (1978). At this point this school is very "hot" in the marketing theory arena with numerous conceptual and empirical articles being published in marketing's leading journals. What we must question now is how long it will retain the intellectual curiosity of marketing scholars and what its long-term contributions will be toward a general theory of marketing.

Another interactive-noneconomic school of thought to emerge in recent years is the *systems school*. The most distinguishing tenet of the systems school is the wholistic belief that the total is more than the sum of the parts, and that we are losing something if we do not remain wholistic in our theory and research. Unlike psychology and to some extent economics, systems philosophy has been more prevalent in sociology and ecology. It is, therefore, not surprising that the systems school has borrowed heartily from social systems and living systems perspectives. Systems as a word began to enter into the marketing literature in the middle 1960s, and several textbooks in the late 1960s and early 1970s adopted a systems approach (e.g., Fisk 1967, Lazer 1971, Enis 1974). However, it is hard to identify any one individual as the pioneer of this school of thought in marketing. Also, too many distinct systems perspectives came into existence in rapid succession. On the one hand, Forrester (1959) and Amstutz (1967) provided the operations research and simulation perspective and, on the other hand, Bell (1966) offered the social systems perspective. More recently, Reidenbach and Oliva (1981) have offered the general living systems approach to marketing, while Montgomery and Weinberg (1979) have discussed and developed marketing information systems. Perhaps the marketing discipline jumped on the systems approach too quickly, adopting a loose and superficial interpretation of systems. It is somewhat surprising to note that the broadest and most generic perspective to developing marketing theory has not found a strong champion to forcefully argue for the systems approach. However, Rethans (1979), has suggested that the systems approach should be adopted as an integrative framework for theory development in marketing.

Finally, the *social exchange school* of marketing thought seems destined to be labeled as the most controversial school in the history of marketing. Although Alderson (1965) initiated this perspective when he set forth his Law of Exchange, the controversy did not erupt until Kotler and Levy (1969) suggested, quite forcefully, that marketing was applicable to all social transactions, not just economic transactions. While it was fairly obvious that marketing techniques were being applied in nontraditional areas, such as politics and religion, the more conservative elements in the marketing community were disturbed by the thought that marketing should broaden its boundaries beyond the friendly confines of the business world. This dispute has now subsided, but it is by no means dead.

Also, there is an additional side to the volatile nature of the social exchange school. Specifically, marketing scholars are not quite sure how potent the notion of exchange really is. Some scholars (Bagozzi 1979, Kotler 1972a) maintain that the exchange concept forms the foundation for a general theory of marketing. Houston and Gassenheimer (1987) have suggested that exchange should serve as the theoretical hub around which other marketing theories connect, but point out that it has yet to fulfill its promise of providing such coherent structure for the discipline. Other scholars have argued that, although exchange is an important element of marketing, it is much too shallow and transparent to sustain a strong theoretical tradition.

METATHEORY CRITERIA FOR THE EVALUATION OF THEORIES

One of the weaknesses in the development of marketing thought has been the lack of metatheory evaluation and noncritical acceptance of previously proposed theories. Marketing theorists do not consistently attempt to critique other theories to identify their particular strengths and weaknesses when they formulate their own theories. Thus, we believe that many of us in the marketing theory arena are guilty on two counts. First, quite often we are unaware of the existence and content of major schools of thought from marketing's past. Second, even if we are cognizant of these previous theories, we all too often accept them at face value without subjecting them to careful review to isolate their virtues and flaws.

Although one of our main objectives, as noted in the preceding pages, is to review the major schools of marketing thought and thereby increase the awareness level, we also want to evaluate these theories and suggest what each of them may offer for future theorizing. For this evaluation phase, we have chosen to utilize a metatheory approach.

As a point of departure, we should first answer a question that many readers may ask: "What exactly is metatheory?" Fortunately, the subject of metatheory has received attention from such notable scholars as Halbert (1964), Bartels (1970), and Zaltman, Pinson, and Angelmar (1973). More recently, it has received attention from Zaltman et al. (1982) and Leong (1985). According to Bartels (1970, p. 4), "metatheory is here understood to pertain to the requirements of theory formulation, with particular reference to the structure of thought and to utilization of language for the communication of meaning." Zaltman et al. (1973) expound a bit further by noting:

> Metatheory is the science of science or the investigation of investigation. Metatheory involves the careful appraisal of the methodology of science and the philosophical issues involved in the conduct of science. It is concerned with such topics as the operationalization of scientific concepts, the logic of testing theories, the use of theory, the nature of causality, and procedures for making predictions. Broadly defined, metatheory is the investigation, analysis, and the description of (1) technology of building theory, (2) the theory itself, and (3) the utilization of theory. (p. 4)

The metatheoretical criteria we have chosen to use for our evaluation can be classified into three distinct categories with two criteria in each of these three areas:

1. Syntax	2. Semantics	3. Pragmatics
A. Structure	A. Testability	A. Richness
B. Specification	B. Empirical support	B. Simplicity

The three broad categories of syntax criteria, semantics criteria, and pragmatics criteria were initially discussed in marketing by Halbert (1964).

Syntax (Organization) Criteria. A "good" theory should be structurally sound with a precise *organizational pattern*. As defined by Halbert (1964, p. 32), "syntactics has to do with the legitimacy of the operations that can be performed on the elements that form the theory." Therefore, two essential syntax criteria, structure and specification, may be used to evaluate theories.

Structure basically questions whether the theoretical concepts are properly defined and integrated to form a strong nomological network. Zaltman et al. (1973) discussed this same basic notion under their criterion of "coherence or systematic structure:"

> Thus information gathered or knowledge acquired should not be found in random relationships. Instead, items of knowledge should be grouped together in some logical way. Thus, related concepts should be grouped to form hypotheses and related hypotheses grouped to form theories. (p. 11)

Bartels (1970) also discussed this structure criterion when he proposed a metatheory criterion that he termed "subject identification":

> A first requirement which a metatheory makes is that a theory should deal with a specific, definable subject and be related to it throughout. This is a requirement of subject identification and unity. Stated conversely, a theory should not be built upon uncertain or conflicting concepts of a subject, unless to deal with the uncertainty or to resolve the conflict. (p. 5)

The second of the syntax criteria is the *specification* criterion, which states that the relationships among the theoretical concepts must be specified in a manner to clearly delimit the hypotheses. In other words, a theory demonstrates weakness on the specification criterion when relationships among the concepts are usually couched in a contingency framework where A is related to B but only if other concepts (C, D, etc.) are absent or present. Bartels (1970) called this requirement the "interconcept relationship" criterion:

> A second type of difference in ideas is that between basic conceptual categories, in contrast to that within those categories. Basic concepts are subdivided for the purpose of identifying their concepts, but the differences between dissimilar concepts are noted for the purpose of relating them. The establishment of such relationships is essential to the construction of theory . . . A presumption of causality is basic to prediction. The causality presumed in theory, however, is conceptual rather than physical. It is a presumed condition in the relationship between two concepts, whereby one is deemed an independent variable, the other a dependent variable. The dominance of the one and the subordination of the other defines determinism or causality. (pp. 9-10)

Semantics (Reality) Criteria. Semantics criteria evaluate the theory's relationship to reality by analyzing the *testability* and *empirical support* of the theory. A theory may satisfy the syntax criteria requirements but still fail to meet the test of the semantics criteria, as noted by Halbert (1964):

> A theory may fulfill all of the syntactical requirements with complete adequacy, and still have serious faults. The statement of the primitive notions, the operators, and the permissible manipulation of the symbols in which the theory is stated may all be complete and logically correct. The difficulties may lie in the way in which the theory is related to the real world . . . If we are to use a theory to tell us what observations to make, then we must be clear, precise, and complete in our description of what constitutes a relevant observation and how to interpret such observation so as to test the theory. This area of the philosophy of science is called semantics. (p. 33)

The *testability* criterion is the first of the two semantics criteria. A strong theory, according to the testability criterion, is one in which precise and direct operational definitions of the theory's concepts are provided to ensure testability and intersubjective consensus (Zaltman et al. 1973). Therefore, if a theorist developed a new theory of channel member behavior using the concepts of power, conflict, and cooperation, he or she must indicate how those concepts are to be operationally defined and measured in the "real world" of marketing channels. If the operational definitions are satisfactorily presented in the theory, the theorist should be able to entrust the actual testing of the theory to other scholars without having to worry that they will misinterpret how to measure the key theoretical concepts. Thus, often when a theory's originator complains about the poor results that other scholars obtained when testing his or her theory, the blame should be properly placed upon the author of the theory for not adequately meeting the testability criterion.

Empirical support, the second of the semantics criteria, evaluates the degree of confirming evidence that has been gathered to support the theory's hypotheses. Regarding this criterion, Zaltman et al. (1973) wrote:

> . . . the criterion of reliability is difficult to meet. Apart from establishing that a particular observation is not very likely to have occurred on a random basis, there is the more demanding question concerning the reliability of a particular explanation or interpretation. There will frequently be a competing explanation for the phenomenon observed that has not been ruled out by the particular test. This might be called the problem of interpretative reliability: The larger the number of plausible alternative interpretations, the lower the degree of reliability. (p. 11)

Therefore, any newly proposed theory must inevitably fail on the empirical support criterion because it has not yet been subjected to empirical verification. However, as more and more tests of the theory are completed with uniform and positive results, the theory's empirical support becomes more convincing. It should be pointed out that a theory or school of thought may have significant empirical support for its constructs even though the theory itself may not be subjected to empirical research.

Pragmatics (Relevance) Criteria. Simply stated, the pragmatics criteria question the relevance of the theory to the "users." In the case of marketing theories, the users of the theories are marketing practitioners, public policymakers, and consumers who actually function in the marketplace to overcome the separations between producers and consumers. If a theory is not beneficial to them, then the theory does not satisfy the pragmatics criteria. Once again, Halbert (1964) points out that the three categories of syntax, semantics, and pragmatics are fully independent:

> Even if a theory is adequately described in semantic and syntactic aspects, it still may not be a very good theory. The way in which it fails to be good may be because of a lack of attention to the richness or fruitfulness of the theory in terms of the needs, desires, and problems of the people who may have use for it. The aspect of the analysis of theory concerned with the use of theory is called pragmatics. We require of our theories that they be rich, fruitful, and useful and apply to important problems as well as that they be formally adequate and definitionally precise. (p. 35)

The first pragmatics criterion is the *richness* criterion, which asks how comprehensive and generalizable the theory is. Generally, a theory is more useful or relevant to a marketing practitioner, a policymaker, or a consumer if it covers a large expanse of problems or situations typically encountered. Bartels (1970) named this criterion the "generality of relationships":

> ... the greater value of a theory is in its suitability to explanation of experience on a broader scale. Universality is an ideal seldom achieved, especially in the fitting of theories to social or behavioral circumstances. It is nevertheless, a status to which generalization tends in scientific reasoning. (p. 11)

Similarly, Zaltman et al. (1973) note:

> ... comprehensiveness or scope of knowledge is a desirable criterion. It is a goal of science and ultimately an unachievable one in most instances, to develop statements or laws having wide applicability. The larger the number of different contexts a given theory or subtheory can encompass, the more powerful—that is, the more comprehensive—it is. (p. 12)

Finally, we come to the second pragmatics criterion and the last of six metatheory criteria that we will utilize in this book. The *simplicity* criterion has not received much explicit attention from the marketing scholars who have discussed metatheoretical issues. However, the simplicity criterion is of paramount importance because it evaluates the communication and implementation potential of the theory. That is, can the theory be easily explained to others and can the theory's recommendations be readily implemented by others?

It should be obvious that a theory could perform very well on the richness criterion but still fail to pass minimal acceptance standards for the simplicity criterion. In fact, there may be a counterbalance effect between these two pragmatics criteria such that, for example, when the theory becomes richer (is more comprehensive and generalizable), it also becomes more difficult to explain and implement.

In our review of the major schools of marketing thought in the next four chapters, we will utilize these six metatheory criteria to evaluate the strengths and weaknesses of each of the twelve major schools. The potential evaluation scores range from 1 (poor) to 10 (excellent). The ratings represent our personal viewpoints regarding each school's performance on the metatheory criteria. While we recognize that our process is subjective, we have attempted to provide a rationale for our ratings. Of course, we do not expect that all our readers will agree with our judgments and, if anything, we view differences of opinion as a positive sign demonstrating that more and more marketing scholars are taking the time and effort to critique seriously the merits of our discipline's diverse storehouse of marketing theories. Therefore, we encourage the reader to debate our ratings.

At the same time, we acknowledge that a more logical-positivist approach would be to ask a representative sample of scholars to rate each school of thought on the six metatheory criteria and then present a statistical analysis of their viewpoints. This approach was taken by Hunt and Burnett (1982) in defining macromarketing.

SUMMARY

This chapter has provided the introduction to the book. It has suggested two main reasons for writing this book on marketing theories. First, a resurgence of interest in marketing theory has generated a need for a review and evaluation of known theories and schools of thought in marketing. Second, the discipline of marketing is going through an identity crisis due to a number of critical shifts and changes. Indeed, marketing is on the verge of becoming fragmented into subdisciplines unless marketing scholars make an effort to bring together various perspectives and domains of marketing under one roof. A review of past theories provided in this book may become highly useful in providing both a sense of security and richness on which to build future theories of marketing.

In this book, we have identified twelve major schools of thought that have emerged from the inception of marketing in the early nineteen hundreds to the most recent times. Utilizing a two-dimensional map anchored to interactive-noninteractive perspectives and economic-noneconomic perspectives, we have classified these twelve schools of thought as follows:

1. *Noninteractive-Economic* perspectives dominate in the classical commodity, functional, and regional schools of thought.

2. *Interactive-Economic* perspectives are more commonly found in the institutional, functionalist, and managerial schools of thought.

3. *Noninteractive-Noneconomic* perspectives underlie the buyer behavior, activist, and macromarketing schools of thought in marketing.

4. *Interactive-Noneconomic* perspectives, the most complex approaches, are the underlying processes for the organizational dynamics, systems, and social exchange schools of marketing theory.

In addition to providing a substantive and a historical perspective of these twelve major schools of thought, we will also provide a metatheory evaluation of each school of thought so that future marketing scholars can assess how to build new theories of marketing. We selected six metatheory criteria that reflect the syntax (organization), the semantics (reality), and the pragmatics (relevance) criteria of judging a theory.

The criteria chosen for organizational aspects are *structure* and *specification*. Structure refers to the definition and integration of concepts into a nomological network. Specification refers to the lack of contingent relationships between two or more concepts.

The two criteria selected for reality aspects of a theory are *testability* and *empirical support*. Testability means the operational definitions of the theory's constructs are provided to ensure adequate empirical testing and intersubjective consensus. Empirical support refers to the amount of empirical research that has been carried out in support of the theory.

The last two criteria, *richness* and *simplicity*, are selected to measure the relevance of a theory. Richness, as the name implies, means the comprehensiveness of the theory in terms of the domain of marketing it is able to describe, explain, and predict. On the other hand, simplicity refers to the communication and implementation of the theory to users such as marketing practitioners, policymakers, and consumers.

2

NONINTERACTIVE–
ECONOMIC
SCHOOLS OF
MARKETING

In this chapter, we will describe, summarize, and evaluate the following three schools of marketing thought: the commodity school, the functional school, and the regional school. As stated before, these three schools of thought are all based on economic concepts and, therefore, contain very little behavioral (social or psychological) perspective in theory building. At the same time, all three schools of thought exclusively focus on the marketer's perspective rather than on the interaction between marketers and buyers. In other words, all three schools of thought were created to provide a theoretical foundation for marketing practitioners.

THE COMMODITY SCHOOL OF THOUGHT

As marketing emerged as a separate discipline in the early 1900s, the pioneering scholars in the embryonic stage of the discipline were interested in the question: "How do we make sense of this new field of marketing?" After having argued that marketing was sufficiently important and unique to be worthy of a separate and distinct discipline, these pioneers were under pressure to come up with a logical and compelling system for describing and advancing the field of marketing.

While there was certainly no unanimity among these pioneering scholars regarding what to pursue, a sizable group emerged to form the foundation for what came to be referred to as the "commodity" school of marketing. Their rationale was deceptively simple. Given that marketing is concerned with the movement of goods from producers to consumers, the commodity theorists proposed that marketing scholars should concentrate on the *objects* of transactions, namely the products. Because the marketing discipline largely emerged from agricultural economics and agricultural marketing, the approach came to be known as the commodity school, even though its proponents primarily discussed manufactured packaged goods not agricultural commodities.

As we reflect back on their advocacy for products as the focus of attention, we can appreciate why this approach was so attractive to these early scholars. As these commodity school proponents surveyed the content of other disciplines that were well-respected, they realized that these more advanced disciplines all were based on a comprehensive classification system. As E. L. Rhoades (1927), one of the early supporters of the commodity approach, wrote:

> In the learned fields, scholars are primarily interested in behavior and classify their materials in the way most satisfactory to furnish proper comparisons of behavior. In the marketing field we are primarily interested in behavior, or market functions (how commodities behave in the market). We may then take our cue from the biologist and work back from behavior or functions to a system of classifications of commodities which will be most helpful in a systematic study of the range and variety of those functions. (p. 8)

Thus, these scholars believed that, if the goods exchanged in the marketing process could be classified into some sort of a rational system, marketing would take a giant stride toward gaining scientific legitimacy. However, these early proponents of the commodity school were not only looking inward to the scientific community, they were also peering outward to the applied world of marketing practice. They realized that, even if marketing was accepted within the academic realm, it still would not survive unless it was appreciated by marketing practitioners. In other words, what can marketing theorists tell the producer of paint in Cleveland that will help him do a better job of selling his product to paint stores in Ohio?

The commodity theorists believed that, once a commodity classification system was developed and refined, it would become clear that each market commodity is *not* unique. They wanted to demonstrate that many commodities are really very closely related to each other. So closely related, in fact, that they may be combined into one relatively homogeneous category in which the same marketing procedures and techniques could be utilized for all products in that particular category. This notion of a fairly limited number of categories that are internally homogeneous and externally heterogeneous created a great deal of excitement among the commodity school scholars because they began to have visions of a grand "marketing cookbook." They believed that, when a marketing practitioner was in need of advice regarding the marketing of a specific product, he could simply find which category his product was in and then follow the prescribed marketing recipe for that category. As evidence of this optimism, Melvin Copeland (1925) asserted:

> The classification of a product into one of these groups facilitates the determination of the kind of store through which the market for a specific product should be sought, the density of distribution required, the methods of wholesale distribution to be preferred, the relations to be established with dealers, and in general the sole burden which the advertising must carry. (p. 14)

Therefore, members of the commodity school vanguard were exceedingly upbeat about their perspective because a classification system for products would establish academic respectability and also generate practitioner benefits. However, it is one thing to say that a classification system is the solution to the problems, and it is quite a different matter to actually create this classification system.

As might be expected, a plethora of classification systems were proposed for consideration and adoption during the first few years of the commodity school's ascendency. Charles Parlin should be given credit for generating in 1912 the initial classification system that captured much attention (Gardner 1945). Parlin and his classification system are intriguing for at least three reasons. First, Parlin was not a member of marketing's academic fraternity. Instead, he was the Manager of Research for the Curtis Publishing Company. Second, his proposed system was published in the *Department Store Report*, Volume B, in October 1912 (Gardner, 1945), and for this reason is not readily accessible to present marketing scholars. Finally, if you ask most marketing students who is the founder of the commodity school, they usually cite Melvin Copeland (1923). For a variety of reasons, Parlin has never received due credit for being the creator of the first true commodity classification system. As to the actual content of Parlin's proposal, he suggested that there were three categories of "women's purchases":

> Convenience goods are articles of daily purchase such as groceries, apron gingham, children's stockings and, in general, those purchases which are insignificant in value or are needed for immediate use. These goods are, to a considerable extent, bought at the most convenient place without a comparison of values and the fact that they are bought as a matter of convenience rather than of shopping makes possible the suburban dry goods stores, grocery stores and the cross roads general stores. An examination of the stock of one of the suburban stores will give one who is interested in pushing the inquiry further, an exact list of convenience goods.

> Emergency goods comprise medicines and supplies which some unexpected happening has rendered immediately necessary. These lines enable a subur-

ban drug store to be something more than a peddler of candy and other convenience goods. Shopping lines include all those purchases which are of sufficient importance to require thought and which will permit of delay, such as suits, dresses, high grade dry goods of all kinds. These things a woman lists on her mental shopping tablet which she never forgets, and when next she visits the city, the articles, one by one, are investigated; values are compared and a serious effort is made to secure the best value for the money. (Parlin 1912, portions reprinted in Gardner 1945, pp. 275-276)

The next prominent classification was offered by Melvin Copeland in 1923. Writing in the *Harvard Business Review*, Copeland made reference to Parlin's earlier work and suggested how his proposed system was an improvement. Also employing three broad categories, Copeland argued that all consumer goods could be labeled as either convenience goods, shopping goods, or specialty goods:

Convenience goods are those customarily purchased at easily accessible stores . . . the consumer is familiar with these articles; and as soon as he recognizes the want, the demand usually becomes clearly defined in his mind. Furthermore, he usually desires the prompt satisfaction of the want . . . The consumer is in the habit of purchasing convenience goods at stores located conveniently near his residence, near his place of employment, at a point that can be visited easily on the road to and from his place of employment, or on a route traveled regularly for purposes other than buying trips. (p. 282)

Shopping goods are those for which the consumer desires to compare prices, quality, and style at the time of purchase. Usually the consumer wishes to make this comparison in several stores . . . The exact nature of the merchandise wanted may not be clearly defined in advance in the mind of the shopper; this is in contrast to the usual attitude in purchasing convenience goods. The purchase of shopping goods, furthermore, usually can be delayed for a time after the existence of the need has been recognized; the immediate satisfaction of the want is not so essential as in the case of most convenience goods. (p. 283)

Specialty goods are those which have some particular attraction for the consumer, other than price, which induces him to put forth special effort to visit the store in which they are sold and to make the purchase without shopping . . . For specialty goods the manufacturer's brand, the retailer's brand, or the general reputation of the retail store for quality and service stands out prominently in the mind of the consumer. (p. 284)

It is imperative to note that Copeland's classification system basically relied on the consumers' needs, knowledge of need-satisfying alternatives, and willingness to delay need satisfaction. In this respect, Copeland's approach shows signs of being a distant ancestor of the more recent buyer behavior school of thought. However, Copeland stopped far short of ever questioning exactly *why* the consumers acted as they did. Rather, he was content to accept the behavior of consumers as a given state of affairs and use it as a foundation for grouping the wide variety of marketing goods.

While Copeland based his method of classifying on the needs and actions of consumers, Rhoades (1927) presented a commodity classification system founded on three factors. Although Rhoades agreed that "characteristics of the use of the commodity" were important, he argued that commodities could also be classified based on "physical characteristics of the commodity" (relative degree of perishability, concentration of value, size of the physical unit) and "characteristics of the production of the commodity" (scale of production, place of production, concentration of production, method of production, length of production period). Even though his scheme seems to have its merits, rarely is Rhoades' work mentioned when the commodity school is discussed.

Other than Copeland, the most prominent scholar in the commodity school has been Leo Aspinwall (1958), who launched a classification system using five characteristics to differentiate three types of goods. What immediately strikes the reader of Aspinwall's work is that, unlike Parlin and Copeland, who used terms like convenience goods and shopping goods to describe their categories, Aspinwall named his three categories the red goods, the orange goods, and the yellow goods. Although this seems strange, Aspinwall (1958) had an answer:

> The choice of color names may be inept in some respects, but the idea of an array of goods, based upon the sum of relative values of characteristics of goods, is important. The length of light rays for red, orange, and yellow, in that order, is an array of light rays representing a portion of the spectrum. For our present purpose it is more convenient to use the three colors only, rather than the seven of the full spectrum. The idea of an infinite graduation of values can be envisioned by blending these colors from red to yellow with orange in between. This is the idea we wish to convey as concerning all goods. (p. 441)

For the selection of the classifying characteristics, Aspinwall established several explicit guidelines. First, every characteristic selected must be applicable to every good. Second, every characteristic selected must be relatively measurable in terms of its relationship to every good. And, finally, every characteristic must be logically related to all the other characteristics. Given these parameters, Aspinwall (1958) chose five characteristics for classifying goods:

1. *Replacement rate:* "The rate at which a good is purchased and consumed by users in order to provide the satisfaction a consumer expects from the product" (p. 437).
2. *Gross margin:* "The money sum which is the difference between the laid in cost and the final realized sales price" (p. 438).
3. *Adjustment:* "The services applied to goods in order to meet the exact needs of the consumer" (p. 439).
4. *Time of consumption:* "The measured time of consumption during which the good gives up the utility desired" (p. 440).

5. *Searching time:* "The measure of average time and distance from the retail store" (p. 440).

As a final result, Aspinwall (1958) produced the following system, which he called the "Characteristics of Goods Theory":

Color Classification

Characteristics	Red Goods	Orange Goods	Yellow Goods
Replacement rate	High	Medium	Low
Gross margin	Low	Medium	High
Adjustment	Low	Medium	High
Time of consumption	Low	Medium	High
Searching time	Low	Medium	High

In comparing the Copeland and Aspinwall classification systems, it appears that Copeland's "convenience goods" matches very well with Aspinwall's "red goods." Although the remaining matches are not as tight, "specialty goods" are similar to "yellow goods" and "shopping goods" are somewhat related to "orange goods."

Aspinwall, as did many of his predecessors in the commodity school, firmly believed that this approach would be the panacea for most of the marketing practitioners' problems. All that was required was the rather simple task of plugging the product into the classification system and then following the standard marketing directions for that category of goods. As Aspinwall (1958) wrote:

> The marketing characteristics of a product determine the most appropriate and economical method for distributing it. To fix its position on the scale, representing the variation in these characteristics, is to take the first major step toward understanding its marketing requirements. To know these characteristics is to be able to predict with a high degree of reliability how a product will be distributed, since most products conform to the pattern. Serious departure from the theoretical expectations will almost certainly indicate the need for change and improvement in distribution methods. These considerations apply both to physical distribution and to the parallel problem of communications including the choice of promotional media and appeals. (p. 435-436)

Although Aspinwall's classification system has not received as much scholarly support as the Parlin-Copeland system, Miracle (1965) did attempt to advance and refine Aspinwall's approach. Whereas Aspinwall delineated only the distribution and promotional implications of his classification system, Miracle proposed a modification to Aspinwall's orginal system and then discussed the product and pricing implications of this revised system.

As we review the history of the marketing discipline, we have noticed that periodically debates among several marketing scholars emerge in the academic literature. Usually these debates focus on a rather narrow, but nonetheless significant, conceptual point. Just such a debate surfaced in the commodity school during the late 1950s and early 1960s. The catalyst of this particular controversy was Richard Holton (1958), who maintained that the definitions of the categories of convenience goods, shopping goods, and specialty goods were in need of revision. According to Holton (1958), greater emphasis should be placed on the role of the consumer in order to differentiate between convenience goods and shopping goods:

> Since items which are shopping goods for some consumers may be convenience goods for others, convenience goods and shopping goods can be defined accurately only from the standpoint of the individual consumer. It may be sufficient to say that, for the individual consumer, convenience goods are those goods for which the probable gain from making price and quality comparison among alternative sellers is thought to be small relative to the consumer's appraisal of the searching costs in terms of time, money, and effort. Shopping goods then, are for the individual consumer, those goods for which the probable gain from making price and quality comparisons among alternative sellers is thought to be large relative to the consumer's appraisal of the searching costs in terms of time, money, and effort. (pp. 53-54)

The perceptive reader will undoubtedly note that Holton's emphasis on the consumer carefully weighing the benefits and costs of additional search for information is closely related to many of the later "search theories" that were developed in the consumer behavior literature (Newman 1977, Punj and Staelin 1983).

Holton also argued that specialty goods, in essence, were not a discrete category that could be clearly differentiated from the other two categories:

> Can specialty goods be distinguished from convenience goods and shopping goods on the basis of the individual consumer's outlook toward the good? . . . Here one must distinguish between the willingness to make a special effort, on the one hand, and the necessity of making that effort on the other . . . Would it not follow, then, that a distinguishing feature of the specialty good is the necessity of making a special purchasing effort, rather than just the willingness? The fact that it is necessary to make a special effort to buy the good in question must stem from a limited market demand . . . Specialty goods, if the above reasoning is justified, are the convenience or shopping goods which face such a limited market that outlets are relatively few, necessitating a "special purchasing effort" on the part of the buyers . . . Therefore, it would seem that the specialty-good classification overlaps both the other groups and

cannot be distinguished either from the shopping goods or from convenience goods. (Holton 1958, pp. 55-56).

Therefore, Holton was suggesting that one of Copeland's original three categories, the specialty goods, should be demoted to a secondary status in the classification system. It will probably come as no great surprise to the reader to hear that not everyone in the marketing theory community was enthralled with Holton's suggestion. After all, Copeland's three categories had survived for thirty-five years and had developed numerous devotees before Holton challenged it.

The sharpest counterattack was mounted by David Luck (1959), who believed that Holton should have placed more emphasis on the consumer's willingness to make a special effort and less emphasis on the necessity of this effort:

> The theory that Holton puts forth comprehends only the existing distribution of a good and the necessity of consumer shopping, both static phenomena. His theory does not explain the dynamics of consumer behavior or of marketers' objectives.
>
> In contrast, a theory that recognizes the willingness of consumers to make special purchasing efforts is explanatory, consumer oriented, and useful. Advertising and merchandising commonly are dedicated to creating specialty goods characteristics for a given brand or good. It would indeed be folly to exclude the "specialty" type of good from marketing theory and literature. (p. 64)

The next major entrant into this definitional dispute was Bucklin (1962), who sought to resolve the disagreement by proposing his own, somewhat modified, interpretation of Copeland's original system. Bucklin suggested that, as a first point of differentiation, a distinction should be made between "shopping goods" and "nonshopping goods":

> Shopping goods are those for which the consumer regularly formulates a new solution to his need each time it is aroused. They are goods whose suitability is determined through search before the consumer commits himself to each purchase. (p. 52)
>
> Turning now to nonshopping goods, one may define these as products for which the consumer is both willing and able to use stored solutions to the problem of finding a product to answer a need. (p. 52)

Then, according to Bucklin, the nonshopping goods may be further subdivided into convenience goods and specialty goods. To clarify the difference between convenience and specialty goods and to support the inclusion of specialty goods as a unique category, he offered the following rationale:

Clearly, where the consumer is indifferent to the precise item among a number of substitutes which he could buy, he will purchase the most accessible one and look no further. This is a convenience good. On the other hand, where the consumer recognizes only one brand of a product as capable of satisfying his needs, he will be willing to bypass more readily accessible substitutes in order to secure the wanted item. This is a specialty good. (p. 52)

As a result of Bucklin's influence, the three-pronged classification system of convenience, shopping, and specialty goods was once again firmly entrenched as the dominant perspective for commodity school theorists. However, as new concepts and theories evolved in marketing and also in other allied disciplines, marketing scholars continued to reanalyze and challenge this classification system. For example, Kaish (1967) attempted to apply Festinger's theory of cognitive dissonance from psychology to the commodity school in marketing. What captured Kaish's interest was the prior emphasis on the consumer's shopping effort. He perceived a potential flaw because:

> ...in singling out shopping effort as the prime consideration, these definitions fail to distinguish explicitly between two types of effort. There is the special physical effort that purchasers of specialty goods are willing to make in going out of their way to insist on a particular good, and there is the mental effort of pricing, comparing, and distinguishing among shopping goods. (pp. 28-29)

By incorporating the implications of the theory of cognitive dissonance, Kaish proposed yet another set of definitions for the three basic categories:

> Convenience goods are goods in which purchase is not important to the consumer, either because of low price, low durability, or low ego-involvement. Usually, there is consumer acceptance of a number of suitable substitutes for the utilities sought, and, as a result, there is a minimum of prepurchase anxiety that the purchase decision will later prove to be inappropriate and another would have been better.

> Shopping goods are goods that arouse high levels of prepurchase anxiety about the possible inappropriateness of the purchase. This anxiety can be allayed by the consumer through information-gathering and subsequent decision-making. These goods are high in economic and psychological importance, contain significant performance differences, and have physical qualities that are readily related to the performance characteristics...

> Specialty goods are goods that are economically or psychologically important enough and have different enough performance characteristics to qualify as shopping goods, but have physical qualities that are not readily related to the performance characteristics sought. In addition, the alternatives may be so limited that the consumer is forced to purchase a good that will be potentially unsatisfying. Prepurchase anxiety is high here also, but not readily reducible by shopping behavior. (p. 31)

The commodity school is particularly fascinating because marketing scholars seemingly never lose interest in it. After the flurry of activity in the decade of 1958-1967 by Holton, Luck, Bucklin, Kaish, and others, the outside observer might expect an extended, if not permanent, avoidance of this school of thought by marketing theorists. However, such was not the case because significant articles concerning the commodity school continued to surface during the 1970s and even into the 1980s.

Ramond and Assael (1974) suggested that the prior classification systems all had significant deficiencies. As an improvement, they proposed that three different approaches to product classification should be explored as fertile ground for future theorizing:

> All three find it necessary to define a product as a relation between two kinds of information. First, they must view the product as a relation between physical ingredients and psychological responses (a psychophysical definition). Here a measure of classification might be developed by clustering techniques. Second, they must define the product in terms of consumer actions and channel response (or what might be termed a distributive velocity definition). We later propose that such measures might be the lag between factory shipment and retail sales. Third, they need a relation between awareness, attitude change or other communication effects, and purchase behavior (or what might be defined as a mental velocity measure). (pp. 348-349)

By concentrating on these three approaches, Ramond and Assael reiterated the uncertainty among commodity theorists regarding exactly what dimensions should be used to classify products. Should it be from the perspective of the consumer or the producer/distributor? If from the consumer's viewpoint, should it be based on physical shopping effort or mental effort devoted to brand comparison and dissonance reduction?

The next significant step forward was provided by Holbrook and Howard in 1977 when they challenged the traditional three categories originally proposed by Copeland. Although other scholars had disagreed about the definitions of these three categories of convenience, shopping, and specialty goods, Holbrook and Howard suggested that a fourth category, preference goods, should be added to the basic classification system. They combined three dimensions — (1) product characteristics (magnitude of purchase and clarity of characteristics), (2) consumer characteristics (ego-involvement and specific self-confidence), and (3) consumer responses (physical shopping and mental effort) — to create the classification of goods diagram shown on pg. 45.

Clearly, the intention of Holbrook and Howard was to reconstruct the classification system by stressing the importance of the linkage between consumer actions and marketers' activities. Referring to their revised categories, they wrote:

> In particular, it distinguishes between two dimensions representing the consumer's utilization of marketing inputs. The top-bottom split continues to

Holbrook-Howard Commodity Classification System

	High clarity	Low clarity
	High self-confidence	Low specific self-confidence
	Mental effort during shopping via brand comparisons	Mental effort prior to shopping via information seeking
	No brand insistence	Brand insistence
Low magnitude Low ego-involvement Low physical shopping effort	CONVENIENCE GOODS	PREFERENCE GOODS
High magnitude High ego-involvement High physical shopping effort	SHOPPING GOODS	SPECIALTY GOODS

represent the degree to which the consumer saves his physical shopping effort by relying on intensive patterns of distribution to make the product readily available ... But the left-right distinction refers to the timing of mental effort in arriving at a brand choice. To the extent that a product falls on the right-hand side of this breakdown, a consumer may seek information from advertising, word of mouth, or other sources prior to the shopping trip. This implies a reliance by the consumer on the seller's promotional efforts and the existence of this reliance for both durables (specialty goods) and nondurables (preference goods). (pp. 214-215)

Enis and Roering (1980) adopted the four-category system proposed by Holbrook and Howard, but they sought to improve it by addressing more explicitly the question of consumer perspective versus marketer perspective. Given the emergence of the interactive or dyadic viewpoint in marketing, they asserted that "a classification scheme that incorporates both the buyer's and the seller's perspective holds the greatest promise for illuminating the exchange process, since exchange only occurs when there is sufficient congruence between these perspectives" (1980, p. 187). Therefore, from the marketer's perspective, they said the four categories could be formed based on the two dimensions of product offering differentiation (the capacity to develop perceived variation among products) and marketing program differentiation (the capacity to individualize the elements of a marketing program to better serve divergent groups within a market). Likewise, from the consumer's perspective, the two relevant dimensions are perceived risk (the belief that the consequences of a purchase decision may be more unpleasant or unfavorable than the buyer perceives them to be) and expected effort (the amount of effort the buyer must exert to complete the exchange transaction).

By combining the marketer's and consumer's perspectives, Enis and Roering developed a new set of definitions for the four categories:

Enis-Roering Commodity Classification System

Specialty products are those bundles of attributes which the buyer perceives might involve high risk with respect to performance and/or interpersonal influence, and are worthy of significant shopping effort; thus the marketer of such products can differentiate both the product offering and its marketing program.

Shopping products are those attribute bundles which the buyer perceives are not likely to involve high performance or interpersonal risks, but are worth considerable shopping effort; thus the marketer's task is to differentiate via the marketing program a commodity—a core concept and product offering rather similar to that of competitors.

Convenience products are those attribute bundles perceived to be low risk and expected to be worth little effort, thus the marketer must efficiently produce and distribute a product which is difficult to differentiate in terms of either product offering or marketing program.

Preference products are those attribute bundles which the buyer perceives to possibly involve high risk, but expects to exert only limited shopping effort; thus the marketer can differentiate the product offering, but must then mass market that offering efficiently. (1980, p. 188)

The four-category commodity classification system (shopping, convenience, specialty, and preference) was clarified in a subsequent article by

Murphy and Enis (1986). Using the dimensions of effort and risk related to price, Murphy and Enis argued that their classification system could be applied to all marketing transactions, products, services, or ideas. They provided the following definitions for their four categories:

> *Convenience products:* "... convenience products are defined as lowest in terms of both effort and risk. That is, the consumer will not spend much money or time in purchasing these products, nor does he/she perceive significant levels of risk in making a selection" (p. 25).

> *Preference products:* "These products are slightly higher on the effort dimension and much higher on risk. In fact, the distinction between convenience and preference products is primarily one of buyer perceived risk. The reason that the consumer perceives this higher level of risk is often through the efforts of the marketer, particularly branding and advertising" (p. 26).

> *Shopping products:* "The name implies much about the characteristics of these products. Buyers are willing to spend a significant amount of time and money in searching for and evaluating these products. Increased levels of risk are also perceived by consumers for these high involvement products" (p. 26).

> *Specialty products:* "Those products that are defined to be highest on both the risk and effort dimensions ... are called specialty products. The major distinction between shopping and specialty products is on the basis of effort, not risk. The monetary price is usually higher, as is the time ... At the limit, the buyer will accept no substitutes" (p. 29).

A particularly fascinating aspect of the commodity school is that scholars in this area always emphasize the potential managerial importance of developing a "marketing management cookbook." Murphy and Enis (1986) are no exception:

> One purpose of any product classification scheme is to guide managerial decision making. A comprehensive and consistent marketing strategy should be based upon product characteristics as perceived by buyers. The product classification suggested here provides a managerial road map for strategy development: buyers' perceptions, marketers' objectives and basic strategy, and specific strategies for each element of the marketing mix. (p. 35)

In summary, the commodity school has been one of the most robust schools of marketing thought. The possible development of a comprehensive framework that links marketing mix decisions to product categories is intriguing to marketing scholars and practitioners. Even though some critical definitional issues are unresolved, this school has generated many stimulating concepts that continue to interest current marketing theorists.

EVALUATION OF THE COMMODITY SCHOOL

STRUCTURE: Are the concepts properly defined and integrated to form a strong nomological network?

Although the basic categories first proposed by Copeland in 1923 have undergone remarkably little revision in over sixty years, we are still searching for definitional clarity for the terms of convenience, shopping, specialty, and preference goods. Should these definitions be based on the physical properties of the goods, or on the behavior of the consumers? If the latter option is preferable, should the focus be on the consumer's mental effort or on his/her physical effort?

In recent years there is a movement toward adopting four categories by adding preference goods to the original three categories. However, are we likely to witness an "intellectual battle" for the inclusion of this new category, much like what we saw in the late 1950s with the dispute over the suggested removal of the specialty goods category?

The commodity school seems to have the potential to establish good structure, but it is not there yet. Perhaps what is needed to firmly establish the definitions of the commodity categories is a special session at one of the marketing discipline's major academic conferences highlighted by several papers that specifically scrutinize the vitality of these definitions. If a reasonable level of agreement is achieved at this type of session, the commodity school will have a stronger foundation for future theorizing.

Our score on structure = 3.

SPECIFICATION: Are the relationships specified in a manner to delimit hypotheses or are they highly contingent?

This metatheory criterion presents major problems for the commodity school because, if the categories of goods are defined based on consumers' behaviors, how should a good be classified if Person A's behavior suggests that it is a convenience good and Person B's behavior indicates it is a specialty good? In other words, the specification of hypotheses becomes *contingent* upon the diversity and individual differences among consumers. If only the majority or average behaviors are used for the good's classification, do we simply ignore the behavior of the minority or the "outlier" consumers and hope they will respond to the marketing programs designed for the majority? This is certainly not a new issue because Converse and Huegy in 1940 noted:

> The line of demarcation between the various types of goods is not always clear cut . . . However, the fact that the two classes of goods are not clearly differentiated does not mean that the distinction is useless. The great majority of people buy many articles in the same way. (p. 145)

Beyond the potential variability among consumers, there is also the question of the possible change in any one consumer's behavior over time. For example, a consumer may regard a product, such as jogging shoes, as a shopping good for the first purchase of that product. However, over time, loyalties may develop and the consumer may treat the purchase of jogging shoes as a specialty goods task. This common movement of a consumer through stages based on increased learning and experience is closely related to the Howard and Sheth (1969) categories of extensive problem solving, limited problem solving, and routinized response behavior. Thus, it is possible, assuming the acceptance of the four basic categories of commodities, that *all* products could be classified in *all* four categories. That is, any product would have to be placed in all four categories if some consumers regard it as a convenience good, other consumers treat it as a specialty good, still others believe it is a shopping good, and finally some consumers see the product as a preference good. As a result of this potentiality, it is fairly obvious that the hypotheses for marketing of any product must be highly contingent based on the specific targeted group of consumers.

It may, therefore, be necessary to specify classifications with criteria that are invariant or noncontingent. This may require abandoning the consumer perspective and utilizing some other perspective such as physical flow of goods, turnover ratios, store locations, and profit margins. For example, products that demand a high degree of shopping effort for consumers will have a low turnover ratio. At the same time, products with a high degree of perceived risk will require the retailers to perform a number of value-added services resulting in high margin ratios. In other words, it may be possible to classify products into specialty, shopping, convenience, and preference goods based on less contingent but highly correlated surrogates such as turnover and margin ratios.

Our score on specification = 4.

TESTABILITY: Are the operational definitions provided to ensure testability and intersubjective consensus?

Although numerous scholars have debated extensively the proper conceptual definitions of the various commodity categories, very little attention except for Aspinwall's efforts has been directed at establishing operational definitions for these categories. Specifically, how do we measure "shopping effort" and distinguish between "limited" and "considerable" levels of this shopping effort? Also, how do we measure "risk"? Unfortunately, most writers in the commodity school have apparently presumed that the inclusion of examples of products that fit into each category is a sufficient demonstration of the categories' operational definitions. Examples are helpful, but they clearly do not satisfy the requirement for operational definitions.

Obviously, what is needed are fairly structured measurement scales with which to quantify the indicators of each underlying force that differentiates one commodity from the other. For example, physical shopping effort might be measured by the number of stores customers visit before making a purchase decision and the time spent at each store. Similarly, we might measure perceived risk toward a product class by creating a psychometric scale that measures risk toward the product class.

Our score on testability = 3.

EMPIRICAL SUPPORT: **What is the degree of confirmation in terms of empirical support?**

Apparently, there has been little, if any, attempt to actually test the commodity theory. Several excellent research studies would be feasible in this area. First, a researcher interested in the commodity school could develop a set of operational definitions for the goods categories and then test the validity and reliability of these definitions using a cross-sectional study of products and consumers. Second, a theory related to the managerial relevance of the commodity classification system could be created and then used to modify the marketing mix for a test product to determine whether market performance for the product could be enhanced.

At the same time, there is ample empirical evidence of the use of the commodity approach in marketing practice at both the manufacturing and the retail distribution levels. Furthermore, the classification is as commonly prevalent in practice as the concept of upper-middle-lower socioeconomic classes is in social stratification. In short, there is considerable empirical support but it is not scientifically tested or validated.

Our score on empirical support = 6.

RICHNESS: **How comprehensive and generalizable is the theory?**

As noted earlier, the commodity theory has demonstrated remarkable vitality with over seventy years of rather consistent attention from marketing theorists. A strong argument for this enduring interest can be found in the potential richness of the theory. Many scholars have apparently felt that, once the rough edges are removed, the commodity school could be truly robust. However, while the possible richness of the commodity school is undeniable, several rather formidable obstacles remain that must be dealt with before this criterion is satisfied. First, the main emphasis in previous theorizing has been consistently on consumer goods. Very little attention has been directed at the applicability of the commodity theory to other categories of goods, such as industrial goods, services, and social goods.

Second, if the basis for category definition is to be the behavior of consumers, most scholars implicitly assume that this is typical "American" behavior. However, it is probable that the behavior of consumers varies across diverse cultures, suggesting that the classifications must be adjusted accordingly. As global markets become increasingly critical for corporate survival, this issue must be addressed to ensure greater richness for the commodity school.

Third, can the commodity school cope with changes in behavior based on the introduction of new technology, such as the growth of electronic shopping? The richness of the theory will be substantially improved if it can be shown that the theory can accommodate the impact of new technology and still maintain the tripartite classification.

Fourth, how generalizable are the results that are obtained from the extensive study of just one specific product class? This is a question that has long perplexed marketing scholars, as evidenced by C. S. Duncan's comment in 1921:

> Thus, one may trace the course of cotton, or wheat, or corn, or cattle, or steel, or leather, or any other commodity bought and sold on the market from its source to the consumer, and study the commercial problems connected with it. This will give a specialized knowledge that is invaluable so far as the specific commodity is concerned. Such as analysis will not, however, demonstrate broad principles. From such a basis of knowledge, one cannot know for himself why there is an organized exchange for cotton and wheat and not for wool; he cannot know whether staple goods can be advertised as well as style goods. One may know thoroughly that one subject, but he cannot generalize from it. A single commodity is only an illustration, and it may be a pertinent and vivid one, too, but it will not establish a principle. (p. 8)

What seems to be needed is a conscious effort to extend the traditional classification into industrial products, services, and social programs. Perhaps this may be easier to do by utilizing the more generic classification and the underlying criteria proposed by Aspinwall. In other words, can we classify industrial products, services, and social programs into red, orange, and yellow categories based on such criteria as replacement rate, gross margin, adjustment, time of consumption, and searching time? A little reflection suggests that except for gross margin, it is possible to apply Aspinwall's generic classification to all these sectors of the economy.

Our score on richness = 8.

SIMPLICITY: **How easy is it to communicate and implement the theory?**

This criterion may be the commodity school's strongest point. As mentioned previously, commodity theorists have always been enthusiastic about the possibility of creating a "marketing cookbook" based on a commodity classification system. The leading proponent of this trend was Aspinwall (1958), who suggested what specific forms of distribution and promotion should accompany various types of goods. Of course, in recent years, much less attention has been given to developing a set of marketing guidelines directly related to product categories. But if such a "cookbook" could be developed, it could be very beneficial to marketing practitioners who seem to be generally more interested in "how to do" than in "why to do" issues.

Our score on simplicity = 8.

Table 2.1 gives a summary of scores we have given to the commodity school and our rationale for them. As can be seen, the commodity school performs best in terms of relevance (pragmatics), next best in terms of reality (semantics), and very poorly with respect to organization (syntax). Therefore, scholars interested in the commodity school of thought may want to apply their talents toward the syntax aspects of the theory.

Table 2.1 Evaluation of the Commodity School*

Criterion	Rationale	Score
Structure	What criterion to use for classification is the biggest weakness	3
Specification	Highly contingent at present but has the potential to be specified on a noncontingent basis	4
Testability	Extremely weak on operational definitions except Aspinwall	3
Empirical support	Good empirical support but not scientifically tested for its validity	6
Richness	Extremely rich and capable of encompassing all areas of marketing	8
Simplicity	Very easy to communicate and implement in general	8
	TOTAL	32

* *Scores range from 1 (poor) to 10 (excellent).*

THE FUNCTIONAL SCHOOL OF THOUGHT

The commodity school proved to be extremely popular, especially with many of the earlier marketing theorists. However, not everyone who was actively involved in shaping the discipline of marketing in the early 1900s was a hearty supporter of the commodity school. In fact, a formidable group of scholars, probably equal in size if not larger, convened to form what came to be known as the functional school of marketing. Like the commodity theorists, the functional theorists also appreciated the need for marketing to attain academic legitimacy and to demonstrate the practical applicability of marketing. However, while the commodity school chose to develop a classification system based on products or the objects of exchange, the functional school decided instead to focus on the activities needed to execute marketing transactions. Thus, these two early schools stand in sharp contrast, with the commodity school based on the "what" element of marketing and the functional school founded on the "how" element of marketing.

While there is some confusion over who should be deemed the "father" of the functional school, marketing historians generally credit Arch Shaw (1912) with launching the functional perspective in an article in the *Quarterly Journal of Economics*. This article is particularly interesting because stylistically it is dramatically different from the typical article published in modern marketing journals. Although Shaw attacked a variety of issues in the sixty pages of the article, he actually devoted only about ten pages to the discussion of marketing functions. Shaw introduced the first classification of marketing functions by writing:

> To understand what seems to be a present tendency to go around the middleman as well as to consider the problem of the merchant-producer with reference to the use of middlemen in distribution, it is necessary to analyze the functions performed by the middleman. Roughly the general functions may be listed as follows:
>
> 1. Sharing the risk.
> 2. Transporting the goods.
> 3. Financing the operations.
> 4. Selling (communication of ideas about the goods).
> 5. Assembling, assorting, and reshipping. (Shaw 1912, p. 731)

L. D. H. Weld, an early marketing scholar who published numerous influential books and articles during the emerging years of marketing, wrote an article in 1917 in which he offered an alternative classification of functions. According to Weld (1917), these functions are not necessarily performed only by middlemen as suggested by Shaw:

1. *Assembling:* "The term 'assembling,' as used here, does not mean the actual physical transportation of commodities from one place to another, but rather the seeking out of sources, the making of business connections whereby commodities may be bought, and the study of market conditions so that they may be bought at the lowest prices possible. Assembling therefore involves all the services connected with buying" (p. 307).

2. *Storing:* "Storing, in its broad sense, means the holding of stocks of goods at convenient points" (p. 308).

3. *Assumption of risks:* "Inasmuch as commission merchants, brokers, and agents do not take title to goods, they assume very few of the merchandising risks; but practically every other middleman, as well as the manufacturer, especially when he produces for stock, has to consider the element of risk. The principal kinds of merchandising risks may be enumerated as follows: (1) price fluctuation, (2) destruction by fire, (3) deterioration in quality, (4) style changes, and (5) financial risks" (p. 311).

4. *Rearrangement:* "Rearrangement of commodities involves sorting, grading, breaking up large quantities into small units, packing, etc." (p. 311).

5. *Selling:* "Selling is the most important of the marketing functions, as well as the most costly one to perform. Salaries of salesmen (plus traveling expenses in many cases) constitute the most important single item in merchant's expense account. Selling involves both creating a demand for the goods and getting the goods into the hands of the purchaser. Though both of these phases of selling are performed largely by personal salesmen, demand creation is being accomplished more and more by means of advertising" (p. 312).

6. *Transportation:* "As explained by Shaw, merchandise middlemen formerly attended to the actual carriage of goods from one place to another more than they do now; but this function has been largely taken over by railroads and other transportation agencies that are specialized middlemen in this field. Transportation, however, is still an important function of merchants" (p. 313).

As with most other schools of thought, critics surfaced in the functional school to offer critiques of prior contributions from such writers as Shaw (1912) and Weld (1917). One such critic was H. B. Vanderblue, who, in 1921, suggested that there was a potential risk of isolating each functional component, when in fact the functions were often interdependent:

> Sale is frequently dependent upon standardization; finance upon storing; risk upon selling and financing; and there is the close interrelationship of transporting, risking, storing, and financing, illustrated in the use of the order bill of lading and the warehouse receipt as collateral. (Vanderblue 1921, p. 683)

The functional school proved to be very popular. Franklin Ryan in 1935 produced a review of the writings in the functional area and discovered that at least twenty-six books and articles had been published that dealt extensively with marketing functions. As evidence of the disparity of opinions regarding the selection of appropriate functions among these early scholars, Ryan found that fifty-two different functions had been proposed by various authors. Ryan summarized the state of art in the functional school as follows:

. . . the lists of functions presented by most of these writers on marketing are usually meant to be brief summaries of functional categories and are not organized to give a complete and detailed picture of the distributive process. Most of these lists seek to find answers to two implied general questions in regard to the productive-distributive process. These two implied questions are:

1.   What general functions add time, place, ownership, possession, and other kinds of utilities (want-satisfying powers) to physical goods as they gradually move toward the point where they are sold to final customers?

2.   What distinctive functions are performed by entrepreneurs or business executives and their employees who carry on the work of distribution?

In answer to the first questions, these books and articles typically list five functions, as follows: (1) assembling, (2) storing, (3) standardization, (4) transportation, and (5) selling. The distinctive functions of the functionaries in the productive-distributive process are usually listed as: (6) the assumption of risks, and (7) financing, which is the providing of capital for the marketing enterprise. (Ryan 1935, pp. 211-212)

The next major contribution to the functional school following Ryan's review article was provided by Earl Fullbrook in 1940. Fullbrook (1940) was rather critical of what had been accomplished in the functional school:

In spite of the length of time the functional concept has been in use and in spite of its wide currency at the present time, it appears that little has been accomplished since the early years toward any significant refining of the concept. It is apparent from any careful survey of the material in the field that there is no very clear-cut and generally accepted interpretation of, or method of handling, marketing functions. The writer believes the functional approach can be a very useful device but contends that a great deal must be done in further developing it before its real possibilities can be realized. (p. 299)

Fullbrook's main goal in this article was to argue that the functional school should recognize the distinction between a functional requirement and the actual performance of that function:

A function of marketing should be regarded strictly as a step, task, or service to be performed in getting goods from producers to consumers. This is in accord with the usual definition. That the performance of a function requires activity is granted. That it is logical to regard a function as an activity to be performed is also granted. To so regard it, however, increases the probability that attention will center upon the activities performed instead of upon the nature and extent of the job which has to be done and gives rise to the activities . . . By regarding a function solely as a task or service that requires performance, it can be analyzed entirely distinct from its actual performance and if the functional treatment is to yield significant results, such procedure is essential . . . Only after gaining a clear understanding of the nature of a task and of what its performance requires, can one evaluate agencies or methods that are used, or might be used, in doing the job. (p. 234)

Ten years after the Fullbrook article, Edmund McGarry (1950) offered yet another review of previous classification systems for the functional school. And, like his predecessors, he maintained that improvement was still needed before marketing theorists could be satisfied with the content of the functional school:

> From the beginning of the systematic study of marketing, a great deal of attention has been given to the analysis of marketing functions. A large number of articles have been published on the subject in various professional journals, and practically every textbook on marketing attempts to make some use of such an analysis in its presentation. Yet, despite all these writings, there is little agreement as to what the functions are or as to the purpose of defining them. (p. 263)

To remedy these shortcomings, McGarry presented his own recommended classification system, which was composed of the following six functions:

1. The *contactual function,* which has to do with the searching-out of potential customers or suppliers and the making of contact with them.
2. The *merchandising function,* which comprises the various activities undertaken to adapt the product to the users' ideas of what is wanted.
3. The *pricing function,* which has to do with the prices at which goods are offered or at which they will be accepted.
4. The *propaganda function,* which includes all the methods used to persuade the potential users to select the particular product and to make them like the product once they have it.
5. The *physical distribution function,* which comprises the transportation and storage of goods.
6. The *termination function,* which has to do with the actual change in custody of and responsibility for the goods and is the culmination of the process. (p. 279)

At this point we will briefly pursue a tangential point closely related to the development of the functional school. Many marketing students tend to believe that the so-called Four Ps of marketing, which were popularized by McCarthy (1960), were a revolutionary breakthrough for the marketing discipline. Obviously, however, the Four Ps of product, price, promotion, and place are actually only derivatives from earlier classification systems presented by functional school theorists, such as Shaw, Weld, Ryan, and especially McGarry.

Unlike the commodity school, which has been the subject of several excellent papers in the past decade, the functional school has received very little attention since McGarry's 1950 article. The one noteworthy exception is an article by Lewis and Erickson (1969) in which they attempted to link together the functional and systems perspectives. As to the classification of marketing functions, Lewis and Erickson maintained that marketing had really only two broad functions—to obtain demand and to service demand. Then, as subsets of each of these functions, they argued there were several activities. Under the obtaining demand function, they listed the activities of advertising, personal selling, sales promotion, product planning, and pricing. Activities connected to the servicing demand function were warehousing, inventory management, transportation, and order processing and handling. With respect to the systems approach to marketing, they concluded:

> ... marketing is a system within the total system of a firm. It is a man-made, open system which attempts to move toward a closed system by feedback-control. It faces internal restrictions of policy, goals, and finances from within the total system of the firm and external restrictions from the environment in such forms as governments, competitors, and customers. (p. 13)

Combining the functional and systems perspectives, they asserted that the functions of obtaining and servicing demand are actually the output objects of the marketing system, while the previously mentioned activities are the input objects of the marketing system. Although their article could have benefited from a more extensive explanation of the most salient points, Lewis and Erickson should be commended for attempting to reveal the relationships between two distinct perspectives. Perhaps if more scholars endeavored to review the similarities and dissimilarities of two or more schools of thought, it would serve to open up new ways of thinking about these various perspectives. Quite often the marketing discipline suffers not from a paucity of interest in theory, but from a lack of cross-disciplinary viewpoints.

EVALUATION OF THE FUNCTIONAL SCHOOL

STRUCTURE: **Are the concepts properly defined and integrated to form a strong nomological network?**

The functional school's major strength with respect to structure is identification, listing, and classification of various functions to be performed by marketing. These functional lists do tend to identify value-added services that provide time, place, and possession utilities to the product or service. Although the functional school seems strong on the definitions, it is weak on forming a nomological network among the concepts. In other words, it does not go beyond the listing and categorization of functions. For example, what functions can be eliminated because they are redundant or do not add values in proportion to the incremental costs of performing them? Similarly, what are the interdependent or complementary relationships among various functions? Do they behave like the domino effect or are they capable of standing on their own? Finally, how can one shift functions from the manufacturer to the middleman to the consumer or vice versa?

Perhaps it might be advantageous to do a historical investigation of the consolidation and shifting of functions in specific product categories and assess how functions relate to one another as an interdependent system. For example, how far is the shift toward self-service or "do it yourself" likely to go before the pendulum begins to shift the other way? Or how much of time, place, and possession utilities can be integrated in product design and manufacturing to eliminate the need for any middlemen?

Our score on structure = 5.

SPECIFICATION: Are the relationships specified in a manner to delimit hypotheses or are they highly contingent?

It is interesting to note that specification issues in the functional school of thought have been limited to understanding the impact of each function rather than the relationships between functions. For example, we have a number of hypotheses related to price elasticity, advertising effectiveness, and salesforce management, but we have no hypotheses for such issues as which promotional activities or functions are better suited with a particular distribution system. This is in sharp contrast to the commodity school of thought, which has at least attempted to suggest hypotheses across marketing activities once a product is categorized as a specialty, shopping, or convenience good. Also, it is important to remember that most hypotheses at the functional level have been generated more through the managerial school proponents rather than directly by the functional school proponents. In our opinion, the more exciting aspects of future research in the functional school of thought remain with issues such as the interdependence and shifting of functions.

Our score on specification = 3.

TESTABILITY: Are the operational definitions provided to ensure testability and intersubjective consensus?

The functional school ranks higher on this criterion. Most of the functions can be operationally measured and the methods used to measure reality have strong face validity. For example, functions such as assembling, sorting, transportation, storing, financing, and so on are overt behavior measures that result in less disagreement than more psychological variables such as risk and effort proposed in the commodity school. Indeed, this criterion may be the strong point for the functional school's popularity; it is measurable and functions can be catalogued with agreed-on measures.

Our score on testability = 7.

EMPIRICAL SUPPORT: What is the degree of confirmation in terms of empirical support?

Similar to the commodity school, the empirical support for the functional school comes from observations, case histories, and anecdotes. Marketing organizations do tend to be configured to perform various tasks identified as marketing functions. At the same time, there is no strong scientific evidence about the impact of shifting or consolidation of functions on market behavior. What is scientifically tested and known are the findings related to each specialized function such as advertising, promotion, financing, shipping, insurance, and the like.

Our score on empirical support = 7.

RICHNESS: How comprehensive and generalizable is the theory?

The functional school is very rich. It has identified major categories of functions as well as individual subsets in each major category applicable across all products, services, and markets. Although functions such as storing and transportation may not be appropriate for intangible services, the functional classification is still fundamentally relevant. In other words, the six major functions (contactual, merchandising, pricing, propaganda, physical distribution, and termination) proposed by McGarry (1950) seem to be relevant across all products and services. Therefore, we must conclude that the functional school of thought is very strong on the richness dimension.

Our score on richness = 8.

SIMPLICITY: How easy is it to communicate and implement the theory?

The functional school is extremely easy to communicate because it is highly descriptive and has a strong reality base, and readers can personally relate to their own experiences. A functional marketing organization is also simple to implement. In fact, most marketing organizations tend to be functional. It is rumored that at Procter and Gamble, the functional organization generated the title "marketing manager" for the person in charge of coordinating and integrating specialized marketing functions such as advertising, physical distribution, and sales force.

However, the functional school has not attempted to provide guidelines or hypotheses about how these functions ought to be organized or implemented. Each marketing organization has tended to learn on a trial and error or ad hoc basis rather than being driven by a well tested recipe.

Our score on simplicity = 8.

Table 2.2 provides a summary of scores given to the functional school and the rationale for them. As can be easily noted, the functional school performs much better with respect to the relevance (pragmatic) and reality (semantic) criteria but performs poorly on the organization (syntax) criterion.

In that respect, the functional school is similar to the commodity school. Indeed, this similarity makes sense because both theories were based on extensive observation of marketing practice. They were, therefore, inductively driven rather than deductively driven, resulting in better scores on the pragmatic side but lower scores on the syntax side.

Table 2.2 Evaluation of the Functional School*

Criterion	Rationale	Score
Structure	Strong on definitions but weak on interrelationships among functions	5
Specification	Some specification at each functional level but lacking in shifting and consolidation of functions	3
Testability	Good on testability because operational measures are overt behavioral scales	7
Empirical support	Very good empirical support in general but lacking in scientific validation	7
Richness	Very rich and can easily encompass all domains of marketing	8
Simplicity	Very easy to communicate and implement within a function but relationship between functions is more difficult	8
	TOTAL	38

* *Scores range from 1 (poor) to 10 (excellent).*

THE REGIONAL SCHOOL OF THOUGHT

The regional school of thought is often overlooked when the subject of marketing theory is discussed. The reasons for this school's lack of popularity are difficult to identify, but it does appear that, with E. T. Grether's 1983 article in the *Journal of Marketing* special theory issue, there may be an increased awareness of and interest in this intriguing theoretical perspective.

To provide the uninitiated reader with a quick introduction to the regional school of thought, we may say that regional theorists perceived marketing as a form of economic activity designed to bridge the geographic, or spatial, gaps between buyers and sellers. While regional theorists certainly agreed that the goods being exchanged were important to study (the commodity school) and the activities used to facilitate exchanges were worthy of investigation (the functional school), they felt more attention should be paid to the role of the physical separations between buyers and sellers. Thus, they were fascinated by questions such as "What role does distance play in a consumer's decision to patronize store A rather than store B?" and "How can we explain the flow of goods among various geographical regions that have diverse resources and needs?"

In some ways, the regional school of thought is difficult to encapsulate. On the whole, however, the regional perspective has, throughout its history, been rather quantitatively driven with extensive utilization of mathematical formulas and data. Also, the regional school has been promoted and nurtured by a rather small group of scholars who have tended to remain closely affiliated with this perspective for most of their academic careers. Finally, the regional school is not really a creation of the marketing discipline but is instead an offshoot from earlier work done in the fields of geography and economics that examined the interplay between economic activity and physical space.

Whereas the commodity and the functional schools surfaced in the second decade of the twentieth century, the regional school did not emerge until the 1930s. Although E. T. Grether had begun to adopt the regional perspective in his economics course entitled "Theory of Domestic Trade" at the University of California, Berkeley, in the 1930s (Grether 1983), the publication of William J. Reilly's book *Law of Retail Gravitation* in 1931 was probably the main stimulus for the growth of the regional approach in marketing.

Reilly's goal was to explain the relative attractiveness of two different cities' shopping areas for those consumers who lived in a town between these two cities. According to Reilly, the following formula provided the solution:

$$\frac{B_a}{B_b} = \left(\frac{P_a}{P_b}\right)\left(\frac{D_b}{D_a}\right)^2$$

where:

B_a = the proportion of the trade from the intermediate city attracted by city A

B_b = the proportion attracted by city B

P_a = the population of city A

P_b = the population of city B

D_a = the distance from the intermediate town to city A

D_b = the distance from the intermediate town to city B

Therefore, based on this formula, a consumer forms a choice of desirable shopping areas using the two factors of population of the alternative cities (a surrogate measure of the number and quality of retail stores) and the distance from the two cities.

Reilly's method captured the interest of P. D. Converse, who actually conducted numerous tests of Reilly's so-called law of retail gravitation. Although Converse found Reilly's approach quite useful, he also proposed his own modifications in the form of "new laws of retail gravitation." One of Converse's (1949) main contributions was the development of a formula to determine the boundaries of a trading center's trade area:

$$D_b = \frac{D_{ab}}{1 + \sqrt{P_a / P_b}}$$

where:

D_b = the breaking point between city A and city B in miles from B

D_{ab} = the distance separating city A from city B

P_b = the population of city B

P_a = the population of city A

As to the usefulness of identifying a town's trade area, Converse (1949, p. 380) wrote :

> Once the trade area is determined, the merchants know where to concentrate their merchandising efforts, and the newspapers know the territories which they should cultivate intensively. To illustrate, a department store was advertising over a considerable area. Its attention was called to the formula for determining the town's trade area. The area was computed and the store found that it was spending much of its advertising appropriation outside its trade area. By concentrating its advertising inside the trade area, it experienced a considerable increase in sales with no increase in advertising expenditures.

This stream of research generated by Reilly and Converse received still more attention from David Huff (1964). Like his predecessors, Huff proposed another model to predict shopping patterns:

$$P_{ij} = \frac{S_j / T_{ij}^{\lambda}}{\sum_{j=1}^{n} S_j / T_{ij}^{\lambda}}$$

where:

P_{ij} = the probability of a consumer at a given point of origin i traveling to a particular shopping center j

S_j = the size of a shopping center j (measured in terms of square footage of selling area devoted to the sale of a particular class of goods)

T_{ij} = the travel time involved in getting from a consumer's travel base i to a given shopping center j

λ = a parameter to be estimated empirically to reflect the effect of travel time on various kinds of shopping trips

In comparing the later work of Huff to the earlier works of Reilly and Converse, we can highlight specific advances that demonstrate a greater degree of sophistication in this analysis of retail trading areas. First, Huff moved to eliminate the surrogate measure of population and instead focus on the actual size of the shopping center for that particular good. Second, Huff recognized that, given the complexity of modern metropolitan transportation systems, consumers concentrated more on travel time rather than on actual distance from alternative shopping sites.

Within the regional school, some scholars chose to shift the focus from the retailing sector to the wholesaling sector. Probably the leading theorist who considered the effects of physical space on wholesaling institutions was David A. Revzan. In his 1961 book, *Wholesaling in Marketing Organization*, he provided the following overview of his approach to regional variable analysis:

> Area structure, in its present content, has reference to the extent to which there are to be found systematic patterns of relationships between the various components of the wholesaling sector and the pertinent spatial units. The initial impact arises from the spatial gaps between where supplies of basic raw materials can be made commercially accessible and the locational patterns of the using manufacturing industries and related business. These initial impacts are enhanced further by the geographic layout of the transportation system by means of which such gaps are bridged. A second level of structure arises in the patterning of spatial arrangements between various components of the wholesale middlemen agency structure. Further spatial arrangements of retailing agencies and of ultimate consumers act as modifying influences at the other end of the commodity flows. (pp. 74-75)

In an effort to move closer to a theory of wholesale area structure, Revzan (1961) proposed that eight factors affect the size of a wholesale market area:

1. *Product weight relative to value:* "Where transportation costs are a small percentage of the total value of the product because the products' value is high relative to its bulk and weight, the supply and distribution areas may be expected to have wider boundaries than if the reverse were the case" (p. 98).

2. *Relative perishability:* "Where such protective devices as canning, fast freezing, and storage are not available or are differentially available, perishability restricts the size of both the supply and distribution areas" (p. 98).

3. *Product differentiation techniques:* "To the extent that manufacturers are successful through their marketing programs in establishing strong national brands for their products, to that extent will the areas of distribution for these products be widened" (p. 98).

4. *Factors affecting plant location:* "The net resultant of the operation of such factors is the differentiation of the orientation of plant locations at sites accessible to raw materials sources because of perishability, labor supply, and transportation cost factors, for example; to consuming marketing sites because of cost factors, size of market, customer preferences for freshness, or for similar reasons; at intermediate locations because of the balancing of inbound and outbound cost factors against the advantages of an intermediate location; or on the so-called footloose basis because of the desire to maximize the amenities aspect of location against the economic factors" (p. 99).

5. *Price and price policies:* "In uncontrolled, organized markets, differential prices become . . . the primary determinants of potential supply and distribution areas. For unorganized markets, price and price differentials are much more difficult to determine, the competitive structure of the industry has a marked effect upon the boundaries of the wholesale trading area" (p. 99).

6. *Transportation rates and services:* "The structure of freight rates in terms of the presence or absence of special commodity rates, the type and amount of progression of rates with distance, the relationship between rail and truck rates, the relationship by quantity levels, the relationship between raw materials and finished product rates, and the differential between rates and transit privileges, all affect the differential relationships between competing markets" (p. 99).

7. *Individual firm's marketing methods:* ". . . the decisions of the individual firms as to marketing functions and channels of distribution either enhance or reduce the significance of particular trade centers" (p. 99).

8. *Auxiliary services:* "Finally, the influence of organized wholesale markets is expanded by the use of methods of systematic circulation of price and related market information; by providing specialized physical facilities in which the activities of middlemen may be housed; and

by providing for specialized financial and other types of institutions and services" (p. 100).

Besides discussing the theoretical aspects of the regional perspective as it relates to wholesaling, Revzan also produced two volumes in 1965 and 1967 in which he analyzed, by means of data from sources such as the U. S. Census, the geographical variations in wholesale/retail sales ratios.

The scholar most closely associated with the regional school of thought is E. T. Grether because he sought to use the regional approach to generate a fairly broad theory of marketing, unlike the narrower theorizing spawned by Reilly, Converse, Huff and, to some extent, Revzan. Grether's contributions to the regional perspective span approximately a half century beginning with his teaching of the regional approach in the 1930s at the University of California, Berkeley, and marked most recently by his 1983 *Journal of Marketing* article.

In a 1950 article, Grether described his viewpoint on marketing:

> One of the reasons why much of current marketing analysis is considered sterile is that it has been cut loose from the full investigation of the behavior of the firm as a whole, as well as from the economy. Specialization in courses has developed its counterpart in the highly artificial, separate treatment of marketing and selling activities. We forget too easily that business, economic, and social phenomena are organic in nature. Market analysis should be integrated with the other aspects of functional behavior. The behavior of the firm should be investigated not only in a price and marketing sense, but, under the conditions of its physical and social environment, in its determination of its location, its spatial outreach in selling and in buying and its relationships in the marketing channel with suppliers on the one hand and the buyers on the other. (p. 116-117)

Then, in the classic 1952 textbook entitled *Marketing in the American Economy,* Grether, along with his co-authors Roland Vaile and Reavis Cox, further explained the concept of interregional marketing (Vaile, Grether, and Cox 1952):

> Space, like time, is omnipresent. Its impact upon buyers and sellers and commodities is not uniform, however, for the amount occupied by a firm or by a process varies enormously. Space provides opportunities for production, marketing, or other activities at various sites and locations. It also erects obstacles in the form of costs of movement that must be borne by buyers and sellers. (p. 487)

Among the hypotheses proposed by Vaile, Grether, and Cox (1952) was a set of hypotheses designed to explain why some goods are produced and consumed within the same economic region whereas other goods are consumed outside of the region in which they are produced. Using their terminology, "home-market goods" may be restricted to their home regions because of:

1. Lack of transportability.
2. Inability to obtain them separately from the person or business establishment supplying them.
3. A degree of perishability sufficient to hold normal distribution within small areas.
4. High costs of movement.
5. The absence of advantages in obtaining goods from exterior sources sufficient to lead to their importation, as is true of most commodities produced in regions with diversified resources. (p. 491)

Vaile, Grether, and Cox (1952) also drew upon the previous work of Bertil Ohlin (1931) in economics to present a set of hypotheses to explain the volume of interregional marketing. According to their theory, the volume of goods entering trade among regions is determined primarily by:

1. The relative inequality of regions as regards the supplies of agents of production. Regions will tend to export products based upon their abundant, cheap resources.
2. The relative prosperity of regions. Other things being equal, regions with high total and per capita incomes will tend to generate more trade than poor regions.
3. The direction of the reciprocal demands among regions. There will be a larger total volume of trade if two trading regions have a strong demand for each other's characteristic products.
4. The relative effectiveness of competition. The basis for interregional exchange should normally be stronger when competition within regions is active and effective, although there may be individual exceptions. Restraints upon competition would be expected to reflect themselves in smaller interregional movements as well as in a lower total output within a region. (p. 509)

As mentioned earlier, Grether produced a paper for the 1983 *Journal of Marketing* special issue on marketing theory in which he summarized his views on the regional perspective. In this paper, he took great care to demonstrate how the regional approach could be particularly beneficial to the study of marketing strategy:

Often the identity, number and importance of the competitors vary as between regions. This factor alone may assist in the delineation of regions for purposes of analysis and control. And demands, whether ultimately those of consumer, business, or government, despite the alleged homogenization of markets, can and do vary widely between regions. For many years Revzan has stressed the "myth of the national market." It is not that enterprises do not sell throughout the national market or world markets, but that results often vary widely between regions and even subregions. From the standpoint of a given enterprise, this in itself may be a reasonable basis for regional delineation. Planning marketing strategy is tremendously improved when related to regional breakdowns of both competition and demand. (pp. 40-41)

For those readers who desire to delve deeper into the regional school of thought, we refer them to Ronald Savitt's (1981) review article, "The Theory of Interregional Marketing." Savitt does a particularly fine job of synthesizing Grether's contributions to this theoretical perspective. Another useful article is Goldstucker's (1965) review of the earlier literature pertaining to retail and wholesale trading areas.

In recent years a promising movement is underway among a small group of marketing scholars who are intent on enhancing the mathematical sophistication of trading area models. For example, Huff and Rust (1984) developed methods for assessing the boundary coincidence of two market areas. Similarly, Black, Ostlund, and Westbrook (1985) formulated a set of models relating to retail store location issues. This continued interest in defining geographic influences in marketing suggests that the regional school is still a fertile area for theoretical development.

EVALUATION OF THE REGIONAL SCHOOL

STRUCTURE: Are the concepts properly defined and integrated to form a strong nomological network?

Among the three schools presented in this chapter, there is no question that the regional school performs better on the structure criterion. It has attempted to define most of the terms in as precise a manner as possible. For example, Vaile et al. (1952) define an economic region as follows:

> For purposes of formal analysis, an economic region may be defined as a relatively large geographical area with the following four characteristics: (1) it has more than one center of economic control, (2) it has greater internal homogeneity than would be present if it were merged with other contingent areas, (3) it exports a characteristic group of products to other areas, (4) it imports the characteristic products of other areas. (p. 488)

Part of the reason for generating more precise definitions and relationships among concepts is clearly due to the mathematical approach taken by this school of thought. Another reason seems to be the strong influence of the disciplines of economics and geography. Finally, the phenomenon under study, namely the market or the region, is much more amenable to a precise definition because it is based on economic rather than behavioral characteristics.

At the same time, we must point out that there are several other concepts in this school of thought that remain ill-defined and, therefore, highly controversial. These include "characteristic products," "internal homogeneity," "product differentiation," and "centers of economic control." Overall, however, the regional school of thought is more rigorous in its structure than either the commodity or the functional school.

Our score on structure = 7.

SPECIFICATION: **Are the relationships specified in a manner to delimit hypotheses or are they highly contingent?**

The major hypotheses suggested by Revzan (1961) and Vaile et al. (1952) are highly delimited in nature. Similarly, the hypotheses generated by Reilly (1931), Converse (1949), and Huff (1964) related to retail location are extremely precise and highly specified. As we stated earlier, part of the reason is the quantitative orientation present in this school of thought, and the other part of the reason probably lies in their interest in prediction rather than explanation of a given phenomenon.

At the same time, we do feel that there is some degree of contingency inherent in their theories. For example, what effects do such exogenous factors as a product's weight to value ratio (granite stones), perishability (fresh fish), and product differentiation (digital PBX) have on the size and structure of economic areas in addition to geographical distances? Similarly, is it not reasonable to expect that factors that have impact on the consumer's choice of a shopping center may be also contingent on whether the product in question is a convenience, shopping, or specialty good? However, there is no question that despite these concerns, the regional school scores well on the specification criterion.

Our score on specification = 6.

TESTABILITY: **Are the operational definitions provided to ensure testability and intersubjective consensus?**

Specific theories related to retail or wholesale trading areas have done a very good job on the testability criterion. For example, laws of retail gravitation have utilized published data from government sources, and the operational definitions of population sizes and geographic distances are less subject to measurement errors.

On the other hand, the regional school exemplified by Grether and his colleagues suffers from inadequate operationalization of variables. In fact, they have often ended up using surrogate measures, following the tradition in economics, for such constructs as "characteristic products" and "internal homogeneity."

This does not mean that the concepts of the regional school are not testable. However, they may require data banks that were not available in the early history of marketing. Indeed, it should be much easier to score high on the testability criterion today in light of on-line electronic data banks that are easily available.

Our score on testability = 7.

EMPIRICAL SUPPORT: **What is the degree of confirmation in terms of empirical support?**

Once again, empirical research carried out by Reilly, Converse, and Revzan has generated strong confirmation of the regional school concepts. Indeed, Reilly has elevated these to the category of a "law of retail gravitation." Similarly, Grether and his colleagues, as well as international trade researchers, have provided good empirical support to the basic propositions of the regional school.

The recent empirical research by Huff and Rust (1984) and Black, Ostlund, and Westbrook (1985) clearly indicates that the body of empirical support for the regional school is growing. In addition, the level of mathematical sophistication introduced by these most recent efforts is light years beyond the simplistic formulations originally offered by early scholars such as Reilly and Converse. However, in comparison to many of the other major schools of marketing thought, the empirical work in the regional school has been confined to a fairly small group of researchers.

In summary, although there is a relatively limited degree of empirical support for the regional school, whatever has been tested has been confirmatory in nature.

Our score on empirical support = 7.

RICHNESS: How comprehensive and generalizable is the theory?

The regional school may be the weakest with respect to the richness dimension. This is primarily due to the narrow area of study chosen by the school, namely the spatial separation between buyers and sellers. But what about the psychological separation or the post-purchase separation that may exist between the two parties? Unfortunately, the regional school apparently cannot accommodate the broader and more pervasive issues of marketing.

Similarly, the regional school has sacrificed richness for the sake of formal precision. This is particularly visible in the mathematical orientation in testing the proposed hypotheses.

Our score on richness = 4.

SIMPLICITY: How easy is it to communicate and implement the theory?

The regional theory is somewhat uncomplicated because it focuses on the spatial separation between sellers and buyers. Thus, the practitioner is urged to analyze geographically where his supply markets are located and where his demand markets are located. Such analysis may be very instructive for practitioners in terms of improving the efficiency of their operations.

Unfortunately, the regional school is heavy on analysis but light on prescriptions. It is not a cookbook to marketing practice.

Our score on simplicity = 7.

Table 2.3 summarizes our evaluation of the regional school of thought. Unlike the functional and the commodity schools of thought, the regional school gets much higher scores on the syntax or organizational dimensions and somewhat lower scores on the pragmatic or relevance dimensions. This makes sense in that the regional school has been deductively driven based on some accepted concepts and principles in geography and economics.

Table 2.3 Evaluation of the Regional School*

Criterion	Rationale	Score
Structure	Very good definitions and relationships among concepts	7
Specification	Very well specified hypotheses especially in the retailing area	6
Testability	Very well tested propositions due to excellent operational measures	7
Empirical support	Limited number of studies but good support for the theory	7
Richness	Too narrow because of focus on only spatial separation	4
Simplicity	Relatively easy to communicate and use but not prescriptive enough	7
	TOTAL	38

* *Scores range from 1 (poor) to 10 (excellent).*

SUMMARY

This chapter has summarized the three noninteractive-economic schools of marketing thought. They are the commodity, the functional, and the regional schools of marketing thought.

The commodity school pioneered by Parlin and Copeland focused on the objects of market transactions and has provided the classification of goods into specialty, shopping, and convenience goods. This classification has been questioned by some and further refined by others. Perhaps the most thoughtful work has been by Aspinwall, who has provided a color-based classification of products and services into red, orange, and yellow goods.

The commodity school is based on the inductive process of observing market realities and case histories. It is a highly relevant school of thought with strong empirical support, at least in terms of marketing practice. Unfortunately, it is very weak with respect to the organization dimensions of structure and specification.

The functional school of marketing pioneered by Shaw and Weld has been researched by many more scholars. The primary emphasis has been on identification, listing and classification of marketing functions that must be performed in market transactions. Although the specific list of activities varies from author to author, it seems that there is a consensus on several fundamental types of functions to be performed by the producer, the middlemen, or the consumers. Perhaps the most comprehensive and meaningful classification is attributed to McGarry, who suggests six functions: contactual, merchandising, pricing, propaganda, physical distribution, and termination functions. It is unfortunate that the functional school has received only limited attention in recent years.

The functional school is also based on the inductive process of case histories and observations. Therefore, it has a high degree of relevance and strong empirical support, at least in terms of marketing practice. It is probably more practical than the commodity school because of the prevalence of the functional structures of marketing organizations. Unfortunately, the functional school also suffers from a very weak syntax with respect to structure and specificity.

The last school of marketing thought described in this chapter is the regional school. Instead of focusing on the objects and activities inherent in market transactions, it has concentrated on the narrower area of spatial separations between sellers and buyers. The regional school has been influenced by geography and economics. The main areas of understanding have been retail locations, wholesale markets, and centers of economic activity such as regions or nations. The regional school has been surprisingly mathematical in orientation with a strong drive to quantify and measure its constructs. Unfortunately, the theory has had only a handful of scholars committed to its ideas.

The regional theory is based on the deductive process of borrowing concepts from well established disciplines and applying them to the marketing arena. Therefore, it is very good in its organization or syntax, moderate in its empirical support, and somewhat limited in relevance.

3

INTERACTIVE–
ECONOMIC
SCHOOLS OF
MARKETING

We have identified three schools of marketing that fit the description of economic but interactive perspectives. They are the institutional school, the functionalist school, and the managerial school. These three schools of thought are all based on economic principles and concepts and are influenced very little by the social and psychological variables inherent in market transactions. To that extent, they are similar to the commodity, the functional, and the regional schools of thought.

At the same time, these three schools of thought acknowledge the interdependent relationships between the sellers and the buyers, and, therefore, take the interactive perspective. This belief in the interdependent relationship, as opposed to the dominance of the suppliers in a transaction, makes these schools different from the functional, the commodity, and the regional schools of thought.

THE INSTITUTIONAL SCHOOL OF THOUGHT

The institutional school of marketing thought holds a central position in the development and growth of the marketing discipline. In the earliest days of the emergence of marketing as a separate discipline, the institutional school shared center stage along with the commodity school and the functional school. As discussed in Chapter 2, the commodity school proposed that marketing could be best understood by analyzing the types of goods being exchanged, while the functional school asserted that the focus of analysis should be on the activities conducted in the course of the exchange. While institutional theorists appreciated the arguments advanced by their colleagues in these other two schools, they nonetheless believed that the marketing discipline could benefit by paying greater scholarly attention to the *organizations* that actually perform the functions required to move the goods from the producer to the consumer.

The role of the institutional school is further enhanced when one notes the current interest in the organizational dynamics school of thought. As the direct descendent of the institutional school, the organizational dynamics school is attempting to analyze the relationships among channel members using a behavioral orientation. Thus, the clear distinction between these two related schools is the institutional school's concentration on economic, rather than behavioral, concepts as explanations for the actions of organizations involved in marketing.

The institutional school emerged in the 1910s largely because of a perception among consumers that the prices they were paying at retail stores for agricultural products were unjustifiably high. Specifically, consumers could not understand the necessity for the size of the markup between the prices paid to the farmer and the retail prices in stores. This feeling of mistrust and confusion is understandable when one realizes the rapid and extreme sociological transitions occurring during the early decades of the twentieth century. Many consumers were moving away from the rural areas of the United States, taking jobs and establishing residences in the booming urban areas. These new city dwellers were accustomed to very short and direct marketing channels, where they either produced their own food products or bought them directly from the producers. They were unprepared for the higher prices attendant with the more elaborate marketing channels needed to bring the same food products to their new homes in the cities of America.

In response to this growing dissatisfaction with the perceived wastefulness of the marketing channel members, several marketing scholars decided to evaluate the functions and efficiency of the organizations involved in transporting and transforming goods from the producer to the consumer. Although it is certainly open to debate, a strong case can be made that L. D. H. Weld deserves credit as the founding father of the institutional school. In his 1916 book, *The Marketing of Farm Products*, Weld addressed the issue of marketing channel efficiency:

> When the statement is made that there are too many middlemen, it may mean one of two things: either that the process of subdivision already described has gone too far so that there are too many successive steps, or that there are too many of each class, such as too many country buyers, too many wholesalers, or too many retailers.

The discussion in the preceding paragraphs bears directly on the question as to whether there are too many successive steps, and this is what most people mean when they glibly state that there are too many middlemen. It was pointed out that such subdivision is merely an example of the well-known doctrine of division of labor, and that economies result from specialization by functions. Although it is perhaps impossible to say definitely whether there are too many middlemen in this sense, it is at least true that there is ample economic justification for a subdivision of the marketing process among specialized classes of dealers; that in some cases lower cost and greater efficiency may be gained by further specialization; and that in other cases it may be possible to reduce the cost by combining the functions of two or more middlemen into the hands of one single middleman. The functions of marketing have to be performed, however many separate middlemen there are; the problem is to find the most economical combination of functions.

This is a matter that can be determined only by careful investigation in each separate trade. Those who have really made firsthand studies of the marketing system in an impartial and unprejudiced way realize that on the whole the system of marketing that has developed is efficient, rather than "extremely cumbersome and wasteful," and that there are very good practical reasons for the form of organization that has developed. It is necessary to realize these fundamental facts before the reader can approach a study of the marketing problem with a sane point of view. (pp. 21-22)

In 1923, Ralph Starr Butler, who at the time was the advertising manager for the United States Rubber Company, made a significant contribution to the early development of the institutional school when he authored *Marketing and Merchandising*. Like Weld, he took considerable care to justify the role of middlemen in the modern marketing system. His approach was to emphasize the utilities that middlemen create for producers and consumers:

Another great function of middlemen is to create utilities. There are four kinds of utilities. Elementary utility is illustrated by the qualities in wheat which enable it to support life. Form utility is given to wheat when it is ground into flour in order to make it palatable. Although these two kinds of utility are essential to everyone, the fact that flour, possessing both elementary and form utility, is in the miller's warehouse in Minneapolis, is of little interest to the hungry man in New Orleans. Place utility must be added to it. Even with the addition of place utility, however, the New Orleans man may not be able to use it. If it is brought to his place in January and he needs it in July, it is of no use to him unless it is stored by someone so it will be available to satisfy his July needs. Even possessing elementary, form, and place utility, the flour can not be used unless it also has time utility—the quality of being available for use when it is needed. With elementary and form utility the market organization has nothing to do, but with place and time utility it has very much to do. Middlemen produce place and time utility; they carry things from the place where they are produced to the place where they are needed, and put them at the disposal of consumers at the time when they are needed. (Butler 1923, pp. 20-21)

Many other scholars joined the ranks of the institutional school and offered their views on marketing. However, we will jump forward in time to the 1930s and 1940s to highlight the contributions of Ralph F. Breyer, Paul D. Converse, Edward Duddy, Harvey W. Huegy, and David Revzan. Breyer, a faculty member at the Wharton School at the University of Pennsylvania, wrote an influential book entitled *The Marketing Institution* in which he chronicled the historical evolution of the marketing process to demonstrate how the current marketing structure came into existence. In the third and fourth chapters of his book, Breyer (1934) persuasively explained the need for marketing institutions:

> To perform the work involved in carrying out the marketing functions demands the construction of a huge, highly complicated piece of business machinery. We have already seen that the functions of marketing have to do with overcoming obstacles and resistances to the exchange of goods. This requires a vast expenditure of time and effort which calls for considerable drafts upon our land, labor, capital, and enterprise resources. These factors must be assembled, apportioned in quality and quantity, and coordinated and correlated into a working machine. The parts of this machine are the various business concerns having to do with marketing. (p. 24)

In addition, Breyer (1934) stressed the importance of markets as the foundation of marketing and the institutional approach:

> The need for marketing depends upon the existence of a market. The amount, nature, and combination of services marketing must perform, and the kind, quantity, and coordination of marketing machinery required are conditional upon the nature of the potentialities which any one market may present. And these vary widely. Hence, the marketing problem, as a whole and in all its details, is colored, conditioned, and hedged about by markets. It is also true that the marketing institution itself reacts upon markets and thus changes the aspects of them. For instance, marketers are able to stimulate the desires of people for their respective products by persuasive and apt salesmanship and advertising. Thus they are actually shaping the potentials that go to make up their markets. It is just this interplay of forces between markets and marketing that constitutes the most purposeful and fruitful vantage point from which to attack an analysis of the marketing institution . . . (p. 55)

Paul D. Converse and Harvey W. Huegy were among the first marketing scholars to consider critically the potential benefits and risks of vertical integration in the marketing channel. In their popular textbook *Elements of Marketing*, they wrote (1940):

> Vertical integration means the joint operation of two or more stages in production or distribution by one company. It has two advantages: a reduction in marketing expenses and the assurance of a supply of materials or an outlet for the goods. Marketing expenses may be reduced by the elimination

of successive buying and selling operations between what otherwise would be separate companies . . . Integration offers one of the most hopeful and most successful methods of reducing marketing costs, but it introduces serious problems of management and coordination. Integration is difficult when the attempt is made to produce a variety of raw materials for a finishing mill, or when a factory attempts to operate retail stores. Retailing is a highly competitive business and one that seems to require specialized management for success. Experience appears to indicate that retail and wholesale functions can be successfully combined but that basic manufacturing operations cannot be combined successfully with retailing. (pp. 800-801)

Duddy and Revzan (1947) added a slightly different perspective to the institutional school of thought, and in a sense foreshadowed the emergence of the organizational dynamics school, when they advocated that marketing managers should be sensitive to environmental influences, as well as economic forces that had been traditionally stressed by earlier institutional scholars:

The institutional approach views the economic order as an organic whole made up of a great variety of economic structures, whose functioning is coordinated not only by prices and profit margins, but by management using authoritarian and persuasive techniques, by government regulation, and by social convention and custom. The phenomena of value determination through exchange are only part of the scope included in the view of the institutionalist. For him the changing patterns of institutional organization and the cultural environment within which exchange takes place are of equal interest with any laws of price or any idea of economic equilibrium. (p. 14)

The institutional school reached its peak in terms of intellectual advancement and popularity among marketing scholars during the twenty-year period of approximately 1954 to 1973. During this era, marketing scholars began in earnest to utilize economic theories to analyze critical issues such as the emergence of marketing channels, the evolution of channel structure, and the design of effective and efficient institutional frameworks.

Among his many other contributions to marketing theory, in 1954 Wroe Alderson wrote an influential article on "Factors Governing the Development of Marketing Channels." He summarized his views on the purpose and importance of channels of distribution by stating:

. . . intermediaries arise in the process of exchange because they can increase the efficiency of the process. The justification for the middleman rests on specialized skill in a variety of activities and particularly in various aspects of sorting. The principle of the discrepancy of assortments explains why the successive stages in marketing are so commonly operated as independent agencies. While economists assume for certain purposes that exchange is costless, transactions occupy time and utilize resources in the real world.

> Intermediary traders are said to create time, place, and possession utility because transactions can be carried out at lower cost through them than through direct exchange. In our modern economy, the distribution network makes possible specialized mass production on the one hand and the satisfaction of the differentiated tastes of consumers on the other. (Alderson 1954b, pp. 13-14)

As shown in this particular quotation, Alderson clearly demonstrates the view of most institutional theorists that economic efficiency criteria are the primary factors affecting channel design and evolution. However, in 1963 Bert McCammon, one of the leaders of the institutional school during this era, argued that several factors, not all of which were based on economic efficiency criteria, should be considered as possible determinants of channel evolution. Specifically, McCammon asserted (1963):

> Economic analysis of institutional change can be and has been carried much further. This type of analysis, however modified, inevitably assumes that the firm's behavior is determined by cost/revenue considerations, and thus it leaves unanswered some or all of the following questions:
>
> > Why is change resisted by marketing institutions even though it appears to offer economic advantages?
> >
> > Why do "uneconomic channels of distribution" persist over extended periods of time?
> >
> > Why do some firms accept change rapidly, while others lag in their adaptation or refuse to change at all? (p. 479)

To answer those perplexing questions, McCammon suggested that institutional scholars should investigate various sociological and psychological variables. For example, he offered the following hypotheses:

1. The rate of diffusion depends upon the innovation itself. Innovations that involve a substantial capital investment, a major restructuring of a firm's relationship with its customers, and a sizable number of internal realignments are more likely to be accepted slowly than those that involve relatively minor intra- or inter-firm changes . . .

2. The innovator is likely to be an "outsider" in the sense that he occupies a marginal role in a given line of trade and is on the outskirts of the prevailing sociometric network. Such individuals are interested in innovation because they have the most to gain and the least to lose by disrupting the status quo . . .

3. A firm will respond incrementally to innovation unless its core market is threatened. If the latter is the case, the response to innovation will proceed swiftly . . .

4. The higher the entrepreneur's aspirations, the more likely he is to initiate or accept innovation . . .

5. The acceptance of innovation is not always permanent . . .

6.   Innovation will be accepted most rapidly when it can be fitted into existing decision-making habits . . .

7.   Influentials and innovators are not always the same firms. Institutional innovators, since they tend to be "outsiders," have relatively little influence among their entrepreneurial colleagues . . .

8.   Greater energy is required to transmit an innovation from one channel to another than is required to transmit it within a channel. (pp. 489-490)

Because he advocated the inclusion of behavioral variables in the analysis of channel evolution, McCammon attempted to pull his fellow institutional theorists away from their attachment to the economic perspective. For this reason, a strong case can be made for including McCammon among those very few scholars who successfully bridged the gulf between the institutional and organizational dynamics schools of thought.

Chronologically, the next noteworthy contribution to the institutional school was provided by F. E. Balderston (1964). He pursued a more normatively based approach to the institutional school by seeking to explain how marketing channels should be designed for optimal benefit to marketing practitioners. Discussing the special problems of channel design for the individual firm, Balderston stated:

> The individual firm faces the channel problem in three ways, which differ from the preceding efforts at "global" analysis of an entire marketing channel as a system. First, the goals or objectives of one firm, no matter how far one chooses to complicate these beyond the assumed goal of simple profit maximization, are nevertheless simpler to identify, and simpler to apply in the evolution of alternatives, than is the channel criterion problem when designing channels. Second, if the firm operates, or can operate, as a multiestablishment enterprise, some of the channel alternatives need evaluation in light of the relative efficiency of market participation and internal administration controls . . . The third difference between the single-firm channel problem and that of the "global" channel design is, however, a complicating rather than a simplifying difference. As was shown in a preceding section, models of a marketing channel system are generated by (1) identifying commodities or commodity groups to study and then (2) examining the various issues that arise in assigning functional activities to the participating entities. The single firm, however, is not necessarily restricted to participation in a single channel system. It may—to make matters most difficult of all—use the same facilities and manpower, at one or more establishments, to participate simultaneously in several marketing channels. (p. 184)

In 1965, McCammon picked up the theme of integration advanced earlier by Converse and Huegy (1940). In this article he stated that there are three types of centrally coordinated channel systems:

> Corporate marketing systems . . . combine successive stages of production and distribution under a single ownership . . . (p. 497)

Administrative strategies, as opposed to ownership, can also be used to coordinate the flow of goods and services and thereby achieve systemic economies. Individual enterprises, by exerting leadership, can often influence or otherwise control the behavior of adjacent firms within the channel . . . (p. 498)

Finally, and most significantly, channel coordination can be effected through the use of contractual agreements. That is, independent firms at different levels can coordinate their activities on a contractual basis to obtain systemic economies and market impact that could not be achieved through individual action. (p. 499)

McCammon listed four major reasons for the emergence and growth of centrally coordinated marketing systems:

1. Increased capital requirements and higher fixed costs.
2. Declining profit margins and rates of return on investment.
3. Growing complexity of marketing processes.
4. Potential economies in centrally coordinated marketing systems.

With the possible exception of McCammon's 1963 article, none of the prior writings in the institutional school proposed a theory of channel structure. However, Bucklin (1965) and Mallen (1973) addressed this weakness in the institutional school by offering two separate theories to explain and predict the structure of channels. Bucklin's theory focused on the concepts of postponement and speculation, which he defined as follows:

If one views postponement from the view of the distribution channel as a whole, it may be seen as a device for individual institutions to shift the risk of owning goods to another. The manufacturer who postpones by refusing to produce except to order is shifting the risk toward to the buyer. The middleman postpones by either refusing to buy except from a seller who provides next day delivery (backward postponement), or by purchasing only when he has made a sale (forward postponement). The consumer postpones by buying from those retail facilities which permit him to take immediate possession directly from the store shelf. (p. 27)

[The] converse may be labelled the principle of speculation. It represents a shift of risk to the institution, rather than away from it. The principle of speculation holds that changes in form, and the movement of goods to forward inventories, should be made at the earliest possible time in the marketing flow in order to reduce the costs of the marketing system. (p. 27)

By combining these principles of postponement and speculation, Bucklin (1965) argued that the creation of stages of inventories in a marketing channel could be explained:

The minimum cost and type of channel are determined by balancing the costs of alternative delivery times against the cost of using an intermediate, speculative inventory. The appearance of such an inventory in the channel occurs whenever its additional costs are more than offset by net savings in postponement to the buyer and seller. (p. 31)

Borrowing from the earlier work of George Stigler (1951), an economist, Mallen (1973) proposed that the concept of functional spinoff could be employed to evaluate and predict changes in distribution structure. Specifically, he suggested eight hypotheses founded on the functional spinoff concept:

1. A producer will spin off a marketing function to a marketing intermediary(s) if the latter can perform the function more efficiently than the former . . .

2. If there are continual economies to be obtained within a wide range of volume changes, the middleman portion of the industry (and perhaps individual middlemen) will become bigger and bigger . . .

3. A producer will keep or resume a marketing function from a marketing intermediary(s) if the former can perform the function at least as efficiently as the latter . . .

4. If in performing a marketing function a marketing intermediary finds that for a part of that function (i.e., a subfunction) another perhaps more specialized marketing intermediary can perform it more efficiently, then he will spin off that subfunction to the latter . . .

5. If a producer finds that in marketing to one (or more) of his markets a middleman can perform a given marketing function more efficiently for the reasons noted in hypothesis 1 above, and for another (or others) of his markets he can perform the same function at least as efficiently for the reasons noted in hypothesis 3 above, he will spin off that function in marketing to the first market(s) and keep or resume the function in marketing to the second . . .

6. If marketing intermediaries characterize an industry, their nature will be determined by the mix of functions and subfunctions spun off . . .

7. The greater the market size is in relation to optimum scale size (at each channel level), the greater the number of channel members that will come into being . . .

8. With a change in technology and the growth of optimum scale size, firms may be expected to leave the channel if there is no corresponding change in market size and vice versa. (p. 24)

Since the early 1970s there has been little significant work done in the institutional school of thought. The primary reason for this decline in activity is the emergence of the organizational dynamics school, which sought to employ the basic institutional perspective but with a behavioral orientation. As clearly reflected in the writings of Bucklin (1965) and Mallen (1973), the institutional school relied heavily on economic concepts related to efficiency with almost no acknowledgment given to behavioral variables that may contribute to our understanding of channel structure and performance. Led primarily by Louis Stern (1969), other scholars suggested that behavioral concepts, such as power, cooperation, and conflict, could assist in the development of more valid and reliable theories of marketing channels. As will be shown in a later section devoted to the organizational dynamics school, a promising movement has been under way in recent years to merge the best elements of the economically based institutional school and the behaviorally based organizational dynamics school.

As we progress toward the development of a more robust theory of marketing based on the analysis of institutions, five issues must receive consideration. First, this theory must explain why the performance of a marketing function may be passed from one channel member to another channel member. More specifically, the impact of technological evolution deserves greater attention as a causal variable in this functional transfer process. For example, the current introduction of sophisticated electronic and computerized communications systems into our society makes it easier for consumers to interact directly with producers or wholesale distributors. As a result, the functions formerly performed by retailers are now sometimes undertaken by either the consumers or the producers and the wholesalers.

Second, marketing theorists have tended over the years to myopically assume that the same set of marketing functions must always be performed, although the actual performance may be conducted by various institutions. However, given the recent dramatic technological strides, it appears that some functions may indeed be entirely eliminated in some channels. For instance, the "just in time" inventory system, made possible by the real time transportation and communication systems now available, allows a producer to eliminate the need for an intermediate inventory-holding institution between itself and its suppliers. Therefore, any future theory of marketing institutions must consider when and how certain marketing functions may be bypassed by marketing institutions to improve the effectiveness and efficiency of the total marketing system.

Third, vertical marketing systems, which have become standard practice in many industries, require closer scrutiny. A theory of marketing institutions must be capable of predicting the situations in which a vertical marketing system should be implemented. Further, there is a need to explain when a corporate, contractual, or administered system is likely to be most effective. Each of these three alternatives offers unique advantages and liabilities that must be fully tied to a theoretical framework.

Fourth, comparatively little interest has been shown for the variance of channel structures across cultures. As marketing becomes increasingly international in its orientation, more questions are being raised about the problems associated with using marketing institutions in foreign cultures. A comprehensive theory of marketing institutions must address these managerially relevant problems and offer some theory-based solutions. Although it is tempting to conclude immediately that the level of economic development is the main determinant of variable channel structure across cultures, such a conclusion may be unwarranted. Instead, the analysis of the powerful influence of sociocultural values and traditional norms may be helpful in explaining channel structure variability. For instance, open air markets composed of numerous small-volume dealers persist in many cultures, not because more efficient systems are not available, but rather because tradition dictates that commercial and social interaction should be conducted in this manner.

Finally, marketing institutions have been traditionally defined as including those agents who perform functions that bridge the gap between the producer and the consumer. Thus, from this linear perspective, the producer is the starting point and the consumer is the ending point for theoretical evaluation. With the advent in the 1960s of the concern for environmental quality, there is now a need to develop a circular perspective and analyze those institutions that serve to recycle or dispose of products discarded by consumers. A strong theory of marketing institutions could help to guide the development of the rapidly growing waste management industry and also assist public policymakers as they attempt to regulate these environmentally critical institutions.

EVALUATION OF THE INSTITUTIONAL SCHOOL

STRUCTURE: Are the concepts properly defined and integrated to form a strong nomological network?

The institutional school of thought has done a good job of defining the institutions, their value-adding roles, and their interrelationships between the producers and the consumers. Furthermore, more recent writers such as Bucklin (1965), Mallen (1973), and McCammon (1963) have provided good axiomatic propositions derived from a strong nomological network of concepts. Of course, the basic philosophy is economic rather than behavioral, but the use of functional spinoff principles, diffusion of innovation concepts, and inventory management issues, all indicate that the institutional school has performed better on the structure criterion than either the commodity or the functional schools of thought.

Our score on structure = 7.

SPECIFICATION: Are the relationships specified in a manner to delimit hypotheses or are they highly contingent?

The institutional school also scores well on the specification dimension. The hypotheses are precisely specified and stated to allow for relatively few contingent propositions. They can be easily questioned if you are not an economist and do not believe in the economic propositions, but this should not deter the specification provided by the institutional theorists.

Our score on specification = 7.

TESTABILITY: Are the operational definitions provided to ensure testability and intersubjective consensus?

The institutional theory is surprisingly weak on this dimension. Most authors have taken a very careful approach at defining and specifying the concepts and their relationships but have failed to provide good operational definitions. For example, how should the concepts of "speculation" and "postponement" be measured and will there be intersubject consensus on these measures? Similarly, how do we measure the concept of functional efficiency so crucial to functional spinoffs? Although the authors have tried to utilize the concepts of economies of scale and marginal cost principles, these concepts are easy to criticize and must be replaced by better concepts to measure efficiency and productivity.

Our score on testability = 4.

EMPIRICAL SUPPORT: What is the degree of confirmation in terms of empirical support?

Unfortunately, there is a very limited degree of scientific support for the propositions generated by the more recent authors including Bucklin, Mallen, and McCammon. At the same time, there is a significant amount of observational validity as well as case histories to the concepts of the institutional school. For example, the role of the middlemen as value-adding institutions providing time, place, and possession utilities and the concept of vertical distribution systems (corporate, administered, or contractual) have a great deal of face validity.

Our score on empirical support = 5.

RICHNESS: How comprehensive and generalizable is the theory?

The institutional school initially concentrated on the marketing of agricultural products. Later, institutional theorists also included the distribution of industrial and consumer goods in their analysis.

Unfortunately, the institutional school has not focused on other and perhaps richer dimensions of market satisfaction, product innovations, and conflict and power issues among the channels of distribution. To that extent, the institutional school is not as rich as the functional school. Unless the institutional theorists build more comprehensive frameworks that integrate both behavioral and economic concepts, and treat producers and consumers also as institutions, it is not likely to produce more comprehensive theories.

Our score on richness = 5.

SIMPLICITY: **How easy is it to communicate and implement the theory?**

The institutional school is fairly simple to communicate and implement, especially concepts such as functional spinoffs and vertical distribution systems. It is also easy to communicate and implement the fundamental concepts of value-added functions performed by the middlemen.

Our score on simplicity = 8.

Table 3.1 summarizes our evaluation of the institutional school. It is interesting to note that it scores high on the organization criteria of structure and specification. To that extent, it is similar to the regional school. This is again understandable in view of the fact that the recent theorists have tended to borrow well-defined concepts from economics and diffusion of innovation disciplines. The institutional school, however, is weak with respect to the reality criteria of testability and empirical support. Finally, while it is relatively simple to understand, it is not a very rich school of thought.

Table 3.1 Evaluation of the Institutional School*

Criterion	Rationale	Score
Structure	Well conceived structures and good definitions of the concepts	7
Specification	Good specification of relationships but limited to economic concepts	7
Testability	Very weak in operational definitions	4
Empirical support	Limited scientific support although good case history and practice oriented validation	5
Richness	Limited by a narrow focus on middlemen and by economic emphasis	5
Simplicity	Very easy to understand and implement	8
	TOTAL	36

* *Scores range from 1 (poor) to 10 (excellent).*

THE FUNCTIONALIST SCHOOL OF THOUGHT

This school of thought is radically different from the other schools of thought that preceded it. While it shares many of the perspectives of the institutional school of thought, it differs in two substantially different ways from the commodity, the functional, and the regional schools. It is, first of all, conceptual as opposed to the largely descriptive nature of earlier schools, and, second, it conceives of marketing as a system of interrelated structural and interdependent dynamic relationships.

A broad generalization of the commodity, functional, and regional schools of thought is that they were fostered by researchers whose formal training was in economics and saw marketing as applied economics. While the main proponent of the functionalist approach was trained as an economist, he certainly did not see marketing as applied economics. Rather he saw marketing from a systems perspective where economic processes worked on an interdependent basis. This is not the same as the systems school of thought discussed in Chapter 5. However, the functionalist view of marketing science espoused by Wroe Alderson is certainly consistent with systems analysis as later developed by Amstutz and others in marketing.

This school of thought also differs from most of the others discussed because it is primarily the work of a single scholar. Wroe Alderson was clearly the major intellectual driving force behind the emergence of this school of thought. In a brief review of Alderson and his contributions to marketing, Barksdale (1980) points out the major impact this single individual had on marketing thought. He also points out that Alderson was both a skilled practitioner and a gifted scholar. He started his career in 1925 with the United States Department of Commerce and then with Curtis Publishing Company in the mid-1930s. After a World War II assignment in Washington, he set up his own consulting firm of Alderson and Sessions. He was equally at home in the academic environment and in 1953 served as a visiting professor at MIT. He joined the marketing faculty at the University of Pennsylvania in 1959 and in 1963 was a Ford Foundation Visiting Professor at New York University.

Alderson shaped this school of thought, not only through his writings (1945, 1948, 1949, 1954a, 1956, 1957, 1958, 1965), but also through his active involvement in what were called "Marketing Theory Seminars" (see Wales and Dawson 1979). These seminars were held at the University of Colorado each summer from 1951 to 1963. These "invitation only" seminars were used by Alderson to both encourage those present to think of marketing in conceptual ways and develop marketing theory, and also to develop and explain the functionalist approach to marketing. By his own powerful intellect and his dominating personality, he was clearly "in charge" of these seminars and put his stamp on the introduction of a formal theory approach to marketing science. Since his untimely death in 1965, these seminars have not been a part of the marketing scene and no one has emerged as a spokesperson for the functionalist school of thought.

The work of Alderson is not easy to summarize. Not only does it present the functionalist approach, but often simultaneously, it presents the logic of the formal theory approach to marketing science. It is also no secret that Alderson's writings were often difficult to read. In addition, he often coined terms that many times added to the confusion, rather than clarifying the issue. Nonetheless, the contributions of Alderson to marketing thought are considerable. Alderson has had his critics as well as his devotees. But as Barksdale (1980, p. 3) points out, the number of references to his work has declined sharply. From our perspective, this is most unfortunate as Alderson was not only a creative scholar, but the incorporation of his thinking and the functionalist approach into current marketing science has the potential to greatly enrich our understanding.

Several attempts have been made to summarize and interpret Alderson's functionalist approach. Nicosia (1962) undertook the task in an article that has been widely reprinted. Nicosia's work was very comprehensive and helped clarify many of the issues presented by Alderson. Unfortunately, his review preceded the publication of Alderson's *Dynamic Marketing Behavior* by several years and therefore misses some of the richness that comes from that work. Rethans (1979) also attempted the task but made only modest additional contributions to our understanding of this school of thought. Of some significance, however, is the contribution of Hunt, Muncy, and Ray (1981), who attempted to clarify and integrate the work of Alderson by "formalizing" his functionalist theory. In addition to defining Alderson's three primitive elements (sets, behaviors, and expectations), these authors articulated Alderson's primary propositions:

1. "Marketing is the exchange which takes place between consuming groups and supplying groups." (p. 268)
2. "The household is one of the two principal organized behavior systems in marketing." (p. 268)
3. "The firm is the second primary organized behavior system in marketing." (pp. 268-269)
4. "Given heterogeneity of demand and heterogeneity of supply, the fundamental purpose of marketing is to effect exchanges by matching segments of demand with segments of supply." (p. 269)
5. "A third organized behavior system in marketing is the channel of distribution." (p. 270)
6. "Given heterogeneity of demand, heterogeneity of supply, and the requisite institutions to effect the sorts and transformations necessary to match segments of demand with segments of supply, the marketing process will take conglomerate resources in the natural state and bring about meaningful assortments of goods in the hands of consumers." (p. 271)

For the reader unacquainted with functionalism as presented by Alderson, it is important to understand the basic tenets of this school and how it differs from the functional school of thought discussed in Chapter 2. While the functional school looks at the functions performed in the practice of marketing, "functionalism" looks at a systemic structure, determining the present relationship between inputs and outputs, and laying the groundwork for bringing about an improvement in these relationships (Alderson 1965). This is not a normative approach. It takes the system as given and tries to improve it, similar to the functionalist approach in other fields of inquiry.

An important aspect of the functionalist approach is the systemic structure or the structure of the system within which marketing both operates and influences. In Alderson's (1954a) own words:

> For any subject under investigation it begins with the pragmatic questions "How does it work?" "What human purposes can it serve?" "How can its effectiveness in serving these purposes be improved?" Functionalism is boldly eclectic rather than rigidly systematic. It does not hesitate to draw upon economics, psychology, or any other discipline for facts or conceptual models which will help in finding the solution of a problem. (p. 40)

Two years later, he added:

> An initial word is also required with respect to the term "functionalism." Too often its use in marketing circles has implied scarcely more than identifying and describing the functions of marketing. The classification of marketing activities is worthwhile but it is only one step in the application of the versatile tool which functional analysis should be. Functionalism always starts by trying to understand the goals or functions of a whole system of action and how it operates in discharging these functions. (Alderson 1956, p. 7)

According to Nicosia (1962):

> Alderson's functionalism merits consideration as an approach or frame of reference which . . . offers an all-encompassing integrating perspective of marketing entities and their interrelations—in short, of a marketing system. (p. 404)

Alderson was not the only one to recognize that marketing was a system and the necessity of determining how the total system worked. As discussed earlier in this chapter, Duddy and Revzan conceived marketing as an "organic" whole. Likewise, Breyer focused on the marketing channel and viewed it as a system within the larger marketing system. But Alderson's view was unique in that it drew heavily on the behavioral sciences for many of its conceptualizations of relations between various units in the marketing system. It builds on the commodity, institutional, and functional approaches, but positioned them in a larger totality.

To properly understand this school of thought, it is necessary to appreciate Alderson's key concepts. Alderson clearly states that "the two advanced concepts which project the essence of functionalist theory are the organized behavior system and the heterogeneous market" (Alderson 1965, p. 25). Nicosia (1962, p. 407) had suggested that the two most important concepts of Alderson's functionalism were the organized behavior system and the marketing process. The apparent reason for this discrepancy is that the concept of the heterogeneous market was introduced in Alderson's 1965 work to improve the understanding of the marketing process originally discussed in his 1957 work.

Organized Behavior System

Although this concept was given only brief attention in Alderson's *Marketing Behavior and Executive Action* (1957), it was obviously a key, if unstated, concept. The concept of the organized behavior system was more fully developed in *Dynamic Marketing Behavior* (1965). As pointed out by Monieson and Shapiro (1980), Alderson appears to have been heavily influenced by the thinking of Talcott Parsons. Parsons' theory of social action was intended to be a general theory of action rather than just a psychological or sociological theory of action. His cohesive system emphasizes the interaction of the individual with many factors within a dynamic social environment.

Alderson defines organized behavior systems as "the entities which operate in the marketing environment" (1965, p. 26). "In an organized behavior system the organizing element is the expectation of the members that they as members of the system will achieve a surplus beyond what they could attain through individual and independent action" (1965, p. 25).

The major test proposed by Alderson to determine the boundaries of an organized behavior system is "a common stake in survival" (Alderson 1965, p. 44). This implies that members of an organized behavior system should act to preserve the system if one part of the system or the entire system is threatened. In addition, an organized behavior system has "rules" for determining membership, a rule for determining the assignment of duties within the system, and a criterion for judging the outputs of the system.

Alderson lists five major systems that meet this test:

Public or political systems

Households as systems

Enterprise systems

Undercover systems

Charitable and educational systems

Fundamental to this concept is a system in which interactions take the form of human behavior. As organized behavior systems interact with the market, they "provide the motive power which keeps the marketing process going" (1965, p. 37). They do so by behaving in a manner that maximizes their best interests and survival.

The two organized behavior systems that were the major focus of Alderson's thinking were the household and the firm. Whereas households are a major organized behavior system, the firm seems to be a major subcomponent of enterprise systems.

> The household persists over time because of its expectations concerning future behavior. These expectations must, on the whole, have a positive value for the individuals making up the household. Their expectations concerning the desired patterns of behavior are higher as members of the household than they would be otherwise. The behavior system offers a surplus to its participants which they would not expect to enjoy outside the system. These expectations of desired behavior patterns may not be fully realized. The theory only requires that these anticipations should persist, perhaps with occasional reinforcement, to show that conditions would be no better outside the system.

> The household accumulates goods to sustain the expected patterns of behavior. The household today, or its primary purchasing agent, is engaged in creating or replenishing an assortment of goods to sustain expected patterns of future behavior. Items are added to the assortment because they increased the potency of the assortment. Potency may be described as the quality of the assortment which protects the household against unpleasant surprises. (Alderson 1965, pp. 37-38)

Alderson characterizes the household as the ultimate target of the marketing effort. Therefore, it can easily be argued that this is the most important organized behavior system for Alderson. One has only to compare this thought with the earlier schools of marketing thought to see how different the perspective becomes when an integrated approach such as Alderson's functionalism is taken.

The firm as an organized behavior system is directly related to the heterogeneous market according to Alderson. As markets became more complex and diverse, firms developed specialized skills and knowledge that facilitated exchange and the matching of needs with resources.

> Heterogeneity provided the immediate basis for exchange. There was no possible route for passing directly to anything resembling the homogeneous markets of pure and perfect competition. The underlying principle of market dynamics is that the existence of a market encourages the growth of a technology which gradually causes all products to flow through the market. (Alderson 1965, p. 39)

Of particular interest is the fact that Alderson did not consider the marketing channel an organized behavior system. He did not deny that a marketing channel could be an organized behavior system, but he argues that it generally lacks a common stake in survival, and he raises the question of "whether either side would assume any substantial costs or risks to ensure the survival of the other side" (Alderson 1965, p. 44).

> The marketing channel exists but it would be stretching the point to call it an organized behavior system with a tendency to persist over a long period of time. At best it is a pseudosystem in which there is a fair amount of cooperation over a short interval but with no commitments over the longer run. (Alderson 1965, p. 44)

Heterogeneous Market

> Progressive differentiation of products and services is the key to defining the values created by marketing. This approach is based on the assumption that each individual's need is different from every other individual's need in one or more respects. Thus the basic economic process is the gradual differentiation of goods up to the point at which they pass into the hands of consumers. (Alderson 1957, p. 69)

This is a considerably richer and more comprehensive statement than those that suggest that marketing creates time, place, and possession utilities. It is so because, as Barksdale points out (1980, p. 2) "in contrast to economic models of perfect competition, which assume homogeneous markets, Alderson postulated heterogeneity on both the supply and demand sides of markets."

If, in fact, markets are heterogeneous, then the marketing process is the mechanism by which heterogeneous supplies are matched with heterogeneous demands. Key to the marketing process, for Alderson, is the series of sorts and *transformations* by which the matching is accomplished.

Alderson viewed sorting as the basic function of marketing (Alderson 1965):

> Sorting is the decision aspect of marketing whether seen from the standpoint of the supplier or the consumer. The supplier assigns items to classes which are to be treated in different ways thereafter. The consumer selects an item into her assortment in relation to what the assortment already contains. While the marketing specialist is interested in all of the transformations which take place as goods move to market, including production transformations, his most vital concern is with the sorts intervening between successive transformations. (p. 34)

The term sorting includes four types of sorts. In the following, we see that Alderson saw the process as both "breaking down" and "building up" collections:

	BREAKING DOWN	BUILDING UP
Heterogeneous	Sorting out	Assorting
Homogeneous	Allocating	Accumulation

Adapted from Alderson (1965, p. 34)

Sorting out is used to describe that situation where a heterogeneous collection is broken into several homogeneous groups, that is, all the 2-by-4s from a tree are put in one pile, the 4-by-6s in another pile, and the 2-by-10s in yet another pile. Accumulation is building up of larger homogeneous collections, that is, putting all the 2-by-4s from many trees into a single large pile of 2-by-4s. Allocation is the assignment or dispersal of goods to intermediaries, that is, sending part of the pile of 2-by-4s to a lumber yard in Chicago. Assorting is the building up of a heterogenous collection or assortment, that is, an individual purchases some 2-by-4s along with other sizes of lumber and nails to build a picnic table that will be used to entertain guests.

> The aspect of sorting of greatest interest is assorting or the building of assortments. Assorting is the final step in taking products off the market. The other three aspects of sorting are not unimportant, but their significance lies in what they can contribute to the final building of assortments. The marketing specialist must look at all the earlier sorts to make sure they were necessary for the end result. (Alderson 1965, p. 35)

The ideal or perfect market would perfectly match each element of supply with each element of demand. For Alderson, markets are not perfect. He suggests (Alderson 1965) that imperfections in the market are the result of a failure in communication. Because of this failure, there may be an excess of some products in the channel of distribution and lesser demand for others. This mismatch in the market can be corrected by information. Information needs to be given to the customer, but also information needs to be gathered about the assortments that customers desire to build to enhance their potency.

In the more traditional economics approach of the homogeneous market, the market is matched by price adjustment. Information is taken for granted. Alderson argues that price is only one piece of information, primarily because his concept of the market is that of a highly segmented or heterogeneous market. While some small segment of the heterogeneous market may respond to price as the only necessary information, other segments may not consider price to be important or use it in conjunction with other information variables.

Consequently, markets are dyadic. There is a constant attempt to better match the marketing process against the heterogeneous market.

Advantages are gained and lost in this quest. Alderson captures this in the title of his last book, *Dynamic Marketing Behavior.*

Transvection

While sorts and transformations are the key concepts for understanding the heterogeneous market, the key concept for analysis is the *transvection.* In an attempt to explain the concept of a transvection, Alderson (1965) contrasts the transvection with transactions.

> A transaction is a product of the double search in which customers are looking for goods and suppliers are looking for customers. It is an exchange of information leading to an agreement concerning the marketing of goods. This agreement is a joint decision in which the customer agrees to take the goods offered and the supplier agrees to sell at the stated price and terms. (p. 75)

> A transvection is the unit of action for the system by which a single end product such as a pair of shoes is placed in the hands of the consumer after moving through all the intermediate sorts and transformations from the original raw materials in the state of nature. A transvection is in a sense the outcome of a series of transactions, but a transvection is obviously more than this. A transvection includes the complete sequence of exchanges, but it also includes the various transformations which take place along the way. (p. 86)

The concept of the transvection is undoubtedly the richest of those brought forth by Alderson. It incorporates most, if not all, of the other concepts that Alderson talks about within the framework of functionalism. While the concept of the heterogeneous market focuses on successive differentiation, it is the concept of the transvection that allows analysis of both the efficiency and effectiveness of the process of matching achieved by successive sorts and transformations. For instance, this concept suggests that the best or shortest route to market is some optimal combination of sorts and transformations. Striving for an optimal combination of sorts and transformations allows one to focus on adding or subtracting sorts and transformations, and the consequent homogeneous and heterogeneous collections, using some weighting of cost, time, and risk.

For Alderson, a formal theory should develop a precise language, using primitive terms and definitions.

> The initial task is to develop a terminology which depends on as few primitive terms as possible, is consistent, and exhaustive in the sense of being capable of describing every kind of system relevant to marketing analysis, and which is complete in the sense of allowing for the formulation of theorems concerning transactions and transvections. The three primitive terms adopted here are sets, behavior and expectations. (Alderson and Martin 1965, p. 118-119)

Before his death, Alderson started the process. By using these primitive terms to define other terms, he advanced the complex concepts of the organized behavior system, the heterogeneous market, and the sorting function (Alderson 1965). Although we can only infer the logical process by which Alderson arrived at the point of assembling the elements from which he hoped to develop marketing theory, he did expand on these elements in his 1965 work.

EVALUATION OF THE FUNCTIONALIST SCHOOL

STRUCTURE: **Are the concepts properly defined and integrated to form a strong nomological network?**

Perhaps the biggest strength of Wroe Alderson's functionalist school is its structure. Alderson is able to define the basic concepts including market heterogeneity, sorting, transformation, and transvection. Furthermore, he has done an outstanding job of integrating them to create a theory of marketing that makes sense.

Unfortunately, Alderson's theory has evolved over time. Therefore, concept definitions have changed over time, perhaps as a function of testing his ideas with colleagues at the conferences he used to organize.

Our score on structure = 7.

SPECIFICATION: **Are the relationships specified in a manner to delimit hypotheses or are they highly contingent?**

Alderson's functionalist theory also scores high on the specification dimension. He has attempted to provide several basic constructs and utilize them to build a theory that has few contingent hypotheses. Indeed, the functionalist theory is able to accommodate the market dynamics without impact on the four basic concepts of market heterogeneity, sorting, transformations, and transvections.

Our score on specification = 7.

TESTABILITY: **Are the operational definitions provided to ensure testability and intersubjective consensus?**

The weakest aspect of Alderson's theory is the testability dimension. He has failed to provide any operational definitions of his basic concepts. Furthermore, there is considerable disagreement among his followers as to the specific measures for the constructs in his theory.

It is unfortunate that Alderson, like so many brilliant theorists, paid little attention to testing the theory or providing operational definitions so that others could test it without misrepresenting the theory. Therefore, it is no surprise that Alderson's theory has remained untested so far, despite its organizational elegance in terms of structure and specification.

Our score on testability = 2.

EMPIRICAL SUPPORT: What is the degree of confirmation in terms of empirical support?

Since the theory has not been put to a test, it has no real scientific empirical support. Some of the concepts, especially associated with market heterogeneity and sorting, are real in that there is observational evidence for them in the real world. However, unlike the functional, the commodity, or the institutional schools, the transvectional theory is basically a conceptual framework devoid of empirical support.

Our score on empirical support = 3.

RICHNESS: How comprehensive and generalizable is the theory?

The functionalist theory is extremely rich. It is able to encompass the marketing domain and all of its aspects with no more than three to four basic concepts. Furthermore, the theory is generic enough to accommodate all specialized domains of marketing such as industrial marketing, services marketing, and social marketing. It appears to us that Alderson's theory is also capable of providing a framework for cross-national marketing. For example, concepts of market heterogeneity, as well as sorting and transformation, may easily explain cross-national similarities or differences and how to cope with them in terms of creating the proper assortment.

Our score on richness = 8.

SIMPLICITY: How easy is it to communicate and implement the theory?

Another major weakness of Alderson's theory is the difficulty of understanding the basic concepts. Indeed, a number of researchers have criticized and remained skeptical about the relevance of the functionalist theory because of Alderson's passion to create new words and phrases rather than use common terminology.

Similarly, in our opinion, Alderson's theory may be very useful as an analytical tool, but it is very hard to implement the concepts in terms of the organization structures and functional responsibilities in marketing departments. In that respect, the functional, the commodity, and the institutional schools are much stronger.

Our score on simplicity = 2.

Table 3.2 summarizes our evaluation of Alderson's functionalist theory. It is an extremely rich theory with good structure and specification. Unfortunately, it suffers from lack of simplicity and empirical content. Perhaps the theory can make an excellent contribution if someone attempts formally to test it in a marketing situation.

Table 3.2 Evaluation of the Functionalist School*

Criterion	Rationale	Score
Structure	Very well structured definitions and good integration of basic concepts	7
Specification	Highly specified and devoid of contingent hypotheses	7
Testability	Poor on operational definitions and a clear disagreement on how to measure his concepts	2
Empirical support	No formal test of the theory and most evidence is anecdotal	3
Richness	Extremely rich and capable of becoming one of the few general theories of marketing	8
Simplicity	Extremely difficult to understand due to strange vocabulary and impossible to implement in practice	2
	TOTAL	29

* *Scores range from 1 (poor) to 10 (excellent.)*

THE MANAGERIAL SCHOOL OF THOUGHT

In the late 1940s and the early 1950s, several scholars in economics struck off in a bold new direction. Sensing that economics scholars had generally become too isolated from the practical world of business, scholars such as Joel Dean and William Baumol developed the area of "managerial economics." Their goal, quite simply, was to translate the often abstract theories of economics spawned by academicians into principles of business practice that could be readily used by executives in their everyday managerial tasks.

In his classic textbook, *Managerial Economics*, published in 1951, Joel Dean clearly articulated his views on the importance of managerial economics:

> The purpose of this book is to show how economic analysis can be used in formulating business policies. It is therefore a departure from the main stream of economic writings on the theory of the firm, much of which is too simple in its assumptions and too complicated in its logical development to be managerially useful. The big gap between the problems of logic that intrigue economic theorists and the problems of policy that plague practical management needs to be bridged in order to give executives access to the practical contributions that economic thinking can make to top-management policies. (Dean 1951, p. vii)

Following the lead established by the managerial economists, some marketing theorists in the 1950s also began to advocate a more managerially based approach to marketing. For example, in 1957 John Howard published his widely accepted textbook entitled *Marketing Management* (revised in 1963b) and in 1958 Eugene Kelley and William Lazer edited the popular readings book *Managerial Marketing: Perspectives and Viewpoints*.

The real core of the managerial school of thought in marketing, however, emerged in a series of influential articles written during the late 1950s and early 1960s. In these works, scholars like Ted Levitt, Neil Borden, and Wendell Smith introduced such concepts as "marketing myopia," "marketing mix," and "market segmentation" for application by marketing executives. Interestingly, these concepts of marketing management have proven to be remarkably resilient, as demonstrated by their prominent inclusion in current marketing management textbooks.

Although space limitations prohibit a complete review of all of the writings in the managerial school published during its formative era, the following few pages will highlight those articles that registered the greatest impact. In addition, some of the more recent scholarly contributions in the managerial school will be highlighted.

One of the most important conceptual breakthroughs during this school's development was the emergence of the so-called marketing mix. Pioneered by scholars such as Ed Lewis, Neil Borden, and E. Jerome McCarthy, the concept of the marketing mix focused on the need for marketing managers to view the marketing task as the process of mixing or integrating several different functions simultaneously. Writing from the perspective of a theorist mainly concerned with advertising effectiveness, Borden (1964) described the marketing mix philosophy:

> Relatively early in my study of advertising, it had become evident that understanding of advertising usage by manufacturers in any case had to come from an analysis of advertising's place as one element in the total marketing program of the firm. I came to realize that it is essential always to ask: what overall marketing strategy has been or might be employed to bring about a profitable operation in light of the circumstances faced by the management? What combination of marketing procedures and policies has been or might be adopted to bring about desired behavior of trade and consumers at costs that will permit a profit? Specifically, how can advertising, personal selling, pricing, packaging, channels, warehousing, and other elements of a marketing program be manipulated and fitted together in a way that will give a profitable operation? (p. 3)

During this particular time period, some scholars began to argue that the pursuit of production efficiencies were perhaps rather shortsighted. Instead, they proposed that marketers should pay greater attention to the ascertainment of the consumers' needs and desires before decisions are made regarding production. Of course, this fundamental principle of the "marketing concept" is probably the most famous axiom developed in modern marketing history. As stated by J. B. McKitterick in his 1957 paper:

Turning the issue around, if business enterprises are to compete successfully in the quicksilver of modern markets, something more than sophistication in means of doing marketing work is going to be required. Indeed, to plan at all, and think adequately of what competition might do and its possible effects before committing multi-million dollar resources, requires knowledge of the customer which penetrates to the level of theory. So the principal task of the marketing function in a mangement concept is not so much to be skillful in making the customer do what suits the interests of the business as to be skillful in conceiving and then making the business do what suits the interests of the customer. (p. 78)

Three years later, Robert J. Keith (1960), then president of the Pillsbury Company, also expressed the requirement for marketers to place the consumers' needs before the production abilities of the company:

In much the same way American business in general—and Pillsbury in particular—is undergoing a revolution of its own today: a marketing revolution.

The revolution stems from the same idea stated in the opening sentence of this article. No longer is the company at the center of the business universe. Today the customer is at the center.

Our attention has shifted from problems of production to problems of marketing, from the product we can make to the product the consumer wants us to make, from the company itself to the marketplace. (p. 35)

More recently, Franklin Houston (1986) critiqued the marketing concept and concluded that marketers have lost sight of the original orientation of this basic concept:

The marketing concept has suffered in two ways: first, it has been established as the optimal management philosophy when it is not necessarily so in all instances, and second, we can see many examples of poor marketing practices which have been adopted in the name of the marketing concept. It is time that we relearn that the marketing concept is one of a set of three concepts— marketing, sales, and production—that form the basis for understanding the management of marketing. And it is time that we remember that, under differing circumstances, each can be the orientation that best furthers the objectives of the organization. (p. 86)

Closely aligned to the marketing concept is the phenomenon of "marketing myopia," which was originated by Ted Levitt (1960) in a classic article in *Harvard Business Review*. Levitt warned that marketers often naively believe that, just because the current situation is profitable, there will always be a market for their particular products that extends indefinitely into the future. According to Levitt, every industry must warily scan the horizon for signs of corporate vulnerability:

In truth, there is no such thing as a growth industry, I believe. There are only companies organized and operated to create and capitalize on growth opportunities. Industries that assume themselves to be riding some automatic growth escalator invariably descend into stagnation. The history of every dead and dying "growth" industry shows a self-deceiving cycle of bountiful expansions and undetected decay. There are four conditions which usually guarantee this cycle:

1. The belief that growth is assured by an expanding and more affluent population.

2. The belief that there is no competitive substitute for the industry's major product.

3. Too much faith in mass production and in the advantages of rapidly declining unit costs as output rises.

4. Preoccupation with a product that lends itself to carefully controlled scientific experimentation, improvement, and manufacturing cost reduction. (pp. 47-48)

With this call for increased sensitivity to the needs of consumers as the basic motivation for marketing effort, there also emerged an awareness that not all consumers possess the same drives and goals. The notion that marketers should segment the market and strive to develop several different marketing mixes to more closely match the diverse needs of the consumers was first proposed by Wendell Smith in 1956. As originally stated by Smith, market segmentation is intuitively appealing:

Market segmentation . . . consists of viewing a heterogeneous market (one characterized by divergent demand) as a number of smaller homogeneous markets in response to differing product preferences among important market segments. It is attributable to the desires of consumers or users for more precise satisfaction of their varying wants. (p. 6)

Over the years, the concept of market segmentation has proven to be a rich and sometimes controversial area for marketing theorists. As noted recently by Winter (1984), some marketers have misinterpreted Smith's original writing and have unfortunately focused on the diversity in consumers' levels of demand, stated usually in terms of the "heavy half and light half" of the market, rather than the diversity in the type of demand among consumers. Also, Winter argues that obsession with demographic identification of consumer segments and preoccupation with product forms instead of product needs have detracted from the original concept of market segmentation proposed in 1956.

The concept of market segmentation continues to be attractive to the current generation of marketing scholars. Dickson and Ginter (1987) demonstrated the similarities and contrasts between market segmentation and product differentiation. Recognizing the increased emphasis on industrial marketing, Doyle and Saunders (1985) discussed the application of market segmentation in industrial markets. Finally, quantitative approaches to market segmentation have recently been considered by Grover and Srinivasan (1987) and Blozan and Prabhaker (1984).

In addition, numerous other scholars in the managerial school proposed principles or theories that concentrated on how marketing managers should deal with specific elements of the marketing mix, such as products, price, promotion, and distribution decisions.

In the area of product decisions, one of the most significant developments was the introduction of the "product life cycle" concept. According to Levitt (1965):

> Most alert and thoughtful senior marketing executives are by now familiar with the concept of the product life cycle. Even a handful of uniquely cosmopolitan and up-to-date corporate presidents have familiarized themselves with this tantalizing concept. Yet a recent survey I took of such executives found none who used the concept in any strategic way whatever, and pitifully few who used it [in] any kind of tactical way. It has remained— as have so many fascinating theories in economics, physics, and sex—a remarkably durable but almost totally unemployed and seemingly unemployable piece of professional baggage whose presence in the rhetoric of professional discussions adds a much coveted but apparently unattainable legitimacy to the idea that marketing management is somehow a profession. There is, furthermore, a persistent feeling that the life cycle concept adds luster and believability to the insistent claim in certain circles that marketing is close to being some sort of science.
>
> The concept of the product life cycle is today at about the stage that the Copernican view of the universe was 300 years ago; a lot of people knew about it, but hardly anybody seemed to use it in any effective or productive way.
>
> Now that so many people know and in some fashion understand the product life cycle, it seems time to put it to work. (p. 8)

More recently, the *Journal of Marketing* devoted its Fall 1981 issue to a series of articles concerning the product life cycle concept. Although the product life cycle is appealing, George Day (1981), the guest editor for the issue, noted the existence of certain conceptual problems:

> There is tremendous ambivalence toward the product life cycle concept within marketing. On the one hand, the concept has an enduring appeal because of the intuitive logic of the product birth -> growth -> maturity -> decline sequence based on a biological analogy. As such it has considerable descriptive value when used as a systematic framework for explaining market dynamics.
>
> However, the simplicity of the product life cycle makes it vulnerable to criticism, especially when it is used as a predictive model for anticipating when changes will occur and one stage will succeed another, or as a normative

model which attempts to prescribe what alternative strategies should be considered at each stage. (p. 60)

Also, Gardner (1987) examined the product life cycle literature published since 1975. He concluded that the product life cycle is not a theory and has many serious shortcomings. Gardner recommended that a major reconceptualization of the life cycle phenomenon is needed to generate a prescriptive, rather than descriptive, concept.

Within the pricing area, Joel Dean (1950) and Alfred Oxenfeldt (1960) strove to translate economic theories of pricing into normative policy guidelines that could be understood and readily implemented by marketing managers. Of Dean's many contributions to the pricing literature, perhaps his most significant effort was the articulation of the pricing policies of "skimming" and "penetration":

> The strategic decision in pricing a new product is the choice between (1) a policy of high initial prices that skim the cream of demand and (2) a policy of low prices from the outset serving as an active agent for market penetration. Although the actual range of choice is much wider than this, a sharp dichotomy clarifies the issues for consideration. (1950, p. 49)

> *Skimming Prices.* For products that represent a drastic departure from accepted ways of performing a service, a policy of relatively high prices coupled with heavy promotional expenditures in the early stages of market development (and lower prices at later stages) has proved successful for many products. (1950, pp. 49-50)

> *Penetration Price.* The alternative policy is to use low prices as the principal instrument for penetrating mass markets early. This policy is the reverse of the skimming policy in which the price is lowered only as short-run competition forces it. The passive skimming policy has the virtue of safeguarding some profits at every stage of market penetration. But it prevents quick sales to the many buyers who are at a lower end of the income scale or the lower end of the preference scale, and who therefore are unwilling to pay any substantial premium for product reputation superiority. The active approach in probing possibilities for market expansion by early penetration pricing requires research, forecasting, and courage. (1950, p. 50)

Oxenfeldt (1960) may be best remembered for advocating that marketers use a "multistage approach" to pricing:

> In order to organize the various pieces of information and considerations that bear on price decisions, a multi-stage approach to pricing can be a very helpful tool. This method sorts the major elements in a pricing decision into six successive stages:
>
> 1. Selection of market targets.
> 2. Choosing a brand "image."
> 3. Composing a marketing mix.

4. Selecting a pricing policy.
5. Determining a pricing strategy.
6. Arriving at a specific price. (pp. 125-126)

The sequence of the stages is an essential part of the method, for each step is calculated to simplify the succeeding stage and to reduce the likelihood of error. One might say that this method divides the price decision into manageable parts, each one logically antecedent to the next. In this way, the decision at each stage facilitates all subsequent decisions. This approach might also be regarded as a process of selective search, where the number of alternatives deserving close consideration is reduced drastically by making the decision in successive stages.

In recent years the topic of pricing has been the subject of three major review articles (Nagle 1984, Rao 1984, Tellis 1986). In addition, a number of articles have addressed a variety of pricing issues, such as price negotiations (Evans and Beltramini 1987), price sensitivity (Huber, Holbrook, and Kahn 1986), and product line pricing (Reibstein and Gatignon 1984, Petroshius and Monroe 1987).

The classic article related to the distribution area was authored by John F. Magee in 1960. Magee, and other scholars like Davidson (1961), were instrumental in encouraging marketing managers to elevate distribution decisions to an equal importance with product, pricing, and promotion decisions. According to Magee (1960):

> Grappling with all of these problems is like untangling a tangled skein of yarn. Each decision has an impact on other choices and for this reason is hard to pin down. The distribution problem is a system problem, and it must be looked at as such. If it is examined in total and if the experience and methods available for studying it are used, the issues just mentioned can be resolved in an orderly, mutually compatible way.
>
> In my experience, three key conditions have, when present, made for a sound distribution system study and an effective implementation program:
>
> 1. Recognition by company management that improving distribution means examining the full physical distribution system.
> 2. Use of quantitative systems analysis or operations research methods to show clearly the nature of trade-offs and the relation between system operation and company policies.
> 3. Cooperative work by men knowledgeable in sales and marketing, transportation, materials handling, materials control, and information handling. (p. 96)

An example of more recent thinking in the distribution management area is Frazier and Sheth's (1985) discussion of the roles of attitude and behavior in the coordination of the distribution channel. By employing these behavioral concepts, they demonstrated the potential application of the organizational dynamics school to the managerial school.

Within the promotion area, marketing scholars in the managerial school offered suggestions to marketing practitioners regarding personal selling and advertising decision making. In a highly influential article in the *Journal of Marketing,* Robert J. Lavidge and Gary A. Steiner (1961) argued that the goal of advertising should be to move consumers through a series of stages that eventually result in product purchase:

> Advertising may be thought of as a force, which must move people up a series of steps:
>
> 1. Near the bottom of the steps stand potential purchasers who are completely unaware of the existence of the product or service in question.
>
> 2. Closer to purchasing, but still a long way from the cash register, are those who are merely aware of its existence.
>
> 3. Up a step are prospects who know what the product has to offer.
>
> 4. Still closer to purchasing are those who have favorable attitudes toward the product—those who like the product.
>
> 5. Those whose favorable attitudes have developed to the point of preference over all other possibilities are up still another step.
>
> 6. Even closer to purchasing are consumers who couple preference with a desire to buy and the conviction that the purchase would be wise.
>
> 7. Finally, of course, is the step which translates this attitude into actual purchase. (p. 59)

The topic of advertising continues to be the subject of a significant number of scholarly articles. Recently, emphasis has been placed on the competitive influences in advertising (Erickson 1985, Gatignon 1984), decision making in advertising (Tull et al. 1986), and determinants of advertising effectiveness (MacKenzie, Lutz, and Belch 1986; Preston 1982).

Marketing has always taken a considerable amount of abuse for the supposedly inconsiderate and deceitful tactics employed by salespeople. During the peak of the managerial school, serious attempts were made to reduce the likelihood that salespeople would feel the need to resort to coercive methods of personal selling. For example, Cash and Crissy (1958) advocated the adoption of the "need-satisfaction theory of personal selling":

> In this theory it is assumed that purchases are made to satisfy needs. Therefore, in order to make a sale the salesman must discover the prospect's needs and show how his products or services will fill those needs. This is a customer-oriented approach as compared with the two previous theories which are, primarily, salesman-oriented approaches.
>
> To be useful in application this theory requires greater skill and maturity on the part of the salesman because he is prevented from talking about his product until he has discovered the customer's needs. This is a sharp contrast to the selling formula, where the salesman is encouraged to point out all the

important features of his product. It also requires that the salesman be sufficiently self-confident to undertake control of the sales interview through questioning rather than by dominating the conversation. (p. 14)

For more serious and complex sales situations, this approach is preferred to the two previously described theories. It is obviously more time-consuming, but the increased likelihood of making a sale by matching the customer's needs with the appropriate product features and benefits makes this approach more attractive, particularly in situations where the potential commissions and/or profits are great enough to warrant the extra expenditure of time.

A considerable amount of scholarly attention has been devoted recently to the subjects of personal selling and sales management. In the personal selling area, Weitz (1981) and Weitz, Sujan, and Sujan (1986) presented conceptual frameworks for understanding selling effectiveness. Along a similar line, Dwyer, Schurr, and Oh (1987) considered the development of buyer-seller relationships, and Williams and Spiro (1985) discussed communication issues in salesperson-customer dyads. In the sales management area, recent articles have addressed the impact of supervisory behaviors on the salesforce (Kohli 1985), salesforce turnover (Lucas et al. 1987), salesperson motivation (Sujan 1986), salesforce socialization (Dubinsky et al. 1986), and stages in a salesperson's career (Cron and Slocum 1986).

As noted earlier, a full review of the managerial school is impossible for obvious reasons. A tremendous volume of conceptual articles, empirical studies, and case studies has been written in the past thirty years concerning this school's key concepts (product life cycle, market segmentation, marketing mix, marketing concept, etc.). Additionally, the managerial school encompasses literature on other topics, including product positioning (Shugan 1987) and the interface of marketing with other functional units within the organization (Ruekert and Walker 1987). In fact, a strong argument can be made for positioning the managerial school as the most comprehensive school among the galaxy of marketing schools of thought. Readers who desire additional information about the managerial school may consult Sheth and Garrett's (1986a) readings book, *Marketing Management: A Comprehensive Reader,* or any recent marketing management textbook, such as Bagozzi (1986) or Kotler and Armstrong (1987).

In summary, the managerial school has had tremendous influence on the marketing profession. Its central concepts continue to be utilized heavily by marketing practitioners in corporate offices and by marketing professors in academic classrooms. In addition to this school's resiliency, another major contribution has been its integrative ability. By emphasizing (1) the marketing concept (which urged practitioners to analyze consumer needs) and (2) the marketing mix (which integrated the functional tasks of marketing), the managerial school established itself as a comprehensive school of thought.

EVALUATION OF THE MANAGERIAL SCHOOL

STRUCTURE: Are the concepts properly defined and integrated to form a strong nomological network?

The managerial school is remarkably good on the structure dimension. It has identified the key policy issues of marketing practice, provided adequate definitions to fundamental concepts such as the product life cycle, the marketing mix and market segmentation, and has even attempted to integrate these concepts into one theory of marketing management, such as by Levitt and Kotler.

Indeed, the managerial school seems even more robust than either the regional or the functionalist schools in terms of structure. This can probably be explained by the fact that "there is nothing more practical than a good theory." In other words, there is a considerable payoff to theorists in terms of recognition and income from industry when they generate a good theory of marketing practice.

Our score on structure = 8.

SPECIFICATION: Are the relationships specified in a manner to delimit hypotheses or are they highly contingent?

The managerial school also scores well on the specification criterion if we examine each marketing function individually. For example, the managerial school has provided excellent hypotheses for advertising effectiveness, sales force management, distribution efficiency, and product life cycle management. Although many of these hypotheses are contingent on exogenous market forces of competition and customers, the managerial school has attempted to incorporate them either by a covariate analysis or by controlled experiments.

The only area where the managerial school seems weak with respect to the specification criterion is the interdependent relationships among various elements of marketing mix. For example, we still do not have well established hypotheses to determine whether advertising and distribution are complementary or substitute marketing forces to generate a desirable market response. Similarly, we still do not know whether product and price are related by some underlying process such as value.

Our score on specification = 7.

TESTABILITY: Are the operational definitions provided to ensure testability and intersubjective consensus?

The managerial school clearly ranks highest on the testability criterion among all the schools reviewed so far. This is not surprising in view of the fact that the managerial school is anchored to marketing practice and marketing realities. There are excellent operational definitions for each functional area of marketing practice so that both field experiments and survey research can be carried out. This has been particularly true for the price and promotion areas of marketing.

Furthermore, there is good intersubjective consensus about the testability of specific relationships, perhaps due to industry-wide measures and standards created by market research companies, such as A. C. Nielsen and M.R.C.A.

Our score on testability = 8.

EMPIRICAL SUPPORT: What is the degree of confirmation in terms of empirical support?

The managerial school has generated by far the greatest amount of scientific studies to test its hypotheses. Although there are strong controversies on specific issues such as how advertising works or which promotional deal generates more sales, it is undeniable that the managerial school has more empirical support for its basic concepts than all the previous five schools of thought put together. At the same time, the managerial school has also generated an enormous amount of empirical support in the world of marketing practice.

Our score on empirical support = 9.

RICHNESS: How comprehensive and generalizable is the theory?

The managerial school also scores high on richness because it encompasses all areas of marketing. Its concepts transcend specialized areas such as industrial, international, services, and social marketing. In other words, the basic concepts of product life cycle, market segmentation, marketing mix, and the like seem equally applicable to any specialized area of marketing activity.

The managerial school has only one weakness. It is managerial in its orientation and, therefore, is likely to provide a biased perspective on such areas as consumerism and environmental side effects of marketing activities.

Our score on richness = 9.

SIMPLICITY: How easy is it to communicate and implement the theory?

The managerial school is extremely simple to understand. Its concepts are easy to communicate as evidenced by their dissemination in introductory marketing management classes.

Similarly, the managerial school has been implemented in most organizations, although probably not to the same extent as the functional concept. Unfortunately, many corporations do not fully appreciate the marketing concept and still equate marketing with selling.

Our score on simplicity = 9.

Table 3.3 summarizes our evaluation of the managerial school of marketing. It is impressive to note that the managerial school scores well across all the three areas of metatheory: organization, reality, and relevance. This suggests that the reputation of the marketing discipline is likely to be enhanced more by the managerial school than by the functional, institutional, commodity, or even functionalist schools of thought. It is also not surprising to note that the managerial school has attracted more scholars and researchers than any other school of marketing thought, except perhaps the buyer behavior school.

Table 3.3 Evaluation of the Managerial School*

Criterion	Rationale	Score
Structure	Extremely well-defined concepts and relationships	8
Specification	Excellent specification of relationships at the elemental level but not at the marketing mix level	7
Testability	Excellent operational definitions at the functional level	8
Empirical support	Very comprehensive testing at both the scientific and practice levels	9
Richness	Extremely rich so that it transcends all areas of marketing	9
Simplicity	Very easy to understand and implement in practice	9
	TOTAL	50

* *Scores range from 1 (poor) to 10 (excellent).*

SUMMARY

This chapter has reviewed the institutional, the functionalist, and the managerial schools of thought. All of them are basically economic perspectives but they do acknowledge the interactive processes between the producers, the middlemen, and the consumers. In other words, they believe in interdependence among various marketing actors.

The institutional school has focused on the role of middlemen in marketing and not on the products or the functions of marketing. It began with Weld, Butler, and Breyer but has been enriched significantly by more contemporary scholars including McCammon, Mallen, and Bucklin. The institutional school has generated some intriguing concepts such as the structure of vertical distribution systems, functional spinoff, and the principles of speculation versus postponement. Although the institutional school is very good in structure and specification, it has been lacking in testability and empirical support. However, it has good relevance in terms of richness and simplicity.

The functionalist school proposed by Wroe Alderson is extremely rich. Based on a very few concepts such as market heterogeneity, sorting, transformation, and transvections, Alderson has provided a theory that is generic to all areas of marketing. Unfortunately, the theory has never been tested. Furthermore, Alderson's obsession with coining new phrases and words has compounded the problem of carrying out operationally defined studies to test his theory. Of course, there is no question that Alderson will always be remembered as a major contributor to the development of marketing thought.

The managerial school has focused on marketing practice. In the process, it has generated such widely accepted concepts as the product life cycle, market segmentation, and the marketing mix. The managerial school scores high on all of the six metatheory criteria, which is somewhat surprising in view of the fact that it is a practice- or application- driven school of thought.

4

NONINTERACTIVE–
NONECONOMIC
SCHOOLS OF
MARKETING

This chapter describes and evaluates three noninteractive and noneconomic schools of marketing. As pointed out in Chapter 1, the three schools of thought that fit this categorization are the buyer behavior, activist, and macromarketing schools of thought. All of them take the perspective of the recipients of marketing practice, including comsumers and society at large. At the same time, they provide conceptual frameworks, hypotheses, and empirical evidence based on behavioral and social sciences rather than economic theories.

The noninteractive-noneconomic schools of thought represent a significant shift in the history of marketing thought. First, the traditional and time-honored normative concepts of economics about how markets *should behave* gave way to the more descriptive concepts of the behavioral and social sciences about how markets *actually behave.* This represents a shift from the normative to the positive sciences.

Second, the emphasis also begins to shift away from an earlier focus on more aggregate markets and toward a focus on individual customers in the market or segments of consumers. In that respect, the unit of analysis becomes increasingly microlevel.

In many ways this two-dimensional shift (economic to behavioral and markets to customers) seems to have resulted in a discontinuity between the older schools and the newer schools of marketing thought. Consequently, all the knowledge and thinking generated by the previous six schools of marketing thought seem to be relegated in importance. Indeed, the emergence of the noneconomic schools of marketing thought seem to fit Kuhn's (1962) paradigm of radical shift as the basis for the revolution of a discipline. Only in recent years have several scholars begun to comment that this discontinuity in marketing thought may have resulted in the loss of valuable heritage and richness of knowledge generated by the commodity, functional, institutional, regional, and managerial schools of thought (Sheth 1979b, 1985a).

THE BUYER BEHAVIOR SCHOOL OF THOUGHT

As the name implies, the buyer behavior school has focused on customers in the marketplace. In addition to the demographic information on how many and who are the customers, the buyer behavior school of marketing has attempted to address the question of *why* customers behave the way they do in the marketplace. This emphasis on the why aspect of consumer behavior has resulted in several unique characteristics of the buyer behavior school.

First, consumer behavior is considered a subset of human behavior rather than treated as a unique phenomenon similar to abnormal or deviant behavior. In the process, there has been a strong tendency to borrow explanations of human behavior as possible clues to understanding consumer behavior. As we will demonstrate later, this has resulted in numerous partial theories of consumer behavior, each one based on a unique or specific proposition in psychology, sociology, and anthropology. As Sheth (1967) has amply demonstrated in his review of the field, this pluralistic but parallel borrowing from diverse disciplines of behavioral sciences has generated the phenomenon of the proverbial seven blind men touching the elephant and providing very plausible but different explanations as to why the consumer behaves the way he or she does.

Second, the emphasis in the buyer behavior school has been overwhelmingly on consumer products such as packaged goods and consumer durables. Although there is increasing interest in industrial and services buying behavior, the discipline of buyer behavior is still focused on consumer products. This is partly due to the operational ease with which empirical research may be conducted, but we believe it is also rooted in the presumption that buying behavior is a subset of human behavior.

Finally, the buyer behavior school has also delimited itself to understanding brand choice behavior as opposed to other types of choices such as product class, volume, or timing of choices. Furthermore, it has also limited itself to understanding purchase behavior as opposed to consumption and disposal behavior (Holbrook 1985, Sheth 1985b).

It is no exaggeration to state that among all schools of marketing thought, the buyer behavior school has had the greatest impact on the discipline of marketing with the possible exception of the managerial school of marketing. Consequently, this school of thought has attracted numerous scholars both from within and outside of the marketing discipline. It is, therefore, extremely difficult to provide a chronological and detailed evolution of this school of thought as we did with the other schools of marketing thought. Literally hundreds of scholars and thousands of research papers are in this area. Therefore, we will attempt to provide major highlights of the historical evolution of buyer behavior in marketing and leave it up to the reader to obtain more detailed information from other sources such as proceedings of the Association for Consumer Research (ACR), the *Journal of Consumer Research*, and several books of readings as well as textbooks (e.g., Kassarjian and Robertson 1981; Engel, Blackwell, and Miniard 1986).

The evolution and description of the buyer behavior school of thought is organized as follows:

1. Why did the buyer behavior school become so popular in marketing?
2. Who were the pioneers in the behavioral sciences to make an impact on this emerging field?
3. How did the buyer behavior school evolve and where is it today?
4. What are the major tenets, findings, and generalizations provided by the buyer behavior school?
5. What impact has the buyer behavior school had on the discipline and practice of marketing?

Of course, we will evaluate the buyer behavior school with the same six metatheory criteria as before.

Popularity of the Buyer Behavior School

Our analysis suggests two major reasons for the evolution and rapid popularity of the buyer behavior school: (1) the emergence of the marketing concept; and (2) the established body of knowledge in behavioral science.

Emergence of the Marketing Concept Soon after World War II, the American economy along with the Western European economy had begun to shift from a sellers' economy to a buyers' economy. The extraordinary installation of manufacturing capacity had generated excess capacity and it was becoming harder and harder to sell what was produced. This was further compounded by intense competition in the marketplace as several large competitors began to emerge in each industry.

Both marketing practitioners and marketing scholars began to question the traditional supply-oriented marketing practices including the concept of push marketing. For example, Robert Keith (1960) at Pillsbury represented the sentiment of the practitioners when he stated:

In today's economy the consumer, the man or the woman who buys the product, is at the absolute dead center of the business universe. Companies revolve around the customers, not the other way around. Growing acceptance of this consumer concept has had, and will have, far-reaching implications for business, achieving a virtual revolution in economic thinking. As the concept gains ever greater acceptance, marketing is emerging as the most important single function in business (p. 35).

Similar views were also expressed by several marketing scholars, most notably Philip Kotler. In the first edition of the most popular textbook in marketing, Kotler (1967) sharply contrasted the production, selling, and customer-oriented marketing philosophies with a strong advocacy toward the latter orientation in marketing practice. This academic sentiment was eloquently expressed by Markin (1969):

[The marketing manager] recognizes at the outset that the success or failure of his marketing strategy rests ultimately with the consumer as market for which his strategy has been designed. Consequently, most strategy formulations are based on the assumption that consumer behavior can be either (i) analyzed and understood, or (ii) analyzed, understood and modified. Both assumptions strongly dictate that marketing managers know and learn how consumer impressions, opinions, and images can be modified and how firms can successfully communicate their marketing programs to the consumer. (p. 7)

Although the customer orientation in marketing was at its infancy in the late 1950s and early 1960s and was limited to packaged goods companies such as Pillsbury, Procter and Gamble, and General Foods, it is important to recognize that customer orientation is today considered vital to the survival of corporations in virtually every sector of the economy (Peters and Waterman 1982, Lele and Sheth 1987).

Established Body of Knowledge At the same time, there was also a growing realization that a host of disciplines in the behavioral sciences had generated a body of knowledge that may be very useful to business functions in general and marketing in particular. Indeed, the Ford Foundation allocated large sums of grant money to schools of business for the explicit purpose of increasing the competency in behavioral and mathematical sciences. Consequently, the pure disciplines began to apply their expertise and ideas to the unexplored areas of business, and a number of scholars in the behavioral and social sciences began to shift their research to the business arena.

It is beyond the scope of this book to provide an exhaustive list of the applications of behavioral and mathematical sciences to marketing and business. However, we will provide some illustrative examples to sensitize the reader.

From cultural anthropology, Hall (1960) proposed five silent languages that create barriers in overseas business and marketing negotiations. These included languages of time, space, friendship, material possessions, and nature of agreements. From the field of cognitive psychology, March and Simon (1958) and Edwards (1961) provided a number of concepts that are often in conflict with economic propositions. These include such concepts as subjective utility, bounded rationality, satisficing goals and objectives, and organizational conflicts due to differences in perceptions and goals among corporate employees.

We also began to borrow concepts from cognitive psychology such as cognitive dissonance (Festinger 1957) and cognitive conflict in consumer and organizational behavior. From the field of clinical psychology and personality, the business discipline began to learn the concepts of group dynamics, emotional versus rational behavior, and the more humanistic theories of managing and motivating employees (Maslow 1954, Heider 1958, McGregor 1960, Allport 1961, Homans 1961, McClelland 1961). In the area of sociology, we borrowed such concepts as social stratification, social class, and diffusion of innovations including theories of opinion leadership and personal influence (Warner, Meeker, and Eells 1949, Katz and Lazarsfeld 1955, Rogers 1962).

Along with the substantive body of knowledge, business disciplines including marketing began to apply the methodologies of the behavioral sciences. For example, focus group interviews and unstructured personal interviews became very popular in market research. At the same time, we began to collect data based on longitudinal panels of consumers following the traditions established in sociology, political science, and public opinion research. Finally, we also started the use of experiments as a scientific way to test behavioral hypotheses, especially as they related to cognitive and learning theories in psychology. In marketing, for example, Holloway (1967a) published a bibliography on experiments in marketing (updated by Gardner and Belk 1980). We also began to apply the laboratory methods associated with physiological psychology including sensory stimulation and perceptions of physical realities. This resulted in the use of pupil dilation, galvanic skin pressure, and other physiological measures of consumer responses (see Ferber 1974 for a good review in market research).

In addition to the behavioral sciences, marketing began to borrow from the mathematical sciences. Operations research and management science techniques such as stochastic process, linear programming, and optimization theory began to be applied to buyer behavior research (Bass et al. 1961, Massy, Montgomery, and Morrison 1970).

In short, the buyer behavior school of marketing emerged and mushroomed because marketing practitioners perceived a need to understand the customer. Further, an available body of knowledge was appropriate for that understanding.

Early Pioneers from Behavioral Sciences

As mentioned before, numerous scholars from many disciplines of the behavioral sciences generated enthusiasm among marketing scholars interested in buyer behavior research. It is again impossible to provide an exhaustive list. However, we will discuss the contributions of a few scholars to illustrate the scope and process of their influence in shaping buyer behavior theory and research traditions.

Among the earliest pioneers from the behavioral sciences was George Katona. His classic paper (Katona 1953) on the differences between economic and psychological behavior generated strong interest in buyer behavior. Katona also pioneered the techniques of consumer intentions and sentiments as a way of forecasting their behavior (Katona and Mueller 1953, 1956). His theories of consumption (1960) and focus on the consumer (1964) are still considered major contributions in economic psychology and consumer psychology.

A second pioneer from the behavioral sciences to make a major impact in marketing and buyer behavior was Paul Lazarsfeld. His research on opinion leadership and personal influence (Katz and Lazarsfeld 1955) generated the tradition of research on word of mouth communication in consumer behavior. He also contributed toward the research methodology of longitudinal panels as a method of collecting data and hierarchical cross-tabulations as a method of analyzing data.

The third pioneer from the behavioral sciences was Everett Rogers. His book on diffusion of innovations (Rogers 1962) immediately became popular in marketing, and a number of empirical studies were carried out on the diffusion of new products and brands. Rogers' work is still popular in consumer behavior and marketing, inspiring major works such as those by Arndt (1967) and Robertson (1971), as well as numerous research papers. His recent work (Rogers 1983) serves as a review of well over a thousand research studies on the diffusion concept. More recently, Gatignon and Robertson (1985) have offered twenty-nine theoretical propositions to guide future research in this area, as well as to provide a foundation for those who wish to model various aspects of the diffusion process.

A fourth pioneer for the behavioral sciences was Leon Festinger. His theory of cognitive dissonance (Festinger 1957) began to be applied in the early 1960s, resulting in a stream of publications for the next two decades. Today, cognitive dissonance theory is an integral part of buyer behavior theory.

Similarly, theories of several other well-known psychologists were applied to understand consumer behavior. These included Sigmund Freud (1953), Clark Hull (1952), Charles Osgood (1957a, 1957b), Daniel Katz (Katz and Stotland 1959, Katz 1960), Neal Miller (1959), Carl Hovland (1954), and Martin Fishbein (1963, 1967; Fishbein and Ajzen 1975). However, their work has received segmented rather than universal attention in marketing.

Finally, March and Simon (1958) and Cyert and March (1963) must be acknowledged for their influence on marketing scholars who were focused more on organizational buying behavior. Their work on organizational psychology was directly applied in understanding and modeling industrial buying behavior.

Evolution of the Buyer Behavior School

Unlike the previous schools of marketing thought, it is extremely difficult to identify any one individual as the father of the buyer behavior school of marketing. Furthermore, it is equally difficult to suggest that at any one time period there was only one thought process dominant in the evolution of the buyer behavior school. Instead, several marketing scholars were simultaneously developing separate research efforts often in conflict with one another. In light of this diversity, we have chosen to provide a chronological perspective.

Decade of the Fifties The buyer behavior school of thought, especially with the behavioral emphasis, really began in the early 1950s. In the decade of the 1950s, we have identified three separate areas of research.

The first area of research focused on emotional and irrational psychological determinants of consumer behavior. This research tradition was pioneered by Ernest Dichter (1947, 1964) and it is often referred to as motivation research. The basic assumption underlying this research tradition was that consumers make product or brand choices for emotional and deep-seated reasons they are neither willing to discuss nor aware of. The only way to understand these motivations is to use the methodology and concepts of clinical psychology. Motivation research thus began to rely on focus group interviews and personal nonstructured interviews that needed to be analyzed and interpreted by trained clinical psychologists.

There has been considerable criticism of motivation research on basically two grounds. First, its heavy reliance on Freudian psychology and unconscious motivations has been criticized as more an exception rather than a rule in consumer motivations. It is argued that most consumer behavior is conscious rather than unconscious and most consumers are normal rather than abnormal in their behavior. Second, the interpretation of consumer information is regarded as highly subjective and lacking in consensus validation.

Motivation research responded to these criticisms by utilizing psychometrically developed and numerically measurable personality tests such as the MMPI. These personality tests also broadened the motivational determinants of consumer behavior from abnormal to normal motivations. Unfortunately, most research utilizing personality traits as the basis of consumer choice behavior has remained inconclusive and conflicting in its findings. For an excellent review of personality research in consumer behavior, the reader is urged to read Kassarjian (1971).

A second research tradition focused on the social determinants of consumer behavior. Popular concepts from sociology including conspicuous consumption and reference group influence resulted in a series of empirical studies in buyer behavior. While the results of conspicuous consumption research have been somewhat interesting in terms of products and brands that are visible symbols of social class, they have provided less conclusive results for other products and services.

Perhaps the most popular area of research has been the influence of reference groups on both product and brand choice behavior (Bourne 1957). For example, reference groups were found to determine whether a person will be a smoker or not, as well as what brand of cigarettes he will smoke. On the other hand, reference groups apparently do not determine whether a person will read magazines or buy furniture. However, reference groups were found to be highly influential on what type of magazines or furniture the person bought.

A related area of research that began in the 1950s was on the power of word of mouth communication. Katz and Lazarsfeld (1955) as well as Whyte (1955) had demonstrated that personal influence was more critical than mass media in social choices. This resulted in the examining of the role of advertising, personal influence, and opinion leadership in consumer behavior (Arndt 1967).

The third area of research in the 1950s focused on household decision making. The interest in this area was generated by the DuPont Corporation, which conducted surveys of grocery shopping including the shopping list the homemaker prepared before entering the supermarket. At the same time, Katona (1964) and his colleagues at the Institute for Social Research had developed consumer intentions as a leading indicator of spending behavior for the U.S. economy. This generated significant amounts of research on family buying behavior by home economists and marketing scholars (Sheth 1974b). Perhaps the best summary of this area of research tradition can be found in the four volumes edited by Lincoln Clark (1954, 1955, 1958) and Nelson Foote (1961).

Decade of the Sixties The decade of the 1960s can be characterized as the sunrise of the buyer behavior school. A large number of scholars with very different academic backgrounds began to devote their time and energy to the area of consumer behavior. Out of their efforts, a number of new and innovative research traditions began to emerge in the 1960s.

Perhaps the most incisive and exciting research focused on brand loyalty among consumer grocery products. With the availability of panel diary data from the *Chicago Tribune* and M.R.C.A., a number of scholars began to analyze the purchase patterns of households over time. The early efforts by Ross Cunningham (1956) and George Brown (1952-53) attracted a number of management science experts to the field. This led to the development of brand loyalty models based on the Bernoulli, the Markovian, and other stochastic processes.

Alfred Kuehn (1962) led the way followed by others including Ronald Howard (1963), Ronald Frank (1962), and William Massy (1969) and his students at Stanford University. This research tradition reached its peak in the late 1960s and culminated in the publication of a major book by Massy, Montgomery, and Morrison (1970). Although the application of stochastic and econometric modeling to understand brand buying behavior still continues, it has not been as explosive since the late 1960s.

A second research tradition began to emerge in the early 1960s. This was founded on the use of experimental designs and laboratory based experiments in a number of different areas of buyer behavior. For example, Robert Holloway (1967b) and his students at the University of Minnesota carried out a series of experiments on the application of Festinger's cognitive dissonance theory in brand choice behavior. At the same time, many advertising practitioners began to use laboratory methods to measure the physiological responses of consumers by such electromechanical apparatus as pupil dilation and galvanic skin pressure. Also, the DuPont Corporation developed a top market research department that conducted numerous field experiments on the effects of advertising media and exposure. Finally, it would be a serious error of omission not to recognize some of the best field experiments conducted by the United States Department of Agriculture on consumer preferences for oranges and apples.

A third stream of research began at Harvard University under the leadership of Raymond Bauer (1960), who proposed a theory of perceived risk in consumer behavior. The basic tenets underlying his theory were based on Simon's concepts of bounded rationality and satisficing. Bauer proposed that consumers do not maximize utilities as suggested by economists but instead minimize risks associated with making consumer choices. This simple but elegant theory became very popular in the same manner as Festinger's cognitive dissonance theory. A number of research studies and doctoral dissertations were carried out in order to test various components and perceived risk implications of Bauer's theory. A good summary of these research findings can be found in Cox (1967).

A fourth stream of research in buyer behavior focused on the development of comprehensive theories of consumer behavior. It was agreed that buyer behavior is too complex and highly dynamic to be fully explained by unidimensional and cross-sectional models. What is needed is a process oriented theory that allows for learning over time because buyer behavior is repetitive, and consumers can easily generalize their experiences from one choice situation to another.

A number of marketing scholars proposed their own comprehensive theories of buyer behavior. These included Howard (1963a), Andreasen (1965), Nicosia (1966), and Engel, Kollat, and Blackwell (1968). The latter was more an attempt to provide a conceptual integrative framework for their first textbook in consumer behavior, although eventually it came to be recognized as a theory of consumer behavior. Even though there were some differences among these models of buyer behavior, they all have the same two basic characteristics: process orientation and feedback through learning and experiences.

Perhaps the most well known comprehensive theory of buyer behavior was proposed by Howard and Sheth (1969). For the first time, Howard and Sheth utilized the metatheory criteria in buyer behavior and began to create a comprehensive theory based on several well-known concepts in psychology. These included learning theory, exploratory behavior, and symbolic representations underlying languages and concept formation. The fundamental axioms of the theory were as follows:

1. Consumers like to simplify complex choice situations by a process of learning over time. This results in a psychology of simplication consisting of extensive problem solving, limited problem solving, and, eventually, routinized response behavior.

2. Consumers like to complicate choice situations when the choices are highly routinized and non-challenging. This results in a psychology of complication consisting of novelty and curiosity behavior, as well as active search for new alternatives.

3. Compared to information, experience with products and brands is a more important determinant of future choice. Only when there is no prior experience is the consumer likely to rely on information.

4. Information from the physical product (significative information) is less filtered through perceptual mechanisms of exposure, attention, and retention than information from advertising and personal selling (symbolic information) sources. Also, information from social and neutral sources is perceptually filtered less than information from commercial sources.

5. Consumer satisfaction is psychological and is directly a function of the discrepancy between prior expectations and subsequent experiences. It will, therefore, vary over time for the same consumer as well as across consumers at a point in time. This makes it very difficult for the marketer to achieve universal consumer satisfaction in the marketplace.

6. A number of exogenous factors influence as well as control the process of simplication and complication. These include the consumer's personal characteristics, his/her social environment, as well as his/her scarce resources of money and time. Also, the process of simplication and complication is likely to be different for product categories that vary in their importance or involvement and perceived risks associated with wrong choices.

In our evaluation, the Howard-Sheth theory of buyer behavior became more popular than others for at least three reasons. First, as Zaltman et al. (1973) pointed out, it was more rigorously developed in terms of theory building criteria a la philosophy of science. Second, it attempted to provide construct validity and face validity by consistently incorporating prior research findings from marketing, psychology, and other behavioral sciences. Finally, and perhaps most important, the theory was tested in the real world in several large-scale research projects at Columbia University (Farley, Howard, and Ring 1974). Although the results were not conclusive, these empirical tests demonstrated that the theory was testable.

Decade of the Seventies The decade of the 1970s can be characterized as the coming of age in the buyer behavior field. For the first time, the buyer behavior school began to emerge as a distinct discipline rather than one more school of marketing thought. A number of institutional events occurred in the 1970s that elevated the buyer behavior school to the status of a separate discipline.

The most dramatic was the formation of a separate organization called the Association for Consumer Research (ACR) in 1969. What began as an American Marketing Association (AMA) sponsored workshop on consumer behavior at Ohio State University under the leadership of James Engel turned into the start of a separate organization for scholars, practitioners, and policymakers interested in consumer behavior. According to Gardner (1971), ACR was organized to serve the following purposes:

1. To provide a forum for exchange of ideas among those interested in consumer behavior research in academic disciplines, in government at all levels from local through national, in private business, and in other sectors such as nonprofit organizations and foundations.

2. To stimulate research focusing on a better understanding of consumer behavior from a variety of perspectives.

3. To disseminate research findings and other contributions to the understanding of consumer behavior through professional seminars, conferences, and publications (p. i).

ACR continued to grow throughout the 1970s and today has become an alternative to the American Marketing Association for researchers interested in consumer behavior. Since 1970, ACR has provided a major avenue of publications through its annual conference proceedings, which are respected as scholarly papers.

Another institutional event that reflected the coming of age in buyer behavior was the start of a scholarly journal. The *Journal of Consumer Research* (JCR), organized in 1974, was intended to be an interdisciplinary journal and not just a marketing oriented journal. According to its first editor, JCR was created as a "medium for interdisciplinary exchange over an exceedingly broad range of topics, the common denominator of which is their relationship to the study of consumer behavior" (Frank 1974, p. v).

The decade of the 1970s generated several research trends, some of which reflected the continuation of the 1960s, and others reflected new thinking. For example, the testing of the comprehensive theories of buyer behavior, especially the Howard-Sheth theory, continued into the 1970s (Farley et al. 1974, Howard and Hulbert 1973, Howard 1977, 1988). Similarly, the applications of operations research techniques to buying behavior were also continued by scholars including Blattberg and Sen (1976). Also, the diffusion of innovations research tradition continued under the leadership of more mathematically oriented scholars such as Bass (1969) and Peterson and Mahajan (1978). In fact, it is quite accurate to state that research on personal influence, social class, household decision making, and perceived risk all continued in the decade of the 1970s. Most of this research was published in the *Journal of Consumer Research* and in Association for Consumer Research (ACR) proceedings.

At the same time, several new research streams began to emerge during the decade of the 1970s. The first research area focused on industrial or organizational buying behavior. The groundwork was already established with the publication of a major book by Robinson, Faris, and Wind (1967). Sheth (1973) published a comprehensive model of industrial buying behavior that attempted to integrate and reconcile existing knowledge. Others such as Webster and Wind (1972), Woodside, Sheth, and Bennett (1977), Bonoma and Zaltman (1978), and Johnston and Bonoma (1981) also were active in defining this area. This interest in understanding and empirically researching organizational buying behavior has continued even today.

This area of research has recently been characterized as "still at the conceptual stage" (Anderson, Chu, and Weitz 1987, p. 71). While a research tradition seems to be developing, most of the existing research falls into one of two categories. These categories are clearly not independent, but overlap one another. One category of research pertains to the organizational buying center. It focuses on organizational members who have significant involvement in the decision-making process for a particular purchase. As an example of work in this area, Jackson, Keith, and Burdick (1984) studied the relative influence of buying center members across product categories. They found that influence was generally relatively constant across different buyclasses but varied across product types and decision types. As another example, Krapfel (1985) developed and tested a model to explain the behavior of buying center boundary role persons who take on the additional role of advocate.

A second category of research pertains to organizational buying behavior. This broad category has a general focus on how organizations approach the buying process, without a specific focus on the buying center. As examples of work in this area, Puto, Patton, and King (1985) explored risk handling strategies in the industrial vendor selection process; and Anderson and Chambers (1985) proposed a model of the organizational buying process based on the assumption that ". . . purchasing process participants are motivated to engage in purchasing behavior by the expectation of both intrinsic and extrinsic rewards" (p. 9). Anderson, Chu, and Weitz (1987) conducted an empirical study of the buyclass theory proposed by Robinson, Faris, and Wind (1967). By querying salesforce managers, they found that:

> Much of what salespeople observe is found to correspond closely to the buyclass theory of organizational buyer behavior. Also the "problem newness" and "information needs" dimensions are found to be strongly related, as expected. However, "seriousness of consideration of alternatives" seems to be a separate dimension that does not operate entirely as predicted by the buyclass framework. (p. 71)

Typical of other studies in organizational buying behavior is research by Leigh and Rethans (1984), who focus on a more limited area, applying cognitive script theory to the analysis of industrial purchasing behavior.

A second major area of research in buyer behavior focused on social and public services such as population control, education, health care, transportation, and nutrition (Sheth and Wright 1974). This was a direct result of the emerging interest in applying marketing practice and concepts to nonprofit organizations (Kotler 1975). To a large extent, this focus in buyer behavior toward socially desirable behaviors resulted in increased respect for scholars in marketing. Other disciplines began to realize that buyer behavior can be researched for the benefit of consumers as well as marketers. Consequently, a number of scholars from social psychology and sociology began to notice the field of buyer behavior as a relevant domain for the application of their research concepts and methods. The emphasis toward nonprofit services has now broadened to the services sector in general including the health care, financial, information, and entertainment industries (e.g., Gelb and Gilly 1979).

A third area of research in buyer behavior began to focus on cross-cultural issues. Although Dichter (1962) had tried to sensitize marketing practitioners to the importance of cross-cultural differences in international marketing, conceptual thinking and empirical research did not begin until the early 1970s. The interest was perhaps due to the increased global competition, especially from Japan and Korea, as well as the increasing volume of international trade between the advanced and the lesser developed nations. Despite attempts at developing comprehensive theories of cross-cultural buyer behavior (Sheth and Sethi 1977), cross-cultural buyer behavior was in its infancy in the 1970s and is likely to intensify and grow in the eighties and the nineties.

A fourth area of research to emerge in the 1970s was family buying behavior, including joint decision-making behavior between husbands and wives. Sheth (1974b) generated a comprehensive theory of family buying behavior that was process oriented and somewhat similar to his theory of industrial buying behavior. However, Davis and Rigaux (1974) triggered considerable interest in this area with their insightful research. In particular, the joint decision-making processes and conflict-resolution strategies among family members became an interesting and important area of understanding. This research on family buying behavior also continues to flourish in the 1980s.

The fifth and perhaps the strongest research stream emerged in the area of attitude-behavior relationship and attitude formation and structure. Howard and Sheth (1969) generated a strong theoretical base for suggesting that prior attitudes toward brands become good predictors of future behavior *if there are no inhibitors*. However, Martin Fishbein (1963, 1967; Fishbein and Ajzen 1975)) and his theory of behavioral intentions generated strong enthusiasm in consumer behavior. The Fishbein model was simple, but elegant, with precise operational measures for its variables. The basic thesis of the model was that a person's intention to perform a specific behavioral act (BI) is a function of two factors: the person's personal beliefs about the consequences arising from performing that act and/or the person's beliefs about his/her reference group's norms whether he/she should or should not perform that act. In short, personal beliefs or normative beliefs and their respective saliencies determine individual actions. The Fishbein model generated numerous research studies in consumer behavior, some of which even attempted to extend or modify the Fishbein model. At the same time, several other attitude models in social psychology began to be applied in consumer behavior (Wilkie and Pessemier 1973, Sheth 1974a).

A related area that emerged as a separate stream of research is called information processing. How consumers utilize information, assimilate it, and make evaluative judgments toward products and brands became fascinating to several scholars in marketing (Jacoby, Speller, and Kohn 1974, Wright 1973, Bettman 1979). This resulted in at least three distinct controversies. First, can there be an information overload? In other words, are consumers worse off with too much information when making choice judgments? The second area of controversy related to the issue of whether consumers use compensatory versus noncompensatory approaches to making judgments. Several alternative models such as compensatory, disjunctive, conjunctive, and lexicographic models of information processing were competing against one another. Finally, a third area of controversy was related to the methodology of information collection. More specifically, whether to use protocols (verbal descriptions) or to use scaled statements for gathering data became a hot topic of interest and debate.

Although attitude research overwhelmed other research streams in the 1970s, it also generated strong negative reactions. Several scholars began to object to the narrow focus and cognitive base underlying the multiattribute models (Sheth 1979b, Hirschman 1980, Zielinski and Robertson 1982, Holbrook and Hirschman 1982). It was argued that a number of buyer behavior phenomena may be experiential, emotional, and otherwise noncognitive in nature. Furthermore, the discipline of buyer behavior had many other interesting areas of research (novelty seeking, crowd behavior, deviancy, etc.) that were being neglected by this exclusive focus on cognitive models.

Decade of the Eighties The decade of the 1980s can be characterized as the new dawn of consumer behavior. The backlash against information processing and multiattribute models has generated interesting and highly interactive research interests. These include rituals and symbolism (Rook and Levy 1983, Rook 1985), experiential and fantasy behavior (Holbrook and Hirschman 1982), and the impact of religion in consumer behavior (Hirschman 1983). This has also generated a backlash against the quantitative measurements and a preference for more qualitative research traditions prevalent during the era of motivation research. Finally, there is a strong emerging interest in cross-cultural and subcultural issues in consumer behavior (McCracken 1986). Some even argue that the buyer behavior school of marketing is coming back home after running away from the discipline of marketing.

The diversity of research within this school of thought is both a blessing and a problem. However, more and more, this school of thought is moving toward developing and extending already specified constructs and concepts rather than generating isolated findings. To list but a few examples of recent research, Bloch, Sherrell, and Ridgway (1986) have offered an extended framework for consumer search behavior; Havlena and Holbrook (1986) have explored two competing typologies of emotion; and Pessemier and Handelsman (1984) have empirically examined temporal variety in consumer behavior. Further, Laurent and Kapferer (1985) have extended the thinking in the area of consumer involvement; Hauser (1986) has looked at selecting or eliminating choice alternatives; and Westbrook (1987) has explored dimensions of product/consumption-based affective responses and postpurchase behavior.

Of course, the richness of this school of thought, by its very nature, encourages new ideas. As one example, Alba and Hutchinson (1987) have recently examined consumer expertise. They have argued that consumer expertise differs from product-related expertise and have identified five dimensions of expertise (cognitive effort, cognitive structure, analysis, elaboration, and memory), exploring the interrelationships among these dimensions. They also have offered an extensive appendix that discusses the issues involved in this new approach and have listed over four hundred fifty bibliographic references to guide others interested in this area.

Another new research area in buyer behavior is that of semiotics. As described by Zakia and Nadin (1987, p. 5) semiotics is "... a discipline that provides a structure for studying and analyzing how signs function within a particular environment." As an example of research in semiotics, Mick (1986) explored how consumers comprehend symbolism in the marketplace. Further, a special conference on semiotics, co-sponsored by Northwestern University (Kellogg Graduate School of Management) and Indiana University (Research Center for Language and Semiotic Studies), was held at Northwestern University in the summer of 1986.

Numerous other new areas of research have also appeared. As examples, Rook (1985) has expanded on the ritual construct as a vehicle for interpreting consumer behavior, presenting the results of two studies that investigate the personal grooming rituals of young adults; and Gardner (1985) has presented a conceptual framework pertaining to consumer mood states, depicting the mediating role of mood states and their potential importance for consumer behavior. Biehal and Chakravarti (1986) have examined eight issues relevant to consumers' use of memory and external information in making brand choices. Their study forms the basis for a set of propositions about memory processes in consumer behavior.

EVALUATION OF THE BUYER BEHAVIOR SCHOOL

It is difficult to evaluate the buyer behavior school for several reasons. First, there is enormous diversity of research within the buyer behavior school, which makes it difficult to evaluate without averaging and suggesting exceptions to the average. Second, the buyer behavior school has produced the largest amount of research. The sheer volume of research and concepts in this school makes the job more difficult. Finally, the buyer behavior school has been more interdisciplinary than most other schools of marketing. There are several research traditions embedded in the discipline ranging from highly qualitative to highly quantitative methods. We will provide our evaluation of this school, but we urge the reader to keep in mind the difficulties associated with the evaluative task.

STRUCTURE: **Are the concepts properly defined and integrated to form a strong nomological network?**

The buyer behavior school has several levels of integration. At the one extreme, it consists of straight applications and replication of specific concepts, hypotheses, and research techniques of the behavioral and mathematical sciences. These include personality research, attitude research, and stochastic processes. In the middle are several midrange theories such as perceived risk, information processing, and reference group influences. Finally, at the other extreme are the comprehensive theories of buyer behavior.

The buyer behavior school has generated several specific constructs such as brand loyalty, attitudes, involvement, perceived risk, joint decision making, and buying centers. These are all well defined and properly integrated as needed.

Our score on structure = 8.

SPECIFICATION: Are the relationships specified in a manner to delimit hypotheses or are they highly contingent?

The buyer behavior school scores well in this regard. Even the most comprehensive theories of buyer behavior have provided specific hypotheses that delimit their scope. This is, of course, more true of midrange theories such as the perceived risk theory. Finally, many of the direct applications of behavioral sciences concepts have been based on well-formulated hypotheses. For example, in personality research, certain personality types or traits are hypothesized to produce certain types of buying behavior.

Our score on specifications = 8.

TESTABILITY: Are the operational definitions provided to ensure testability and intersubjective consensus?

On this criterion, the buyer behavior school gets mixed reviews. The operational definitions are excellent when researchers have borrowed standardized and well-tested instruments from other disciplines. These include personality tests and attitude models. Similarly, some of the midrange theories have consciously attempted to evolve toward standardized definitions based on empirical research. These include perceived risk and attitude-intention research. However, there are problems with testability in areas such as motivation research, information processing, involvement, and many of the constructs included in the grand theories of buyer behavior. This is especially true in the areas of organizational, family, and cross-cultural buyer behavior.

Our score on testability = 6.

EMPIRICAL SUPPORT: What is the degree of confirmation in terms of empirical support?

The buyer behavior school has generated the largest amount of empirical research in marketing. There are literally thousands of empirical research studies by both academics and professionals. However, unlike the managerial school of marketing, this school's empirical support has more conflicting results than confirmatory results. In other words, despite the vast amount of research, the degree of confirmation of various research streams is still inconclusive and subject to further testing.

Our score on empirical support = 8.

RICHNESS: How comprehensive and generalizable is the theory?

In this regard, the buyer behavior school scores high. Not only has this school produced comprehensive theories of buyer behavior, but even the midrange theories are regarded as highly generalizable. Furthermore, the buyer behavior school has generated concepts that are usually relevant to both public policymakers and marketing practitioners. Similarly, these concepts are generalizable to both products and services as well as to both consumer and organizational buyer behavior.

Our score on richness = 9.

SIMPLICITY: How easy is it to communicate and implement the theory?

The buyer behavior school gets mixed reviews on this criterion. On the one hand, theories such as perceived risk and attitude models are highly simple to communicate and implement. On the other hand, the process-oriented comprehensive theories such as the Howard-Sheth theory are very complex and difficult to implement in practice. At the same time, consumer behavior is intuitively very appealing since all of us are also consumers and can relate to the concepts based on our own personal experiences.

Our score on simplicity = 8.

Table 4.1 summarizes our evaluation of the buyer behavior school of marketing. It is promising to note that it scores well on all the criteria at least when compared to other schools of thought.

Table 4.1 Evaluation of the Buyer Behavior School*

Criterion	Rationale	Score
Structure	Several specific constructs that are well defined and properly integrated	8
Specification	Theories provide specific hypotheses that delimit their scope	8
Testability	Problems with several midrange theories	6
Empirical support	Much empirical research, but often conflicting results	8
Richness	Produced comprehensive theories and highly generalizable midrange theories	9
Simplicity	Mixed reviews	8
	TOTAL	47

* *Scores range from 1 (poor) to 10 (excellent).*

THE ACTIVIST SCHOOL OF THOUGHT

The activist school of marketing thought represents both empirical research and conceptual thinking related to the issues of consumer welfare and consumer satisfaction. More specifically, it focuses on the imbalance of power between buyers and sellers and on the malpractices of marketing by individual firms in the marketplace.

The activist school is similar to both the buyer behavior school and the macromarketing school in that they all take the perspective of the consumer in the marketplace rather than the marketer. In that respect, they are in sharp contrast to the commodity, functional, and regional schools of thought.

At the same time, the activist school differs from the macromarketing school by focusing on individual consumers and specific industries or companies rather than taking a more macro or institutional perspective. It also differs from the buyer behavior school by taking a more normative and pro-consumer perspective.

The activist school emerged only after several years of efforts by consumer advocates to remedy the imbalance of power. In an excellent summary of the history of the consumer movement, Beem (1973) defines it as follows:

> The expression, the *Consumer Movement*, may be used provisionally in either of two ways. In its more inclusive sense, the term refers historically to the efforts of individuals and groups acting more or less in concert, to solve consumer problems. In this sense, the Consumer Movement refers to activities from the earliest time to the present, and includes the organized activities of consumers themselves, and of other groups and individuals such as teachers, writers, private business and government activities that have worked in the consumer interest. In a second sense, the Consumer Movement refers more particularly to the great burst of activities in behalf of consumers that began in the 1930s and has continued at an accelerated pace (p. 13).

Beem identifies several institutions and individuals responsible in creating and sustaining the consumer movement:

1. Consumers' cooperatives, which began in the late eighteen hundreds and continued to flourish until World War II.

2. Interested organizations such as the American Home Economics Association and pressure groups such as women's clubs, labor unions, and educational institutions.

3. Business agencies such as the Better Business Bureau, the American Standards Association, and many trade associations including the American Medical Association and the American Dental Association.

4. Government agencies such as the Food and Drug Administration, the Federal Trade Commission, and the Department of Agriculture. In

addition, a number of other federal and state regulatory agencies invited consumer representatives to join their advisory boards.

5. Publication of books that depicted consumers as guinea pigs had a strong impact on arousing public attention toward the problems inherent in marketing practices. These include Upton Sinclair's best seller *The Jungle* (1906); *Your Money's Worth*, by Chase and Schlink (1927); *100,000,000 Guinea Pigs*, by Kallet and Schlink (1933); *Skin Deep*, by Phillips (1934); *Eat, Drink and Be Wary*, by Schlink (1935); *Counterfeit*, by Kallet (1935); *Partners in Plunder*, by Mathews and Shallcross (1935); and *American Chamber of Horrors*, by Lamb (1936).

However, the rapid rise of the movement in recent years is more directly attributed to consumers and politicians. For example, John Kenneth Galbraith (1958), Vance Packard (1960), and Rachel Carson (1962) pointed out problems of affluent societies. Similarly, President Kennedy in 1963 attempted to establish the rights of consumers to be informed, to choose, to have safe products, and to be heard (Executive Office of the President, 1963). Also, Senator Warren Magnuson not only introduced a number of bills in Congress, but wrote about the dark side of the marketplace (Magnuson and Carper 1968). But undoubtedly the most influential consumer advocate was Ralph Nader.

> It may be said that one man, Ralph Nader, was really responsible for setting off the new Consumer Movement in 1966 with the publication of his study of the safety of automobiles. His concept of the consumer advocate, of a man well trained in the law, devoting his time and great energies to the public interest was indeed unique. Initially, it inspired cynical disbelief, especially in the corporate boardrooms (what's Nader's angle?) which gave way in time to grudging admiration, if not acceptance (he seems for real!). Indeed, amongst the teenage population and college crowd, Nader took on the dimension of a folk hero, and his panache and influence was strong and persistent and is to this day. (Kelly 1973, p. 49)

As we pointed out in Chapter 1, it is important to recognize that very few marketing practitioners or scholars were interested in this area until the late 1960s, when the consumerism movement became nationally important. Indeed, the early efforts by the marketing practitioners to respond to this movement resulted in the setting up of "hot lines" in their public relations departments. Similarly, only some scholars began to focus on consumerism and develop a stream of research and conceptual thinking.

Empirical Research

The empirical research in marketing regarding consumerism issues can be divided into several distinct areas. Perhaps the largest number of research studies has focused on the malpractices of marketing, especially related to product safety and consumer information. Product safety research has been largely carried out by various federal regulatory agencies including the FDA, FTC, and USDA. Academic researchers have focused on such issues as deceptive advertising and product labeling information (Gardner 1976, Russo 1976, Jacoby and Small 1975, Preston 1976, Armstrong, Kendall, and Russ 1975, Armstrong, Gurol, and Russ 1979, Ford and Calfee 1986).

A second area of empirical research has focused on disadvantaged consumers including the blacks, the Hispanics, the disabled, the poor, and other minority consumers. The classic studies by sociologist David Caplovitz (1963) on the ghetto consumer and his findings that the poor pay more for the same products generated strong interest among several marketing scholars (Andreasen 1975, Ashby 1973, Kassarjian 1969, Bauer and Cunningham 1970, Bullock 1961).

A third area of empirical research has focused on consumer satisfaction and dissatisfaction. Andreasen (1977) provides a rationale for the study of consumer satisfaction as follows:

> Business and nonprofit organizations need measures of how well products and services are meeting client needs and wants so that these organizations can enhance their own and their client's well-being. The government also needs such measures to determine whether the marketplace is functioning well or whether further intervention in the consumer's interest is needed. The extent to which consumer needs and wants are met has come to be called consumer satisfaction/dissatisfaction. (p. 11)

Several conferences were organized in the area of consumer satisfaction/dissatisfaction (Hunt 1977, Day 1977, Hunt and Day 1979, Day and Hunt 1983). Furthermore, many research papers have been published in the Association for Consumer Research (ACR) proceedings. In this area of research, the focus has been largely on empirical studies that measure complaint behavior especially among disadvantaged consumers, such as senior citizens and disabled consumers. At the same time, a considerable number of papers have grappled with the issue of defining and operationalizing measures of consumer satisfaction/dissatisfaction. For example, Cadotte, Woodruff, and Jenkins (1987) compared disconfirmation models of customer satisfaction using causal modeling.

Conceptual Thinking

Only a handful of marketing scholars have attempted to conceptualize the activist school of thought including the role of consumerism in marketing practice. Peter Drucker (1969) defines consumerism as the shame of marketing:

> Consumerism means that the consumer looks upon the manufacturer as somebody who is interested, but who really doesn't know what the

consumer's realities are. He regards the manufacturer as somebody who has not made the effort to find out, and who expects the consumer to be able to make distinctions which the consumer is neither able nor willing to make (p. 60).

Drucker therefore conceptualizes the activist approach as looking at marketing practice from the buyer's viewpoint rather than from the seller's viewpoint. He shows how advertising, product quality, and other marketing mix elements have very different perceptions in the minds of consumers:

> It is our job to make things simple so that they fit the reality of the consumer, not the ego of our engineers. I've long ago learned that when most manufacturers say "quality," they use the engineers' definition, which is "something that's very hard to make and costs a lot of money." That's not quality, that's incompetence. We have not realized that the very abundance, the very multiplicity of choices creates very real problems of information and understanding for the consumer. We have not looked at our business from his, the consumer's, point of view. (p. 61)

Bauer and Greyser (1967) provide a perceptual bias framework for the lack of dialog between business executives and government advocates:

> Why do business and government spokesmen talk past each other in discussing ostensibly the same marketplace? We think it is because each has a basically different model of the consumer world in which marketing operates. This misunderstanding grows from different perceptions about a number of key words. (p. 2)

Bauer and Greyser then summarize these differences as follows:

Two Different Models of the Consumer World

Key Words	Critic's View	Businessman's View
Competition	Price competition	Product differentiation
Product	Primary function only	Differentiation through secondary function
Consumer needs	Correspond point-for-point to primary functions	Any customer desire on which the product can be differentiated
Rationality	Efficient matching of product to customer needs	Any customer decision that serves the customer's own perceived self-interest

Key Words	Critic's View	Businessman's View
Information	Any data that facilitate the fit of a product's proper function with the customer's needs	Any data that will (truthfully) put forth the attractiveness of the product in the eyes of the customer

Adapted from Bauer and Greyser (1967).

Similar to Peter Drucker, Bauer and Greyser also suggest that the best way to reconcile these perceptual differences is for both parties to take the consumer's viewpoint:

> What we propose as a worthwhile endeavor is an independent assessment of the consumer's view of the marketing process, focusing on information needs from his point of view. Thus, rather than businessmen lamenting the critic's proposals for product-rating systems and the critics bemoaning what seems to be obvious abuses of marketing tools, both sides ought to move toward proposing an information system for the consumer that takes into account *his* needs and *his* information-handling capacities while still adhering to the realities of the marketing process. (p. 188)

The most thought-provoking and cogent thinking in this area is provided by Kotler (1972b). Kotler believes that the practice of the marketing concept with its customer orientation is necessary to mesh the actions of business with the interests of consumers:

> Consumerism has come as a shock to many businessmen because deep in their hearts they believe that they have been serving the consumer extraordinarily well. Do businessmen deserve the treatment that they are getting at the hands of consumerists?
>
> It is possible that the business sector has deluded itself into thinking that it has been serving the consumer well. Although the marketing concept is the professed philosophy of a majority of U.S. companies, perhaps it is more honored in the breach than in the observance. Although top management professes the concept, the line executives, who are rewarded for ringing up sales, may not practice it faithfully. (p. 55)

Kotler suggests that customer satisfaction is not sufficient to create a win-win situation between consumers and producers for two reasons. First, it is very difficult to define objectively customer satisfaction. Second, what is desired by consumers may not be good for them. Therefore, the marketer may create a happy customer in the short run but in the long run, both the consumer and society at large may suffer in satisfying the customer. He cites several examples such as cigarette smoking and nonnutritious foods to prove his point. He suggests that it is the responsibility of marketing to generate new products that provide *both* immediate customer satisfaction *and* protect the long-term welfare of the consumers.

Kotler provides a paradigm to classify all current product offerings based on the two dimensions of immediate satisfaction and long-term consumer welfare:

Kotler's Paradigm of Product Categories

		Immediate Satisfaction	
		Low	High
	High	Salutary products	Desirable products
Long run consumer welfare	Low	Deficient products	Pleasing products

... *desirable products* are those which combine high immediate satisfaction and high long-run benefit, such as tasty, nutritious breakfast foods. *Pleasing products* are those which give high immediate satisfaction but which may hurt consumer interests in the long run, such as cigarettes. *Salutary products* are those which have low appeal but which are also highly beneficial to the consumer in the long run, such as low phosphate detergents. Finally, *deficient products* are those which have neither immediate appeal nor salutary qualities, such as a bad tasting patent medicine.

The manufacturer might as well forget about deficient products because too much work would be required to build in pleasing and salutary qualities. On the other hand, the manufacturer should invest his greatest effort in developing desirable products — e.g., new foods, textiles, appliances, and building materials —which combine intrinsic appeal and long-run beneficiality ... The challenge posed by pleasing products is that they sell extremely well, but they ultimately hurt the consumer's interests. The product opportunity is therefore to formulate some alteration of the product that adds salutary qualities without diminishing any or too many of the pleasing qualities. Salutary products, such as nonflammable draperies and many health foods, are considered "good for the customer" but somehow lack pleasing qualities. The challenge to the marketer is to incorporate satisfying qualities in the product without sacrificing the salutary qualities (pp. 56-57).

Kotler's fourfold classification of products based on the two criteria of long-run consumer welfare and immediate customer satisfaction has considerable merit. It is possible to suggest that long-run consumer welfare measures marketing effectiveness, whereas immediate customer satisfaction measures marketing efficiency. Thus, an industry with many desirable products will be both effective and efficient and, in the process, balance the interests of the company and the public. On the other hand, an industry full of pleasing products will be very efficient or profitable, but may not be effective from society's viewpoint; therefore, it may require social regulation. Finally, an industry full of salutary products may be very effective, but not efficient or profitable; therefore, it may require government incentives or public sector ownership.

In recent years, the activist school has focused its attention on the specific subject of marketing ethics. Although sporadic studies of unethical marketing practices by marketing scholars had appeared for many years, in the 1980s a concerted effort has been made to evaluate conceptually the nature and role of marketing ethics. A major development in this regard was the publication of *Marketing Ethics: Guidelines for Managers*, edited by Gene Laczniak and Patrick Murphy (1985). Chapters in this volume focused on ethical issues in advertising, personal selling, marketing research, pricing, and multinational marketing.

Hunt and Chonko (1984), in a survey of nearly 4300 marketing practitioners, found that the marketing profession is definitely *not* considered Machiavellian. Their study suggests that, while there are individuals who are Machiavellian in their orientation toward marketing activities, marketing people are no more Machiavellian than others in society at large. Also, Hunt, Chonko, and Wilcox (1984) have empirically examined the ethical problems faced by marketing researchers.

Laczniak (1983) has suggested a framework for analyzing marketing ethics and reviewed the "ethical maxims" of the golden rule, the utilitarian principle, Kant's categorical imperative, the professional ethic, and the TV test. However, after evaluating these maxims, he concluded (p. 8):

> While not without value, these limited ethical frameworks have hampered the ethical analysis of marketing managers. They have also caused marketing educators some discomfort when discussing ethical issues in the classroom. In short, many marketing educators have shied away from lecturing on the topics of marketing ethics because of the perception that existing frameworks for analyzing marketing ethics are simplistic and lack theoretical rigor. The net result is that the seeming absence of theoretical frameworks for ethical decision-making has retarded the teaching, practice, and research of marketing ethics.

Ferrell and Gresham (1985) offered a contingency framework with which to evaluate ethical decision making in a marketing organization:

> The proposed framework for examining ethical/unethical decision making is multidimensional, process oriented, and contingent in nature. The variables in the model can be categorized into individuals and organizational contingencies. The individual variables consist of personal background and sociali-

zation characteristics, such as educational and business experiences. The organizational characteristics consist of the effects of organizations external to the employing organization (customers, other firms) and intraorganizational influences (e.g., peers and supervisors). These variables are interdependent as well as ultimately affecting, either directly or indirectly, the dependent variable—ethical/unethical marketing behavior. (p. 88)

Robin and Reidenbach (1987) have recently considered the challenge of integrating ethics and social responsibility concerns into the strategic marketing process:

Without the integration of concerns about ethics and social responsibility at the very beginning of the marketing planning process, as well as throughout the process, the organizational culture may not provide the checks and balances needed to develop ethical and socially responsible marketing programs. Corporate values of profit and efficiency tend to dominate most organizational cultures, particularly in the absence of the overt addition of counterbalancing ethical and socially responsible values. This situation arises because the organization reinforces its members at all levels on the basis of achieving profitability or efficiency objectives. Though profit and efficiency must remain central values within the culture, they must be balanced by other values that help define the limits of activities designed to achieve those objectives and by values describing other important ethical and socially responsible behaviors. (p. 52)

Several researchers have recently explored the impact of marketing and advertising on consumers, attempting to offer guidelines for managers and policymakers. For instance, Aaker and Bruzzone (1985) have attempted to identify product categories and advertising copy characteristics that result in higher or lower levels of irritation with advertising. Pollay (1986) went outside the marketing literature to examine the thoughts and theories about advertising proposed by scholars in the humanities and social sciences. He concluded that:

In brief, they view advertising as intrusive and environmental and its effects as inescapable and profound. They see it as reinforcing materialism, cynicism, irrationality, selfishness, anxiety, social competitiveness, sexual preoccupation, powerlessness, and/or a loss of self-respect. (p. 18)

Gaski and Etzel (1986), using the Market Facts mail panel, examined consumer sentiment toward marketing, finding it to be slightly unfavorable. They suggest that consumer sentiment toward marketing should be measured on a regular basis. Finally, Garrett (1987) has studied consumer boycotts, pointing out that boycotting in the 1960s was an early signal of the emergence of the consumerism movement. Based on a study of thirty consumer boycotts, as well as an extensive literature review, he proposed a theory of boycott effectiveness positing three determinants of such effectiveness: economic pressure, image pressure, and policy commitment.

In our review of the activist school, several interesting trends are apparent. First, even though consumer activists not affiliated with the marketing discipline launched the activist perspective, in recent years marketing scholars have taken the lead in the conceptual development of this school. Second, a greater sense of realism has emerged in the activist school. While early writings tended to conclude that unethical marketing practices were perpetrated by greedy and insensitive marketing practitioners, more recent writings have suggested that a complex set of variables may lead even highly responsible and honest individuals to commit ethically questionable acts. Finally, the activist school has moved beyond a simple criticism of improper behavior and has now begun to consider how ethical behavior can be encouraged in an organizational structure through the use of ethical training, guidelines, managerial example, and incentives.

EVALUATION OF THE ACTIVIST SCHOOL

STRUCTURE: Are the concepts properly defined and integrated to form a strong
               nomological network?

Although the activist school was originally very weak on this criterion, progress has been made in recent years to focus attention on the concepts of ethics and social responsibility. Further, some scholars have drawn from the writings in philosophy to introduce to marketing such basic ethical concepts as deontology, utilitarianism, proportionality, social justice, and so on. As a result, the marketing discipline now has a much clearer notion of the parameters that philosophers have utilized to define ethical behavior. However, we still have not developed a conclusive and precise definition of *marketing* ethics. Nonetheless, all signs suggest that this definitional problem may be resolved within the near future.

Perhaps of even more concern is the still unresolved debate regarding marketing's social responsibility. What *exactly* is marketing's social responsibility? And, perhaps more importantly, *who* should answer this thorny question? Almost certainly a precise definition of ethical marketing behavior will be offered before marketing's social responsibility is delineated.

Our score on structure = 5.

SPECIFICATION: Are the relationships specified in a manner to delimit hypotheses or are they highly contingent?

On the positive side, much progress has been made in identifying the variables that may influence a marketer's ethical decision making, such as personal beliefs, organizational pressures, reward systems, and so on.

However, on the negative side, these influencing variables have been combined into contingency frameworks, such as the framework by Ferrell and Gresham (1985). As a result, the relationships among the variables that influence ethical decision making have not been clearly specified. Once again, given the rather dramatic progress achieved in recent years, this major deficiency may be remedied soon.

Our score on specification = 5.

TESTABILITY: Are the operational definitions provided to ensure testability and intersubjective consensus?

Not surprisingly, the activist school encounters critical problems on this criterion. Foremost among these problems is the highly subjective nature of defining ethical behavior. Even with philosophical principles such as the golden rule and utilitarianism as benchmarks, outside evaluators are likely to vary widely in their judgments concerning the ethics of a specific marketing practice. For example, in the highly publicized case in which Nestlé was accused of marketing infant formula improperly in Third World countries (Garrett 1986, Post 1985), opinion was sharply divided regarded the ethics of the company's marketing program. Thus, we are still left with the formidable task of determining what exactly is the demarcation line between ethical and unethical behavior in marketing.

Our score on testability = 4.

EMPIRICAL SUPPORT: What is the degree of confirmation in terms of empirical support?

Numerous case studies have been written by marketing professors that chronicle companies' ethical dilemmas. Also, many news reports in the popular press have detailed, and sometimes sensationalized, the supposedly unethical marketing behavior of corporations. In addition, some studies have evaluated how practitioners of marketing would respond to hypothetical situations that involve ethical judgments. Therefore, a substantial body of empirical data confirms that many marketing practices raise ethical issues. However, a glaring vacuum in the empirical data base is the lack of confirmatory research to support the recent theories of ethical decision making suggested by Laczniak (1983), Robin and Reidenbach (1987), and Hunt and Vitell (1986).

Our score on empirical support = 7.

RICHNESS: How comprehensive and generalizable is the theory?

The activist school suffers on the richness criterion because consumer activists have traditionally focused only on preventing unethical marketing practices. They have been unconcerned with the marketing manager's need to realize certain levels of economic effectiveness and efficiency from his/her marketing program. For this reason, the activist school, at least as portrayed by consumer activists, addresses only a minor portion of the concerns that confront marketing managers.

Conversely, the activist school, as envisioned by marketing scholars in the 1980s, has explicitly accepted the fact that marketing managers are constrained by their corporations' needs to realize economic profits. The next step, which has not yet been accomplished, requires these scholars to develop theories of marketing decision making that *simultaneously* satisfy both ethical criteria and economic criteria. If that can be achieved, then the activist school will be immeasurably richer.

Our score on richness = 5.

SIMPLICITY: **How easy is it to communicate and implement the theory?**

Because judgments regarding the ethics of any particular action must be related to circumstances surrounding the action, ethical decision making is very complex. Indeed, in many case examples of supposedly unethical marketing behavior, the allegedly guilty marketing practitioners have quite sincerely stated that they honestly did not realize that their actions could possibly create ethical problems. The use of marketing codes of ethics and increased ethical training has helped to make ethical decision making easier for practitioners. However, these general guidelines will be of only limited assistance when practitioners are confronted with situations with specific circumstances.

Our score on simplicity = 6.

Table 4.2 summarizes our evaluation of the activist school of marketing thought. It suffers weaknesses on all the criteria, especially testability, but is strongest in terms of empirical support.

Table 4.2 Evaluation of the Activist School*

Criterion	Rationale	Score
Structure	Unresolved debate as to marketing's social responsibility	5
Specification	Many contingency frameworks	5
Testability	Highly subjective nature of defining ethical behavior	4
Empirical support	Lack of confirmatory research in support of theories of ethical decision making	7

Criterion	Rationale	Score
Richness	Need for theories that simultaneously satisfy both ethical and economic criteria	5
Simplicity	Limited usefulness to practitioners	6
	TOTAL	32

* Scores range from 1 (poor) to 10 (excellent).

THE MACROMARKETING
SCHOOL OF THOUGHT

The macromarketing school of marketing refers to the role and impact of marketing activities and institutions on society and vice versa. During the early 1960s there was a growing concern about the role of business institutions in society. Public opinion, which considered business as a viable and necessary institution in a society founded on the free enterprise system, had begun to doubt its intentions and activities. Phrases such as price fixing, industrial-military complex, and monopoly powers were gaining increasing attention in the 1960s. As the society began to critically examine business activities soon after the incidents of thalidomide and defective automobiles, business schools began to encourage seminars on business ethics and stakeholder analysis. Macromarketing emerged as a school of marketing directly as a consequence of the growing interest in the role of business in society.

With the exception of the managerial school of marketing, little consideration was given to the environment of marketing by other schools of marketing thought. Although the managerial school of marketing recognized the presence of exogenous variables, it treated them as uncontrollable factors within which marketing functions and practices must operate. Conversely, the macromarketing school began to analyze and understand societal needs and concerns and their impact on marketing as a social institution.

Although understanding the role of marketing in society began in the 1960s, it was not uncommon to find statements to that effect in earlier writings. For example, Vaile, Grether, and Cox expressed this sentiment as early as 1952:

> The authors of this book on marketing came to the subject from different fields of interest. We have a common meeting ground, however, in our conviction that students can best be introduced to marketing by a textbook whose primary point of view is the transcendent importance of this social institution as a vast and complex function of our free enterprise economy. We believe that students must be given a clear understanding of why marketing exists as well as how it is carved out in the American economy's dynamic mixture of public

and private enterprise, and that they must be able to come to some judgment as to how well it discharges both its social and economic tasks. (p. v)

In some sense, marketing practice has been subjected to social scrutiny even before the industrial age (Steiner 1976). In fact, even today, marketing's image among the average public is that it is a selling activity that entails numerous malpractices of marketing such as deceptive advertising, bait and switch tactics, and pushy salespeople.

However, what is unique about the macromarketing school is the serious and scientific attempts at understanding the role of marketing in society and providing a framework with which to explain the negative perceptions among the average public. In particular, we credit two individuals for their early and pioneering work in this area. They are Robert Holloway at the University of Minnesota and George Fisk at Syracuse University.

Holloway visualized marketing as an activity of society. Consequently, marketing both was influenced by and influenced its society. Together with his colleague Robert Hancock, Holloway conceptualized a "rough schema" to depict "the environment of marketing" (Holloway and Hancock 1964, p. 1). The first statement of this "rough schema" was a collection of readings organized around the broad exogenous environments of sociological, political, economic, legal, ethical, competitive, and technological forces. Further revisions of this popular readings book eventually allocated one fifth of their space to articles raising questions about the performance of marketing in society (Holloway and Hancock 1974).

George Fisk, on the other hand, used a general systems perspective to understand the role of marketing in society. Fisk was heavily influenced by the pioneer thinking of Wroe Alderson and Reavis Cox. His first major book was explicitly based on a systems perspective in which he attempted to describe the interrelationships between "the economics of equalization, the strategy and mechanisms of marketing management, and the social consequences of marketing activity" (Fisk 1967, p. xvii). Fisk makes a distinction between microsystems and macrosystems: "Microsystem behavior consists of directly observable goal-motivated activities of individuals, groups, and organizations, whereas macrosystem behavior consists of statistical aggregations of microsystem behavior" (Fisk 1967, p. 77). In particular, Fisk focused on the social performance of marketing and continued to shape this school of thought in his capacity as the first editor of the *Journal of Macromarketing*.

The macromarketing school became dormant soon after the initial writings by Holloway and Fisk. Holloway became more interested in consumerism and the role of business in society, while Fisk shifted his interests to international marketing. At the same time, many other scholars interested in the area got carried away with the more visible and immediate areas of consumerism and malpractices of marketing for which a great deal of impetus came from the Federal Trade Commission (FTC) and other governmental agencies.

Even during this dormant time period, some work appeared, notably by Reed Moyer (1972), which represented a bridge between the broader issues of macromarketing and the more focused issues of the activist school of thought. Moyer (1972) focused on the larger societal issues and on evaluation of marketing performance from his more macro perspective. Moyer suggested that macromarketing issues should be studied from a societal viewpoint unlike the micromarketing issues. As such, macromarketing refers to the *aggregate* performance of marketing as an element of the entire economic system. Therefore, its performance can be judged, at least at the aggregate level, comparable to the performance of other economic systems such as income distribution (taxation), welfare, and productivity. Furthermore, marketing should be held accountable like all other economic systems for achieving certain social objectives.

The macromarketing school of marketing got a new life when the University of Colorado organized the first macromarketing seminar in 1977 under the leadership of Charles Slater. With his vast experience in applying marketing principles to economic problems of the lesser developed countries, Slater was acutely aware of the interaction between marketing and society. His goal in organizing the annual conference at the University of Colorado was to encourage research and development of marketing systems and institutions with the proper interface with society.

It soon became apparent at these conferences that one of the necessary initial steps was to define the boundaries of macromarketing. In view of the fact that conceivably all marketing aspects could be relevant for study and research, this school of thought consciously attempted to define the nature and scope of macromarketing. Thus, unlike the other schools of thought, there was less evolution and more planned direction in defining the school.

One of the earlier and still very relevant definitions of macromarketing was provided by Shelby Hunt (1977):

> Macromarketing is a multi-dimensional construct and a complete specification would (should) include the following: Macromarketing refers to the study of (1) marketing systems, (2) the impact and consequences of marketing systems on society and (3) the impact and consequences of society on marketing systems. (p. 56).

Several papers have since appeared to clarify the boundaries of macromarketing. For example, Shawver and Nickels (1979) suggested that "when the objective is to describe or enhance aspects of social welfare related to exchange systems the study is macro-marketing" (p. 41).

While there is still some disagreement regarding the exact boundaries of macromarketing, the publication of the *Journal of Macromarketing* has served to define the field, at least for a while. Two alternative approaches are taken to resolve this definitional dilemma. The first is to define what macromarketing is not. For instance, it is not "decision making to produce an intended result for an individual household, business, or public organization" (Fisk 1981, p. 4). In that sense, macromarketing is neither a managerial nor a policy-oriented school of thought.

The second approach is to list topic areas that define "marketing behavior that affects a larger community of society" (Fisk 1981, p. 3). Fisk lists the following topic areas as appropriate for macromarketing:

1.   Marketing as a life supply support provisioning technology.
2.   The quality and quantity of life goods served by marketing.
3.   Marketing as a technology for mobilizing and allocating economic resources.
4.   Societal consequences of marketing in learning societies. (p. 3)

More recently, Hunt and Burnett (1982) carefully reviewed all prior writings on the dichotomy of macromarketing versus micromarketing. Based on this assessment, they generated the following nine propositions to separate the domains of macromarketing from micromarketing (p. 15):

1.   Studies of marketing systems are macro (Moyer 1972).
2.   Studies of networks of exchange relationships are macro (Bagozzi 1977).
3.   Studies adopting the perspective of society are macro (Shawver and Nickels 1979).
4.   Studies examining the consequences of marketing on society are macro (Hunt 1977).
5.   Studies examining the consequences of society on marketing are macro.
6.   Studies of the marketing activities of industrial, profit-sector organizations are micro (Moyer 1972), as are studies that adopt the perspective of individual profit-sector organizations (Shawver and Nickels 1979).
7.   Studies of the marketing activities of individual, nonprofit sector organizations are micro (Hunt 1976b).
8.   Studies adopting the perspective of an individual industry are micro (Hunt 1976b).
9.   Studies of the marketing activities of consumers are micro (Hunt 1976b).

These propositions were tested by preparing a standardized questionnaire sent to a large sample of academic scholars still active in research. As expected, the perceptions of the marketing scholars as measured by the questionnaire reflected the face validity of the nine propositions. Hunt and Burnett (1982) concluded:

In conclusion, marketers can and do categorize marketing phenomena, issues and research by way of the macromarketing/micromarketing dichotomy.

Using the three criteria of level of aggregation, perspectives of and consequences on, a taxonomical model can completely specify the various kinds of marketing studies (p. 24).

In contrast to Hunt and Burnett's efforts to separate and differentiate macromarketing from micromarketing, Zif (1980) attempted to demonstrate that the managerial approach inherent in micromarketing is equally applicable to macromarketing situations and problems. According to Zif, managers in the public sector and in charge of societal issues and problems can and do behave in a parallel manner with their counterparts in the private sector who are in charge of commercial products and services. The major variables of the managerial approach are familiar from studies of micromarketing: (1) managerial responsibilities, (2) managerial objectives, (3) managerial orientations and strategies, and (4) decision making variables. With some adjustment and redefinition, these variables can be adapted to apply to macro phenomena.

Zif (1980) applied the managerial concepts of micromarketing to macromarketing situations and insightfully demonstrated that the process of management is very similar, although the inputs and outputs may differ significantly between micromarketing and macromarketing situations. Zif does suggest some differences. For example, in comparison with micromarketing, most macromarketing situations show a significant decrease in direct competition and an increase in cooperation in the regulation of consumption and in product-line planning. The concept of the marketing manager as a strategist competing against adversaries shifts to that of an integrator concerned with the development of a whole market working with a centralized data bank and affected only by indirect competition.

The literature generated by the macromarketing school is highly diverse, and it is not yet clear what particular areas of interest are emerging. In the 1970s, considerable interest was fostered in social marketing, or the role of marketing in effecting social change (e.g., Kotler and Zaltman 1971). Typical of recent work, however, is the argument by Zeithaml and Zeithaml (1984) that marketing does have an important role to play in the management of its own environment. Related to this argument, Greene and Miesing (1984) have explored the public policy, technological, and ethical issues relevant to marketing decisions for NASA's space shuttle; Enis and Sullivan (1985) have explored the marketing implications of the AT&T settlement; and Heath and Nelson (1985) have examined the corporate and public policy issues surrounding image and issue advertising, with their primary focus on issues addressed by the Federal Trade Commission (FTC), the Federal Communications Commission (FCC), and the Internal Revenue Service (IRS). Further Hutt, Mokwa, and Shapiro (1986) have examined politics of marketing, suggesting that parallel to the distribution channel is a political "network." Their thinking is an extension of the political economy framework:

... economic and political forces coalesce into "organized behavior systems" or "domesticated market domains." Accordingly, market systems can be defined in terms of parties, relationships, and actions which enhance and facilitate both the performance and prevention or prohibition of marketing exchanges. (p. 41)

The authors offer a careful discussion of the implications for clarifying marketing's role in the political market domain, as well as a discussion of associated public policy issues.

Both Arndt (1979) and Kotler (1986b) have argued that marketers must acquire political skills if they hope to operate successfully in today's market environment. Arndt (1979) has discussed the increasing prevalence of "internal" or "domesticated" markets, arguing that:

... the competitive, open market is in the process of being tamed, regulated, and closed. To an increasing degree, transactions are occurring in "internal" markets within the framework of long-term relationships, not on an ad hoc basis. (p. 69)

He describes domesticated markets, and compares them with traditional competitive markets, as follows:

[In domesticated markets] transactions are moved inside a company (when for instance buyers and sellers actually merge) or inside the boundaries of a group of companies committed to long-term cooperation. Transactions in domesticated markets are usually handled by administrative processes on the basis of negotiated rules of exchange. In open, competitive markets, coordination is implemented ex post through the workings of autonomous, spontaneous, centralized decision processes. Domesticated markets, on the other hand, are coordinated ex ante by centralized control procedures. Information is consciously and directly managed. (p. 70)

Arndt points out that domesticated markets offer the advantage of reducing uncertainty in an increasingly turbulent environment. However, operating in domesticated markets also calls for more imaginative marketing, with more attention to the political aspects of economic decision making and more attention to the design, implementation, and maintainance of effective interorganizational marketing systems. This is in contrast to the traditional concentration on the marketing mix or Four Ps (product, price, place, and promotion).

Kotler (1986b) has proposed a broadened view of marketing, explicitly focusing on problems associated with entering blocked or protected markets (markets characterized by high entry barriers). Given the existence of blocked or protected markets, Kotler suggests that marketing is increasingly becoming a political exercise:

There is a growing need for companies that want to operate in certain markets to master the art of supplying benefits to parties other than target consumers. This need extends beyond the requirements to serve and satisfy normal intermediaries like agents, distributors, and dealers. I am talking about third parties—governments, labor unions, and other interest groups—that, singly or collectively, can block profitable entry into a market. (p. 119)

Kotler goes on to argue that, faced with blocked or protected markets, marketers must engage in "megamarketing" in which the concepts of power and public relations are given emphasis:

In addition to the four Ps of marketing strategy—product, price, place, and promotion—executives must add two more—power and public relations. I call such strategic thinking *megamarketing*.

Marketing is the task of arranging need-satisfying and profitable offers to target buyers. Sometimes, however, it is necessary to create additional incentives and pressures at the right times and in the right amounts to noncustomers. Megamarketing thus takes an enlarged view of the skills and resources needed to enter and operate in certain markets. In addition to preparing attractive offers for customers, megamarketing may use inducements and sanctions to gain the desired responses from gatekeepers. (p. 119)

There is every reason to believe that the macromarketing school of thought will continue to grow, but its exact direction and overall contribution to marketing has yet to be determined. However, evidence of the maturation of this school of thought is provided by recent attention to methodological issues in conducting macromarketing research (Venkatesh and Dholakia 1986).

EVALUATION OF THE MACROMARKETING SCHOOL

STRUCTURE: Are the concepts properly defined and integrated to form a strong nomological network?

The macromarketing school is weak on this criterion. It is unfortunate that most scholars in the area have not worked together or organized a conference explicitly to resolve (as opposed to express) differences about the definition of macromarketing. Granted, Hunt and Burnett (1982) make a gallant effort to show that there is a consensus among academic scholars as to what is macromarketing and what is micromarketing. However, it must be pointed out that it is limited to five *specific* domains of macromarketing and four *specific* domains of micromarketing. We really do not know whether one would obtain highly agreed-on definitions if the same respondents were asked to freely describe their own views of macromarketing.

Even if there were a consensus on the definition, it is important to recognize that the structure criterion requires establishment of relationships among the definitional concepts of a theory or school of thought. In other words, we need more than a typology or classification to score high on this criterion.

It is, of course, our hope that scholars interested in macromarketing will generate a theory of macromarketing with explicit propositions similar to what is attempted in the buyer behavior and organizational dynamics schools of thought.

Our score on structure = 4.

SPECIFICATION: Are the relationships specified in a manner to delimit hypotheses or are they highly contingent?

It is unfortunate that the scope and complexity of the macromarketing school forces it to be more contingent than invariant. For example, as an economic subsystem of society, it must coexist in harmony with societal values and concerns, and according to the advocates of this school, it must also serve society's values and concerns. However, societal values and concerns are dynamic, and very few theories of social values can be borrowed to predict the future. This contingency forces the macromarketing school to change its domain, definitions, and relationships as social values changes. Furthermore, at a point in time there are likely to be divergent social values and concerns especially between industrial, preindustrial, and postindustrial societies. The macromarketing school has not articulated the role of marketing (definitions and relationships) in divergent economic societies.

Our score on specification = 4.

TESTABILITY: Are the operational definitions provided to ensure testability and intersubjective consensus?

The Hunt and Burnett (1982) study has strongly indicated that the specific definitions can be empirically tested. Furthermore, they clearly demonstrate that there is a consensus, at least among marketing scholars, as to what is macromarketing and what is micromarketing. Therefore, it is safe to say that the concepts of macromarketing are testable, although the Hunt and Burnett study is a lonely exception.

We also believe that there is an emerging consensus about the domain of macromarketing. As Hunt (1977) has suggested, macromarketing consists of the study of consequences of marketing on society and vice versa. Most scholars tend to agree with this conceptualization. At the same time, it is difficult to go beyond this statement and obtain consensus about the marketing and society interface. For example, social activists such as Sethi

(1971) would take a sharply different perspective than practitioner-oriented people such as Levitt (1958). We believe that as we evolve toward a theory of business policy, we will also evolve toward a theory of marketing policy.

Our score on testability = 6.

EMPIRICAL SUPPORT: **What is the degree of confirmation in terms of empirical support?**

Similar to most older schools of thought, the empirical support for the macromarketing school comes from observations, case histories, and anecdotes. This includes, on the one hand, use of marketing techniques to solve social problems such as alcoholism, traffic congestion, and population control; and, on the other hand, regulatory and legislative normative approaches to make marketing more socially responsive. Both types of observations and case histories have good empirical support for the domain of macromarketing. Unfortunately, it is not generalizable, or at least no one has as yet attempted empirical generalizations to support the macromarketing school.

Our score on empirical support = 6.

RICHNESS: **How comprehensive and generalizable is the theory?**

By definition, the macromarketing school is very comprehensive in its scope and nature. It focuses on the "raison d'être" of marketing as a social institution. Furthermore, it is an important enough social institution to invite comments and criticisms from stakeholders outside the discipline. Finally, as we pointed out earlier, macromarketing issues are ancient and predate the modern industrial states. The inherent danger of the pervasive nature of macromarketing is that it begins to blur its own boundaries. For example, it is not an easy task to separate macromarketing from business policy or from political economy.

Our score on richness = 7.

SIMPLICITY: **How easy is it to communicate and implement the theory?**

The concepts of macromarketing are difficult to communicate to others and implement in practice for several reasons. First, the macromarketing school is a value-laden school and the divergent values of others result in perceptual biases of selective attention and selective retention. Second, it is extremely difficult to get a consensus on the methods to solve social problems and concerns. Furthermore, as Zaltman and Duncan (1977) and Sheth and Frazier (1982) have pointed out, it is not easy to choose between public education, economic incentives, or mandatory rules to bring about harmony between marketing and society. Finally, the issues to be dealt with in macromarketing are not only far reaching in their impact, but often tend to be long term and intangible. All of these forces make macromarketing concepts difficult to communicate and also difficult to implement.

Our score on simplicity = 4.

Table 4.3 summarizes our evaluation of the macromarketing school of thought. It is fairly weak on syntax criteria and simplicity but stronger on semantics criteria and richness.

Table 4.3 Evaluation of the Macromarketing School*

Criterion	Rationale	Score
Structure	Consensus on definition lacking	4
Specification	More contingent than invariant	4
Testability	Specific definitions can be empirically tested. No consensus on marketing and society interface	6
Empirical support	Mainly based on observations, case histories, and anecdotes	6
Richness	Comprehensive, but blurred boundaries	7
Simplicity	Concepts difficult to communicate	4
	TOTAL	31

* Scores range from 1 (poor) to 10 (excellent).

SUMMARY

In this chapter we have reviewed and evaluated the three noneconomic-noninteractive schools of marketing thought: the buyer behavior school, the activist school, and the macromarketing school.

The buyer behavior school has a number of distinct characteristics not matched by any other school. First, it generated a paradigm shift in marketing to the extent that it has emerged as a separate, stand-alone discipline. Second, it generated the largest amount of empirical research and theory building. Indeed, the more scientific approaches to developing a discipline both in conceptualizing and testing have been inherent in the buyer behavior school. Finally, the buyer behavior school has elevated the image of marketing as a more respectable discipline whose tools and techniques can be used for the good of society in such socially desirable behaviors as population control and social programs.

Not surprisingly, the buyer behavior school's evaluation on the metatheory criteria comes out high. It scores well on all three criteria: the organization (syntax), the reality (semantics), and the relevance (pragmatics) dimensions.

The activist school of thought gained momentum in the 1960s, although it has a long tradition going back to the late eighteen hundreds and early nineteen hundreds. Unfortunately, the activist school focused more on ad hoc industry- or product-specific issues of protecting the interests of the consumer and therefore did not develop good conceptual frameworks until very recently. It seems to have limited future promise because the interest of the public policy has shifted from consumerism to international competitiveness. This is unfortunate in timing, because a lot can be accomplished now that some good conceptual frameworks have been proposed.

The activist school scores low on the metatheory criteria on all dimensions except empirical support and simplicity. This is not surprising in view of the fact that it began by focusing on specific consumer problems and proposed highly action-oriented recommendations.

The macromarketing school examines the relationship between marketing and society. It is a relatively new school of thought and is the consequence of a broader interest in the role of business as a social institution. Almost in direct contrast to the activist school, the macromarketing school is richer in concepts and poorer in empirical support. This is of course understandable. As one moves away from the specifics of an issue it is harder to generate and analyze reality. We do expect the macromarketing school to enrich its conceptual base with the recent focus on technology and megamarketing concepts of politics and public relations. It seems that macromarketing may finally create the same excitement as the buyer behavior school did in the early 1960s as we shift national public policy concerns away from consumerism and toward international competitiveness.

5
▭

INTERACTIVE–NONECONOMIC SCHOOLS OF MARKETING

In this chapter we review three more schools of marketing thought. They are the organizational dynamics, the systems, and the social exchange schools. As mentioned in Chapter 1, the two common characteristics of these three schools of marketing thought are as follows:

1. They all take an interactive perspective with respect to market transactions, in which both buyers and sellers are regarded as equally important to understand and analyze. Unlike the economic schools of marketing thought (commodity, functional, and regional), which examine market transactions from the supplier's viewpoint, or the noneconomic schools of marketing thought (buyer behavior, macromarketing, and activist), which examine market transactions from the buyer's perspective, these three schools examine the mutual interdependence and integrated relationships inherent between the sellers and the buyers in market transactions.

2. At the same time, these three schools of thought primarily rely on the behavioral sciences rather than economic sciences. Therefore, the underlying concepts borrowed or developed are significantly different from the classical schools (commodity, regional, and functional) as well as the managerial, institutional and functionalist schools of thought. In that respect, the organizational dynamics, social exchange, and systems schools are much closer to the noneconomic schools of buyer behavior, macromarketing, and activist.

149

These three schools of marketing thought are more recent in their development. Furthermore, they have remained as the specialized interest of a few scholars in marketing, unlike the buyer behavior school, for example, which attracted attention from many scholars. Consequently, our review of these schools will be somewhat limited. Indeed, we have the opposite experience as compared to the buyer behavior where we had a difficult time incorporating all the contributions within the page limits of this book.

THE ORGANIZATIONAL DYNAMICS SCHOOL OF THOUGHT

As discussed in Chapter 3, the organizational dynamics school of marketing thought is the direct descendant of the institutional school in the sense that both of these schools seek to explain the intricate workings of the channels of distribution. However, the fundamental difference between these two schools is their underlying perspectives. The institutional school utilized economic foundations to analyze how a distribution channel could be structured more efficiently for the eventual benefit of the ultimate consumer. In contrast, the advocates of the organizational dynamics school shifted their attention from the welfare of the consumer to the analysis of the goals and needs of the members of the distribution channel, such as the manufacturers, wholesalers, and retailers.

For this reason, the organizational dynamics theorists began to view the distribution channel as a competitive coalition that was based on self-interest. Although, for example, a wholesaler and retailer must cooperate and coordinate their efforts if they wish to have an effective relationship, these two actors also compete with each other to determine who will garner the lion's share of the rewards from their cooperative venture. Thus, these theorists sought to understand how channel members could effectively interact in a complex and seemingly contradictory setting of competitive and cooperative drives.

The organizational dynamics school is a relatively new school of marketing thought with the bulk of the scholarly writings in this area published in the 1970s and 1980s. However, the seeds of this school were actually planted in the late 1950s and early 1960s. One of the first articles written about distribution channel relationships using a behavioral orientation was Valentine Ridgeway's article entitled "Administration of Manufacturer-Dealer Systems." According to Ridgeway (1957):

> A manufacturer and his dealers make up a competitive system which is in need of administration much as is a single organization. Some activities can best be performed centrally, and some are carried out best on a decentralized basis but with a need to coordinate the decentralized activities of numerous dealers. The manufacturer is in the most logical position to perform this administration of the system because of his acquaintance with the products,

his operations in the larger market, and his contact with the numerous dealers. Despite the separation of ownership of the dealers' facilities and the break in the chain of command, the manufacturer seeks power to administer the system by means of rewards and punishments which he can apply to dealers. (p. 483)

After Ridgeway helped to plant the seed for the organizational dynamics school, the next major contribution was made by Bruce Mallen (1963, 1967). Mallen (1963) stressed the interplay of conflict, control, and cooperation in channel member relations:

> This paper will show that between channel members a dynamic field of conflicting and cooperating objective exists; also that if the conflicting objectives outweigh the cooperating ones, the effectiveness of the channel will be reduced. Thus, the efficient distribution of consumer goods will be impeded.
>
> The channel members can meet this problem in three distinct ways. First, they can have a leader (one of the channel members) who "forces" members to cooperate; this is an autocratic relationship. Second, they can have a leader who "helps" members to cooperate, creating a democratic relationship. Finally, they can do nothing, and so have an anarchistic relationship. (p. 24)

Although the efforts by Ridgeway and Mallen set the stage for the emergence of the organizational dynamics school, it was not until 1969 that this school began to truly capture the interest and attention of a large number of marketing scholars. The event in 1969 that thrust the organizational dynamics school into the spotlight in marketing theory was the publication of Louis Stern's readings book, *Distribution Channels: Behavioral Dimensions*. In the introduction to this volume, Stern clearly addresses the inadequacies of the economic perspective formerly proposed by the institutional school:

> The concept of channels of distribution is one of the most original, enduring, and fundamental concepts in the marketing literature. Attempts to understand interfirm relationships within these channels and to generate strategies for their management have traditionally been cast in terms of economic theory. From this perspective, firms join together in trading arrangements because of cost and revenue considerations; their strategies are conditioned by the type of competition extant in the various markets in which they act. This analytical treatment suffices as long as the tools of economics are thought to be wholly adequate in depicting the realities of behavior in marketing channels. It is becoming more and more apparent, however, that conceptualization beyond that supplied by economic theory is needed if marketing students, academicians, and practitioners alike are to gain further insights into the increasingly complex and diverse nature of such channels. (p. 1)

Of the many influential articles contained in this book, two original articles stand out as having laid the groundwork for later theorists in marketing. First, in a paper co-authored by Frederick Beier and Stern, the concept of power, particularly as developed by social scientists such as Emerson (1962) and French and Raven (1959), is analyzed:

> The concepts of dependency and commitment are key to an understanding of power relationships in marketing channels. A channel is generally composed of a set of marketing specialists. The effective linking and coordination of the specialists are prerequisites to the efficient and successful distribution. However, the more extensive is the division of labor among the components of any system in the performance of its functions, the more interdependent the components become. Thus, power is pervasive in the channel, because each member is dependent, at least to some extent, on the others. As one channel member's dependence upon another increases, the greater becomes the power of the latter. On the other hand, as a member's commitment to the system diminishes, the ability of other system members to influence him decreases. (Beier and Stern 1969, p. 112)

The second influential article focused on the concept of conflict in distribution channels. Stern and his co-author of this article, Ronald H. Gorman, again stressed the pivotal function of dependency as a cause of conflict:

> When a channel of distribution is viewed as a social system, the members of such a channel are, by definition, caught up in a web of interdependency. The actions or behavior of any one member have consequences for the level of output (measured in terms of individual goals) achieved by the others. This dependency relationship represents the root of conflict in channels of distribution. In any social system, when a component perceives the behavior of another component to be impeding the attainment of its goals or the effective performance of its instrumental behavior patterns, an atmosphere of frustration prevails. (Stern and Gorman 1969, p. 156)

Following the framework established by Stern, other marketing theorists quickly entered the organizational dynamics school and began to explore more critically the topical subjects of power, conflict, cooperation, and bargaining. Although a complete review of the extensive literature in these areas is clearly beyond the scope of this book, a few of the more compelling research questions will be highlighted.

1. *What are the sources of power?* Hunt and Nevin (1974), relying on the work of French and Raven (1959), proposed that a channel member may possess coercive and noncoercive sources of power:

> In an empirical case, coercive power can be differentiated from the others because it, alone, involves potential punishment. For all the other noncoercive sources of power, i.e., reward, legitimate, expert, and referent, the individual willingly (rather than begrudgingly) yields power to another. (Hunt and Nevin, 1974, p. 187)

Expanding on the Hunt and Nevin framework for coercive and noncoercive power sources, Lusch and Brown (1982) suggested that the use of certain power sources may have a direct impact on the channel members' perceptions of the power relationships:

> The categorization and consequences of various power sources may not be as originally posited by Hunt and Nevin (1974). We develop the logic for categorizing power sources as economic (coercion, reward, legal legitimate) and noneconomic (referent, expertise, traditional legitimate, and informational). As we move from economic to noneconomic sources of power we move from direct outcome control to indirect outcome control. If a channel leader successfully implements noneconomic sources of power, the influenced channel member attributes less, not more, power to the powerholder. This outcome occurs because the channel members adopt the channel leader's norms and values as their own and therefore believe that they are acting independently of the powerholder. Consequently, the higher the quality of assistances (a noneconomic source of power), the lower the influenced channel members' perceptions of channel leader's power. (p. 187)

Gaski (1987) proposed an alternative explanation for what he deemed the "rather counter-theoretical finding" (p. 145) that an inverse relationship exists between a channel member's reward power sources and its actual power. Building on the work of Lusch and Brown (1982), Gaski devised a test for the hypothesis that this "anomaly" can be explained by the interaction between the use of reward and the power subject's attitude. Since his empirical evidence did not support the Lusch and Brown hypothesis, Gaski proposed an alternative explanation — that power had not been validly measured.

2. *How should channel members utilize their available power?* Kasulis and Spekman (1980) added a new normative perspective to the power literature by suggesting how marketing managers should utilize their power sources:

> Channel relations provide frequent opportunities for one member to influence another's behavior. The ultimate objective of any channel management strategy is to develop a degree of cooperation in channel participant behavior. The efficiencies gained from a coordinated channel effort are expected to improve the channel's competitive stance vis-a-vis other distribution networks. This means that the channel administrator should not myopically view half-hearted and forced complicity among channel members as a successful power outcome: but should, instead, strive to cultivate those power bases which tend to elicit an internalization of, and an identification with the system's goals and values. While in some instances firms must rely on coercion, rewards, or contractual agreements, firms should develop, and more extensively use, those bases of power which produce the greatest amount of long run cooperation. (p. 190)

Frazier and Summers (1984) explored the use of various influence strategies by boundary personnel within distribution channel relationships. Gaski and Nevin (1985), in a study using an existing distribution system, reported:

> The results support the proposition that exercise of the coercive power source by a supplier has a stronger effect on dealer satisfaction and channel conflict than the mere presence of that power source. In contrast, exercise of the reward power source seems to have only a marginal impact on these dependent variables. (p. 139)

McAlister, Bazerman, and Fader (1986) have explored the use of a moderately high externally set profitability constraint as a goal-setting mechanism for controlling channel negotiators. In an experimental market situation they found:

> Equal and high power channel members are shown to be made more profitable by the constraint. Low power channel members are shown to be made less profitable by the same constraint behavior. (p. 228)

3. *How should power be measured?* Some of the latest work in the power area has focused on the need to develop valid and reliable measures of the power construct. In this regard, Frazier (1983b) has argued that power is directly linked to role performance:

> When the level of a source firm's role performance is perceived as being high, the target should be highly motivated to maintain the exchange relationship. Furthermore, the higher the perceived role performance of a source, the fewer the alternatives that should be available to the target to replace it sufficiently. By specifying the primary elements of a source firm's channel role, one can identify the domain of elements needed to represent a target firm's dependence in the relationship. (p. 159)

4. *What is the relationship between power and conflict?* Lusch (1976), in an empirical study of the automobile distribution channel, concentrated on the possible causal link between power and conflict:

> It can be concluded that noncoercive and coercive sources of power have significant impacts on intrachannel conflict, at least for the distribution of automobiles in the United States. Noncoercive sources tend to reduce intrachannel conflict whereas coercive sources tend to increase it. (p. 388)

Lusch's provocative conclusions were challenged by Etgar (1978), who questioned the purported cause and effect relationship between power and conflict:

If one recognizes that the use of power in a distribution channel is often an end result rather than a cause of conflict, Lusch's results are viewed in a different light. They imply that use of coercive power is linked with high levels of channel conflict. That is, channel leaders use coercive power when basic rivalries and differences divide the channel members. Such differences apparently cannot be solved by "soft" treatment and by convincing channel members to cooperate. Instead, compliance is achieved through the use of threats, denials of resources, etc. (p. 273-274)

Frazier and Summers (1986) report empirical research to support Lusch's (1976) position:

The results of our field study support the position of those channel theorists who have emphasized the positive role of interfirm power in promoting the effective coordination of channel relationships. Manufacturers' representatives appear to use coercion with great reluctance, only when other types of influence strategies have failed to produce a satisfactory response on an important issue. (p. 175)

They also report in this same study (Frazier and Summers 1986) that:

. . . the negative relationship found between dealers' perceptions of their manufacturers' power and the manufacturers' use of coercion may be primarily due to two factors.

1. The positions of the manufacturer and its dealers tend to be more congruent when the manufacturer has high power based on the dealer's dependence in the interfirm relationship. Furthermore, the manufacturer is able to make more effective use of information exchange under these conditions. These factors tend to reduce the manufacturer's need to engage in overt influence attempts (both coercive and noncoercive) with its dealers.
2. Manufacturers with high power are better able to utilize noncoercive influence strategies (e.g., requests) effectively when overt influence attempts seem appropriate, and thereby avoid the use of coercion. (p. 175)

The question of the relationship between power and conflict has also been addressed by Gaski (1984). Based on a major review of the literature, he developed an integrated overview of the status of this area. Gaski's outline of the conceptual foundations and empirical content of this area is used to point toward unresolved issues. Further, Gaski (1986) found a compound effect of the use of certain sources of power.

5. *How should conflict be measured?* Just as the measurement of power has been an area of scholarly research, the optimal measures of conflict have received some attention recently by organizational dynamics theorists. The most rigorous effort to date was provided by Brown and

Day (1981), who analyzed the validity of several different measures of manifest conflict:

> Conflict in channels of distribution was conceptualized as a dynamic process in which conflict progresses from a latent state of incompatibility to perceived conflict to felt conflict to the behavioral stage of manifest conflict. In manifest conflict the parties interact with each other to cope with frustrating behaviors. The most promising way to measure manifest conflict in field studies appears to be to monitor the frequency with which disagreements occur about different aspects of the channel relationship and the typical strength or intensity of conflictful behavior which occurs when the disagreements are discussed in written or oral communications. (p. 272)

6. *What is cooperation in an interorganizational system?* Although the organizational dynamics literature has been dominated by articles focusing on the topics of power and conflict, some theorists are now beginning to address the issue of cooperation. Childers and Ruekert (1982), drawing on previous definitions of cooperation, proposed a new definition of cooperation within a channel network:

> . . . cooperation is the expectation of a balanced exchange of the resources required to achieve both intraorganizational and interorganizational goals through joint action among two or more actors. Important to this definition are the ideas that cooperation stems from mutual effort (joint action) and that underlying this action is the expectation of a balanced exchange. (p. 117)

7. *How does power affect the bargaining process?* Because channel members must often negotiate the levels of their inputs and rewards from an interorganizational relationship, the subject of bargaining behavior has become more relevant in recent years. Dwyer and Walker (1981) attempted to manipulate the balance of power between bargainers in a laboratory study to determine how this would affect bargaining activities:

> Despite the contrived setting, several specific conclusions can be drawn from this study on the nature of bargaining in an asymmetrical power condition. First, compared to a more balanced power setting, the negotiation process in an asymmetric market is more "efficient." Bargainers tend to reach agreement at the Pareto optimal solution and divide the total rewards equally when power is symmetrically distributed. However, in the unbalanced condition, while the specific terms of agreement are much less predictable, the bargainers tended to take a more "direct" negotiating approach. Their initial offers were closer to the ultimate agreement and, as a result, they yielded less and sent fewer bids before attaining a solution. (p. 111)

In addition to these attempts to clarify specific concepts of power, conflict, cooperation, and bargaining, other organizational dynamics theorists have endeavored to create general models of interorganizational relations. The leading contributors to this general models perspective have been Robicheaux and El-Ansary (1975-76), Cadotte and Stern (1979), Stern and Reve (1980), Achrol, Reve, and Stern (1983), Frazier (1983a), and Gaski (1984). More specialized aspects of these models have been investigated by Anderson and Narus (1984), Anand and Stern (1985), Eliashberg et al. (1986), Anand (1987), and Anderson, Lodish, and Weitz (1987).

Two significant movements have recently emerged in the writings of these general models theorists that deserve special attention. First, Stern and Reve (1980) and Achrol et al. (1983) have advocated that distribution channels be classified as political economies. According to Stern and Reve (1980):

> Basically, the political economy approach views a social system as comprising interacting sets of major economic and sociopolitical forces which affect collective behavior and performance. (p. 53)

The most intriguing claim made by proponents of the political economy perspective is that it will bridge the gulf between the institutional school and the organizational dynamics school:

> . . . channel theory is fragmented into two seemingly disparate disciplinary orientations: an economic approach and a behavioral approach. The former attempts to apply microeconomic theory and industrial organization analysis to the study of distribution systems and has been essentially "efficiency" oriented, focusing on costs, functional differentiation, and channel design (cf. Baligh and Richartz 1967, Bucklin 1966, Bucklin and Carman 1974, Cox, Goodman, and Fichandler 1965). The latter borrows heavily from social psychology and organization theory and has been essentially "socially" oriented, focusing on power and conflict phenomena (cf. Alderson 1957, Stern 1969). Rarely have there been attempts to integrate these two perspectives. Indeed, they should be viewed as complementary, because the former deals mainly with economic "outputs" while the latter is concerned with behavioral "processes." (Stern and Reve 1980, p. 53)

Dwyer and Welsh (1985) developed a theoretical model based on the belief that the political economy framework illuminates the interaction between the internal and external sociopolitical and economic forces of marketing channels. Their model should be useful "for explaining interorganizational responses to uncertainty and dependence constraints of the channel environment" (p. 397).

The second noteworthy movement has been launched by Frazier's (1983a) article suggesting that organizational dynamics theorists have been unnecessarily restrictive in their view of the interorganizational relationship. Specifically, Frazier (1983a) posits that the exchanges among channel members can be divided into a three-stage process involving initiating, implementation, and review:

Previous research in the marketing channels literature has focused on the implementation or coordination of interorganizational exchange relationships and the constructs of interfirm power and conflict. The framework presented herein clearly suggests that a broadening of research effort is required to aid future progress and understanding in the marketing channels area. Attention is especially warranted on why and how exchange relationships are initiated, and how the rewards or losses from the exchange are reviewed and evaluated by each channel member. Indeed, because constructs within the initiation, implementation, and review processes are so highly interrelated with one another, a clear understanding of attempts to coordinate ongoing exchange relationships, including the constructs of power and conflict, is not possible without some understanding of the other two processes, and vice versa. This suggests it would be beneficial for channel researchers to examine both distal and immediate antecedents of existing exchange relationships, analyzing the "history of each exchange" so to speak, in examining and explaining their current nature. (p. 75)

Finally, Graham (1987) has offered a theory to explain the outcomes of negotiations between representatives of buying and selling firms. Graham takes a social psychological perspective, proposing that situational constraints (power relationships) and bargaining characteristics (culture/nationality, interpersonal orientation, and listening skills) influence the process of negotiation (use of questions, initial demands, procedural discipline, impression formation accuracy, and topical control), and that the process of negotiation affects negotiation outcomes (economic rewards, satisfaction, and interpersonal attraction).

EVALUATION OF THE ORGANIZATIONAL DYNAMICS SCHOOL

Our evaluation of the organizational dynamics school must be interpreted with the conscious thought that this is a young and emerging school whose full life cycle is yet to evolve. In some ways, it is even unfair to compare the organizational dynamics school with the same set of criteria as, for example, the classical schools or the buyer behavior school. We will provide an evaluatory summary, but the reader is cautioned to keep the foregoing comments in mind.

STRUCTURE: Are the concepts properly defined and integrated to form a strong nomological network?

Because the organizational dynamics school has heavily relied on well-known concepts from the behavioral sciences especially as they relate to power, conflict, and cooperation, it has reaped the benefit of thinking and development in these borrowed disciplines. Therefore, the basic tenets of the organizational dynamics school seem to be well defined, despite some controversy about the classification or taxonomy of power sources.

On the other hand, it is harder to find agreed on definitions for the outcomes of channel power, conflict, and cooperation. For example, it is not clear whether the outcomes should be measured in behavioral terms or psychological terms. Also, most of the outcomes are noneconomic measures, even though the ultimate goals of competitive coalition are the economic goals of profits and growth.

Most hypotheses and proposed theories do have good integration to generate a strong nomological network. Indeed, in this respect, the organizational dynamic school is as good as the buyer behavior and the managerial schools of marketing thought.

Our score on structure = 8.

SPECIFICATION: Are the relationships specified in a manner to delimit hypotheses or are they highly contingent?

It is refreshing to note that the organizational dynamics school has deliberately focused on one aspect of marketing practice, namely the channels relationship. To that extent, most of the hypotheses have been stated in very specific terms. On the other hand, many of the theories and concepts borrowed from organizational psychology are based on a contingency theory approach. In other words, it is possible that channel behavior may be driven by other forces than those hypothesized by the organizational dynamics school. This is particularly true with the comprehensive theories proposed in the area.

Overall, however, we believe that most publications in the organizational dynamics school provide a good deal of specificity, especially in view of the fact that behavioral sciences in general have limitations of their own with regard to specificity.

Our score on specification = 8.

TESTABILITY: Are the operational definitions provided to ensure testability and intersubjective consensus?

It would appear that the organizational dynamics school is relatively weak on this criterion. Partly, this is due to the lack of empirical studies, at least as compared to the buyer behavior and the managerial schools or marketing. However, it is also true that different scholars have proposed different operational measures for both the independent and the dependent variables. As mentioned before, there is no real consensus on whether the outcomes should be measured in behavioral or psychological terms. Similarly, there is no standardized set of scales to measure the independent variables such as power and conflict.

We believe that this relative lack of testability is largely due to the infancy of the school. In due course, some scholars in the field will develop standardized scales similar to attitude and personality research in order to improve testability and replication. However, even though it may be unfair, we must evaluate the school at this point in its life cycle.

Our score on testability = 4.

EMPIRICAL SUPPORT: **What is the degree of confirmation in terms of empirical support?**

The organizational dynamics school is probably weakest on this criterion. This is primarily due to its specialized nature within marketing. Unlike the managerial and the buyer behavior schools, it has attracted relatively fewer scholars to conduct research and testing. In fact, it is not an exaggeration to state that the organizational dynamics school has more concepts and theories than empirical testing and support. This is somewhat contrary to a more typical trend in discipline development, wherein empirical observations precede theory development. We believe this is due to the heavy reliance by this school on borrowed concepts from the behavioral sciences.

It is obvious that what is needed now is to generate large-scale empirical research comparable to what happened with the buyer behavior and the managerial schools of marketing.

Our score on empirical support = 3.

RICHNESS: **How comprehensive and generalizable is the theory?**

The organizational dynamics school is very comprehensive in explaining the behavioral outcomes of channel members (such as motivation, satisfaction, resentment, and the like). However, it seems to have very limited usefulness in terms of explaining and manipulating the economic behavior of the channel members (such as shifting functions, improving productivity by elimination of functions, or sharing of profits). For example, the organizational dynamics school is not directly linked to the concept of the value chain, and who performs what functions in the chain. Perhaps this is not the intent of the organizational dynamics school. However, it has explicitly rejected most economic concepts as being inadequate to explain channel behavior. Therefore, it should be capable of providing alternative explanations for the same behavior.

Our score on richness = 5.

SIMPLICITY: **How easy is it to communicate and implement the theory?**

The original concepts proposed by Louis Stern and his students are fairly simple and elegant. The fundamental concepts of power, conflict, and cooperation are everyday experiences in both the organizational and the personal worlds of most readers. They are, therefore, easy to relate to, and also easy to implement or apply in the real world.

However, the more recent efforts at developing comprehensive theories of channel behavior remind us of a similar effort at developing comprehensive theories in the buyer behavior school. They are more abstract, harder to relate to, and have too many variables. Furthermore, they are process-oriented rather than outcome oriented, which also makes them more difficult to communicate and implement in practice.

Our score on simplicity = 4.

Table 5.1 summarizes our evaluation of the organizational dynamics schools of marketing. It appears that this school is good in the syntax aspects, but weak in the semantic and pragmatic aspects of theory building.

Table 5.1 Evaluation of the Organizational Dynamics School*

Criterion	Rationale	Score
Structure	Has benefited from the well-defined concepts of the behavioral sciences from which it has borrowed	8
Specification	Has strongly focused on channel relationships and, to that extent, it is well specified	8
Testability	Operational definitions of power, conflict, and outcome variables are highly divergent	4
Empirical support	There are more concepts and propositions than there are empirical tests	3
Richness	Rich in behavioral outcomes but poor in economic or functional outcomes	5
Simplicity	Basic concepts of power, conflict, and cooperation are simple, but the recent process-oriented models are hard to understand	4
	TOTAL	32

* *Scores range from 1 (poor) to 10 (excellent).*

THE SYSTEMS SCHOOL OF THOUGHT

Like many other schools of thought, the systems school of thought emerged in response to the changing environment. However, we observe that many early writers in marketing recognized that marketing must be viewed as a system, even though the systems school did not really emerge until the 1960s. In the 1960s, the systems school of thought in marketing became visible due to the influence of operations research techniques in other disciplines of business. This gave impetus to examining marketing and marketing activities from a systems perspective. Furthermore, widespread use of powerful mainframe computers popularized the word "system" in the management literature.

A review of the proceedings of the educators conferences of the American Marketing Association points to the popularity of at least the term "systems." As will be pointed out later, systems and the systems school of thought are not necessarily the same. The 1965 AMA Conference Proceedings (Bennett 1965) does not contain a single paper with "systems" in the title. However, in 1966 (Hass 1966), there are at least five papers with "systems" in their title. By 1967, the theme of the entire conference was "Changing Marketing Systems" (Moyer 1968). For the next several years, "systems" was a common noun in paper titles and at least one marketing textbook was called *Marketing Systems* (Fisk 1967).

To properly evaluate this school of thought, it is important to have some feel of the basic tenets of the systems school. There is a surprising degree of agreement on this. The reason can easily be traced to the pioneering work of Forrester (1958), Boulding (1956), Kuhn (1963), and Bertalanffy (1968).

The work of Forrester is a direct outgrowth of the operations research approach fostered during World War II. This approach took a multidisciplinary view of problems and viewed the blending of the behavioral and quantitative sciences as necessary for the solution of complex problems. Forrester believed that:

> The company will come to be recognized not as a collection of separate functions, but as a system in which the flows of information, materials, manpower, capital equipment, and money set up forces that determine the basic tendency toward growth, fluctuations, and decline. (Forrester 1958, p. 52)

Boulding (1956) posits in his General Systems Theory that the often bewildering and confusing relationships between production, marketing, and consumption can be organized into a coherent and unified perspective using the analytical framework of systems, especially systems levels for classifying problems. For Boulding, marketing problems belong to a class of systems characterized by communication and adaptation in social organizations.

Similarly, Ludvig von Bertalanffy (1968), in his *General System Theory*, proposed a theory to explain all systems across contexts. He discussed open systems that interact with their environment, receiving inputs, processing these inputs, exporting outputs to the environment, and exchanging information and energy with the environment.

George Fisk (1967), in commenting on the application of general systems theory to marketing, writes:

> By viewing marketing problems in a system context, decision-makers can find a set of problems of which a particular problem is a member sharing at least some common properties. For many sets of problems much is known about acceptable solutions so that if a decision-maker is dissatisfied with his own solution or if he cannot find any solution he can refer to the set of problems to see if existing solutions apply. In this way, a tremendous body of information becomes more accessible (p. 12)

Kuhn (1963) broadened systems thinking to a more macro perspective with his application of system concepts to society. For Kuhn, marketing is a subsystem within society, with its own further subsystems such as the market and channels of distribution.

Systems, for these and subsequent writers, were made up of two classes of variables: the components or elements and the relationships among these components. These elements are generally thought of as interacting within a set of limited conditions usually referred to as the environment.

> Elements are simply the components of the system, and for any particular system they will range over a limited domain. Attributes are properties of elements, and relationships are those things that tie the elements of a system together. It is these relationships that make the notion of a system useful. The environment of any system can be defined as the set of all objects a change in whose attributes are changed by the behavior of the system. Any given system may be further subdivided into systems of a lower order. A system is also a part of a supersystem. That is, there exists a hierarchy of systems. (Dowling 1983, p. 23)

Katz and Kahn did much to familiarize management academics with the systems perspective through their now classic book *The Social Psychology of Organizations* (Katz and Kahn 1966). For them, organizational systems are complex, open, and behavioral. They also suggest that open systems are indeterminant and are frequently referred to as probabilistic systems. In defining complex, open, and behavioral systems, they identify nine characteristics of these systems:

1. *Importation of Energy* — open systems import some form of energy from the environment.

2. *The Throughput* — open systems transform the energy available to them. Work gets done in the system that in some manner reorganizes the input.

3. *The Output* — open systems export some product into the environment.

4. *Systems as Cycles of Events* — the pattern of activities of the energy exchange has a cyclic character. The product exported into the environment furnishes the sources of energy for the repetition of the cycle of activities.

5. *Negative Entropy* — a universal law of nature is entropy, i.e., all forms of organization move toward disorganization or death. To survive, open systems must acquire negative entropy by importing more energy from the environment than expended.

6. *Information Input, Negative Feedback, and the Coding Process* — in addition to energy, the open system also imports information to furnish signals to the structure about the environment and about its own functioning in relation to the environment. The simplest type of information input is negative feedback that allows the system to correct deviations from course. However, the reception of inputs is selected as systems react only to those inputs to which they are attuned. Coding is the term for the selective mechanisms of a system by which incoming information is rejected or accepted and translated.

7. *The Steady State and Dynamic Homeostasis* — any internal or external factor making for disruption of the system is countered by forces which restore the system as closely as possible to its previous state.

8. *Differentiation* — open systems move in the direction of differentiation and elaboration. Generalized patterns are replaced by more specialized functions.

9. *Equifinality* — a system can reach the same final state from differing initial conditions and by a variety of paths (Katz and Kahn 1966, pp. 14-29).

Relating the thinking of Katz and Kahn to marketing, Dowling (1983) states:

> The marketing subsystem exhibits many of the characteristics of a complex homeostatic mechanism because it helps the business enterprise attain a dynamic equilibrium and preserve its character. For example, one traditional function of marketing is to gather information from certain sections of the environment (customers) and transmit this to other parts of the enterprise. In carrying out this function, information is decoded and then reorganized according to the marketing system's perception of the needs of the enterprise. The decoding/recording phase of this operation is crucial to how the information will be used to change the behavior of the enterprise. Obviously, there are limits to the degree to which marketing can act as a homeostatic mechanism. These limits are defined in terms of the enterprise's other internal subsystems, its environment, and the type and number of system/environment exchange relationships (p. 24).

Even before the more formal statements of systems, marketing scholars understood that the various elements of marketing were of necessity related to and interdependent on each other. Such were the lessons of the commodity, functional, regional, and institutional schools of thought. As Mackenzie and Nicosia (1968) point out, in the period from 1920 to the late 1950s, "Major efforts were given to the problem of obtaining a picture of the whole marketing system" (p. 16). The most visible of these attempts were Clark (1922), Stewart and Dewhust (1939), Duddy and Revzan (1947), Vaile et al. (1952), and Alderson (1957).

As marketing scholars explored systems theory for relevance to marketing, the richness of this approach became evident. Bell (1966) provides an excellent discussion of social systems as they relate to marketing. In this discussion, he lays out the characteristics and requirements of social systems and social systems analysis, regarding marketing systems as special types of social systems. This discussion is summarized as follows:

1. A system is a group of interrelated components. All elements outside this relationship are outside the boundaries of the system and are components of the environment.

2. The behavior of a system is affected by the condition of its components. Similarly, system components are affected by environmental conditions.

3. The condition of a system component is variable. A change in the condition of a component or a change in environmental conditions necessitates an adjustment in the behavior of the system.

4. Closed systems can be completely isolated from the environment for analysis. In analyzing marketing systems, perhaps the best that can be hoped for is to temporarily maintain environmental conditions in an unchanged state.

5. In systems analysis, it is desirable to observe relations between a system and its environment under controlled conditions. Thus, it is advisable to use controlled experimentation in marketing research.

6. In systems analysis, attention is primarily focused on dynamics. This is the process whereby a system adapts to change and moves toward a new equilibrium after experiencing imbalance.

7. Systems are dynamic, composed only of variables. A component that does not change is not part of the system. In the analysis of marketing systems, almost everything is included in the analysis because almost everything is dynamic.

Exploring what the systems approach to marketing means, Lazer and Kelley (1962) discussed in some depth the component elements of marketing systems:

1. A set of functionally interdependent marketing relationships among people and institutions in the system—manufacturers, wholesalers, retailers, facilitating agencies, and consumers.

2. Interaction between individuals and firms necessary to maintain relationships including adjustment to change, innovation, cooperation, competition, linkages and blockages.

3. The establishment of objectives, goals, targets, beliefs, symbols, and sentiments which evolve from and reinforce the interaction. This results in determining realistic marketing objectives and instituting favorable programs, images, attitudes, opinions, and practices.

4. A consumer-oriented environment within which interactions take place subject to the constraints of a competitive market economy, a recognized legal and socio-economic climate, and the accepted relationships and practices of marketing functionaries.

5. Technology of marketing including communications media, credit facilities, standardization and grading techniques, marketing research and physical distribution techniques. (Lazer and Kelley 1962, p. 193)

As mentioned in Chapter 3, the functionalist school as advocated by Alderson is heavily dependent on systems thinking and analysis. For Alderson (1957), there were three types of systems: the atomistic, the mechanical and the ecological. The atomistic system is usually closed with no one of the components important enough to influence the entire system. The components are free to move and interact, but similar to the pure or perfect market structure, no one component emerges as the leader. Since there are few, if any, marketing systems that could be described as atomistic, this type of system has not been of much interest.

Alderson dismissed the mechanical system because it tends to be even more closed than the atomistic system. However, he recognized that some aspects of marketing appear to be mechanical systems, especially some aspects of warehousing and distribution. However, by pointing out that a system must be in touch with its environment, he almost dismissed mechanical systems as having much relevance to marketing.

Ecology is the study of an organism in relation to its environment. For Alderson, the organized behavior system is the expression of the ecological concept in marketing. While the organized behavior system has some definite limitations as pointed out in Chapter 3, it appears to have value to explain certain types of marketing phenomena.

We are unable to identify a stream of research similar to what we have found in previous schools of thought. Given the promise of this school of thought to both theory development and the practice of marketing, we had anticipated more. In an attempt to classify and organize the writings on systems thought in marketing, we have taken Dowling's (1983) suggestion and organized the literature into what Hall and Fagan (1968) have called macroscopic and microscopic analysis.

Microscopic analysis focuses on the minute structure of certain subsystems of interest; e.g., advertising and distribution (the traditional marketing perspective). Macroscopic analysis, on the other hand, focuses on the behavior of the system as a whole. Macroscopic analysis does not completely ignore specific marketing phenomena, rather it focuses attention on the patterns of behavior of a system under differing environmental conditions (Dowling 1983, p. 23.)

What follows is not an exhaustive review of the literature. However, it is very typical of the thought to date.

Macroscopic Marketing Systems

While we have discussed the approach of Wroe Alderson under the functionalist school of thought, much of Alderson's work could also be considered as relevant to this school of thought. He definitely viewed marketing from a total systems perspective. His work (1957, 1965) is the only major work directly relating systems to marketing thinking.

Also focusing on the system as a whole, Mackenzie and Nicosia (1968) pointed out that marketing literature had progressively adopted a systems point of view.

> Our view and interpretation of marketing literature shows a fund of knowledge which, although almost exclusively verbal, is very rich and amenable to more precise and analytical treatment. This knowledge can be summarized in three separate but conceptually related groups.

> First, consider a group of ideas that points to the existence of certain dimensions of any marketing system. These dimensions can be called "elementary" in that they ought to be there for any marketing system to exist. They are the objectives, objects and subjects of marketing activities, the marketing activities themselves, and all other entities such as laws, regulatory agencies, customs, social institutions, human and other resources, etc.

> A second group of ideas concerning marketing consists of attempts to conceptualize how the morphology of a system produced by its elementary dimensions leads to the system's behavior through dynamic interactions.

> The final group of ideas . . . consists of attempts to conceptualize and observe empirically the relationships that may exist within and/or across the elementary dimensions mentioned in the first group. (Mackenzie and Nicosia 1968, p. 17)

They also proposed a formal definition of a marketing system in a three-dimensional space: "The three main dimensions of agency, activity, and product define the traditionally more important dimensions of the behavior space known as marketing" (Mackenzie and Nicosia 1968, p. 21).

Amstutz (1967) contributed to the systems approach by developing a computer simulation of competitive market response. Various functions of marketing were operationalized and integrated to simulate the marketing system. Amstutz's model of marketing is the most generic yet developed. Unfortunately, it has not enjoyed further development and refinement.

Farley (1967), using simultaneous equation estimation techniques, demonstrated how marketing systems analysis can be used. He discussed several statistical techniques for estimating parameters of the Jamaican distribution structure. He concludes:

> While the theory in these areas is relatively well-developed, it turns out that there are a number of practical problems—particularly those posed by inter-correlations in explanatory variables of such systems—which lead us to consider less-than-best procedures to deal with the problems. Larger data banks and improved computational procedures may combine to improve the situation. However, in this area, as in many others where branches of technology are brought to bear on marketing problems, a variety of quite practical problems remain to be solved before we can be satisfied with research results. (p. 321)

More recently, Howard (1983) has taken a systems approach in integrating descriptive concepts of demand and supply cycle, product hierarchy, competitive structure, and a customer decision model to form a marketing theory of the firm. According to Howard, marketing management has suffered from the lack of a systematic body of knowledge to guide decisions. He maintains that, to be useful to managers, the "bits and pieces" of marketing knowledge must be organized into a superstructure. Thus, he advocates viewing marketing as a system.

Dowling (1983), in an attempt to formulate propositions about the future of marketing, examines the evolution of marketing systems. In what could become a classic article, he classified the four marketing management philosophies of production, selling, marketing, and societal marketing concepts into four environments originally proposed in the work of Emery and Trist (1965). Emery and Trist used a two-dimensional framework for outlining the characteristics of an enterprise's environment.

> Each level of environmental complexity relies on (a) a different *organization* of the objects within the environment, and (b) various rates of change over time of these objects. Objects can be described as having either positive attributes; i.e., they represent goals or negative attributes; i.e., they are regarded as noxiants or things to be avoided. (Dowling 1983, p. 25)

Based on his conclusions (Dowling 1983, p. 30) that "the evolution of marketing can best be described in terms of the attempt by business enterprises to become more aware of, and to react to, the requirements of their various relevant external publics," he proposes the following observations about the future:

> The future environments of all social systems will be characterized by increasing levels of relevant uncertainty.

Relationship Between Marketing and Its Environment

Environment	Relevant Uncertainty	The Normative Response of the Enterprise (System)	Analogous Marketing Management Philosophies
I Placid random	Low	Automatic reaction	Production concept
II Placid clustered	Low-medium	Strategy	Selling concept
III Disturbed reactive	Medium-high	Strategy, tactics, and operations	Marketing concept
IV Turbulent	High	Initiate systems changes	Societal marketing concept

Adapted from Dowling (1983).

> The marketing (sub)system is best conceptualized as carrying out a complex homeostatic function for its parent system, the business enterprise. This boundary role makes it ideally suited to help monitor environmental change and where necessary to provide information which will help initiate change within the structure of its parent enterprise.
>
> The ability of the marketing system to fulfill its homeostatic functions will determine, in part, how an enterprise perceives and reacts to its environment. (Dowling 1983, p. 30)

As an example of another approach classified as macroscopic analysis, Reidenbach and Oliva (1983) apply the open system characteristics of entropy to an examination of marketing. They conclude, using indifference analysis, that as a society, we face major trade-offs between the macro and micro levels of the environments. They argue that marketing must shift from an emphasis on demand creation to that of synchronizing, maintaining, and even reducing and destroying demand in order to slow down the entropic process of pollution and resource diminution.

> The consequence of not assuming a more aggressively responsible posture is proliferations of government-controlled macro agencies charged with the responsibility of regulating the transformation processes. This brings with it a concomitant reduction in social and economic freedom. (Reidenbach and Oliva 1983, p. 39)

Microscopic Marketing Systems

There are more examples of microscopic systems analysis. A sample of these would include Ridgeway (1957), Staudt (1958), Goldstucker (1966),

Uhl (1968), McNiven (1968), Brien (1968), Gardner (1973), and Reidenbach and Oliva (1981).

For instance, Ridgeway (1957) suggested that a manufacturer and its dealers be considered as a single organization and be administered as a system. Staudt (1958) observed that the firm should be viewed as an integrated system with the market (environment) holding veto power over all its activities. Goldstucker (1966) presented the case for developing a systems framework for retail location. Uhl (1968) commented on the need for marketing information systems. He argued that three general information subsystems appear appropriate: (1) selective dissemination, (2) retrospective, and (3) unsolicited. McNiven (1968) discussed several reasons why marketing information systems are counted as failures and suggested a forward-looking approach. Brien and Stafford (1968) discussed marketing information systems and marketing research, and Brien (1968) chided management for mistaking computers for marketing information systems before management is really systems oriented. Gardner (1973) offered the hypothesis that the concept of "dynamic homeostasis" explains the research tradition and its future use in marketing cases that are brought before regulatory bodies. Reidenbach and Oliva (1981) discussed the application of a "general living systems theory" to marketing and its adaptation to the needs of society.

In the mid-1960s, systems were thought to be one of the most important trends in marketing courses. For example, Lazer (1966) wrote:

> Systems-thinking has affected developments in several disciplines, particularly operations research and engineering. Emphasized are the integration of elements and activities into wholes or total systems, and networks, linkages, interactions, feedback, system-adjustment, survival, and growth. This has led to the widely hailed marketing-management philosophy and the marketing concept, both of which emphasize the coordination, integration, and linkage of marketing ingredients in order to achieve a total system of action. The systems-approach has encouraged the acceptance of functionalism — with its emphasis on adjustment, survival, and growth — and has stimulated the study of input-output and open and closed systems. The systems approach will affect future marketing knowledge in even another way. Systems engineers are now developing new mathematical techniques for modeling and analyzing complex systems. Some of these techniques are applicable to marketing systems, and will result in new conceptual and analytical approaches. (p. 35)

But just two years later, Seymour Banks speculated that the systems concept as applied to marketing may be just another fad that will eventually fade away (Banks 1968). After surveying leading marketing firms, he found very few firms using the systems concept in marketing. From the few positive responses, however, he predicted "a gradual expansion of the application of the systems concept to marketing since the requirements are not too rare and the benefits substantial, at least for early adopters" (Banks 1968, p. 28).

Amstutz (1968), in an excellent appraisal of "systems analysis," discussed the misapplication of the term to a wide range of procedures that are neither systematic nor analytic. For Amstutz, "valid systems analysis separates the complex market environment into constituent elements and describes interactions among elements with empirically verifiable assertions" (p. 305).

There are several reasons why the potential of a systems perspective in marketing is not likely to materialize in the short run. The first relates to its global, all encompassing nature. To date, with the exception of writers like Alderson (1957, 1965), Mackenzie and Nicosia (1968), Dowling (1983), and Reidenbach and Oliva (1983), most writers seem to associate systems with each function of marketing such as product, communication, marketing research, and distribution. It seems apparent that we need to devote considerable conceptual research to marketing as a system versus marketing systems.

The second reason relates to the problems of "doing research" on systems, especially macromarketing systems. We have not yet classified our knowledge into sufficient categories for systems analysis at the macro level. Even if we had our knowledge organized, we lack the appropriate analytic techniques for dealing with the highly probabilistic relationships that are likely to be involved. And if that isn't problem enough, the publish or perish environment in which many researchers find themselves makes it difficult to devote the large block of time necessary to engage in acceptable systems research, especially at the macromarketing level.

There is no question that the systems approach still offers much to the development of marketing thought. Will it ever reach its potential? While the outlook in the immediate future is not encouraging, the recent work of Michael Porter (1980, 1985) offers hope that we can classify marketing knowledge and postulate tentative systems relationships in marketing.

EVALUATION OF THE SYSTEMS SCHOOL

If the organizational dynamics school is in its infancy, then the systems school must be considered in the embryonic stage of development. Therefore, it is unfair to subject the systems school to the metatheory criteria used in this book. Although we will go ahead and evaluate it, the reader is urged to remember that some of the evaluative comments are made in the hopes of encouraging further research in this area.

STRUCTURE: Are the concepts properly defined and integrated to form a strong nomological network?

By definition, a systems perspective is taken to integrate various components or elements into a strong network. Therefore, the systems school must be scored high on this criterion. However, the problem lies with the definition of the elements of marketing. There is no real consensus among the systems school scholars about various elements of marketing. This is not new. We commented on a similar problem encountered by the functional school of marketing. Unless the systems school provides a conceptually rigorous classification of marketing functions that can be operationally organized by marketing practitioners, it is unlikely that we will have a generic marketing system. The only exception to this has been Amstutz (1967) and his simulation of the marketing system. Unfortunately, it has not been adopted by others for further development and refinement.

Our score on structure = 5.

SPECIFICATION: Are the relationships specified in a manner to delimit hypotheses or are they highly contingent?

The systems school of thought scores well on specification. Although various scholars of this school do not agree on a common definition, each one has formulated the relationships among the chosen constructs to specify directionality and sometimes even the magnitude of relationships. It is, therefore, possible to attempt a simulation of the systems perspective and provide certain answers based on "what if" changes in the input variables. Indeed, the systems school has even attempted to quantify its relationships so that one can also attempt to optimize market responses. This is especially true at the microscopic marketing subsystems level.

Our score on specification = 8.

TESTABILITY: Are the operational definitions provided to ensure testability and intersubjective consensus?

Once again, we must reiterate that many systems perspectives have provided operational definitions to test the outputs as a function of inputs. Again, this has been particularly true of the managerially oriented microscopic systems such as new products, advertising, and distribution models. On the other hand, the more generic macroscopic systems that attempt to interface the external noncontrollable societal environment with the internal controllable marketing environment have not provided operational definitions rigorous enough to make the systems testable. Perhaps the recent efforts by Howard (1983) to incorporate the life cycle as the fundamental concept underlying the demand and the supply side of marketing is a good attempt in the right direction.

Our score on testability = 6.

EMPIRICAL SUPPORT: What is the degree of confirmation in terms of empirical support?

On this dimension, the systems school scores low. There are too few attempts to empirically test marketing systems. Some industry efforts, such as measuring advertising effectiveness (DAGMAR model) or new product introduction (DEMON model), generated hope for developing strong empirical support, but it has not fully materialized. This is understandable because it takes a lot money and long-term commitment to develop and implement marketing systems in the real world.

Our score on empirical support = 5.

RICHNESS: How comprehensive and generalizable is the theory?

It scores very well on this dimension. Whatever the level of analysis (micro versus macro), scholars of this school have consciously taken a comprehensive perspective to generate richness of ideas and hypotheses. For example, Amstutz's (1967) model of marketing is the most generic system yet developed by anyone. Similarly, Forrester's industrial dynamics can accommodate any number of marketing functions with infinite possible relationships. Even the econometric approaches to systems have proven to be fairly robust and rich.

Our score on richness = 8.

SIMPLICITY: How easy is it to communicate and implement the theory?

In our opinion, the systems school is relatively simple since it attempts to describe and depict reality by breaking it up into components or subsystems. The only complication inherent in the systems school is that it is more difficult to implement, not because it is complex but because it requires a significant degree of top management commitment.

Our score on simplicity = 8.

Table 5.2 summarizes our evaluation of the systems school of marketing thought. It is relatively weak in structure and empirical support, but scores relatively high on all other dimensions. As we stated earlier, the systems school holds great promise for the advancement of marketing as a discipline. It is quantifiable and testable. Also, marketing practitioners have a vested interest in using its concepts because they are likely to enhance marketing efficiency and productivity. We urge our colleagues to devote more time to this school of thought.

THE SOCIAL EXCHANGE SCHOOL OF THOUGHT

Although marketing scholars from various theoretical perspectives long acknowledged that the fundamental purpose of marketing was to facilitate

Table 5.2 Evaluation of the Systems School*

Criterion	Rationale	Score
Structure	Systems orientation should generate well-defined structure, but lack of consensus on what to focus on in defining the marketing system is a major weakness	5
Specification	Good specification due to functional and sequential decomposition of subsystems of marketing	8
Testability	Good operational definitions for microscopic systems but weak for macroscopic systems	6
Empirical support	Excellent support for each functional marketing system such as new products, advertising, and distribution, but none at the total systems level	5
Richness	Very robust and comprehensive at both micro and macro levels	8
Simplicity	Very easy to understand and implement at subsystem level	8
	TOTAL	40

* Scores range from 1 (poor) to 10 (excellent).

exchanges between buyers and sellers, it was not until the mid-1960s that a group of theorists began to advocate a more explicit emphasis on the social exchange school of marketing thought. The honor for launching this exchange perspective in marketing should be rightly shared by Wroe Alderson and William McInnes.

In a paper in the highly influential volume *Theory in Marketing* published in 1964, McInnes argued that greater attention should be given to the role of the market as the focal point of exchanges between buyers and sellers. According to McInnes, "markets result from the social intercourse of men when the makers and users of economic goods and services seek to satisfy their needs and wants through exchange" (p. 53). Using this foundation of market exchanges, he further argued that:

> Marketing is any "motion" or activity that actualizes the potential relation of producer and consumer. The essential task of marketing is, therefore, always related primarily to the market. The work of marketing always begins with the discovery of market potential . . . A concept of marketing in its widest sense, therefore, is any activity which actualizes the potential market relationship between the makers and users of economic goods and services. (p. 57)

Among his many contributions to marketing, Wroe Alderson, writing along with Miles W. Martin (Alderson and Martin 1965), proposed "The Law of Exchange" to explain why two parties decide to enter into a transaction. His "Law of Exchange" was defined as:

> Given that x is an element of assortment A1 and y is an element of the assortment of A2, x is exchangeable for y if and only if these three conditions hold:
>
> (a) x is different from y
> (b) The potency of the assortment A1 is increased by dropping x and adding y
> (c) The potency of the assortment A2 is increased by adding x and dropping y (p. 121)

A critical feature of Alderson's concept of exchange was the pivotal role played by the *perceptions and preferences* of the exchange actors in determining the optimality of the exchange transaction:

> Viewing exchange from the standpoint of one of the decision makers, we can say that exchange is optimal if he prefers it to any available alternative. Similarly, for the decision maker on the other side of the transaction, it will be optimal for him if he prefers it to any available alternative. It is assumed that if a concrete situation offers an exchange opportunity, the number of alternatives realistically available to either side is not infinite in number but limited to only a few. Faced with a decision, an individual must be guided by his present knowledge of alternatives and the ordering according to his preferences within that set. (p. 122)

The next major boost to the exchange school of thought occurred in 1972 when Philip Kotler presented his "generic concept of marketing." In light of the turmoil during the early 1970s regarding the scope and nature of marketing, Kotler (1972a) sought to clarify his perception of the basic focus of marketing:

> What then is the disciplinary focus of marketing? The core concept of marketing is the transaction. A transaction is the exchange of values between two parties. The things-of-values need not be limited to goods, services, and money; they include other resources such as time, energy, and feelings. (p. 48)

To further fortify his view that transaction or exchange is the core concept of marketing, Kotler discussed how marketers seek to facilitate and mold exchange relationships:

> Marketing is a particular way of looking at the problem of achieving a valued response from a target market. It essentially holds that exchange values must

be identified, and the marketing program must be based on these exchange values . . . The marketer attempts to find ways to increase the person's perceived rate of exchange between what he would receive and what he would give up in freely adopting that behavior. The marketer is a specialist at understanding human wants and values and knows what it takes for someone to act. (p. 53)

In the mid-1970s, Richard Bagozzi assumed the leadership position in the social exchange school of thought. In a series of related articles (1974, 1975, 1978, 1979), Bagozzi refined and elaborated on his conception of exchange as the fundamental foundation of marketing. Beginning in his 1974 article, Bagozzi defined the exchange system as "a set of social actors, their relationships to each other, and the endogenous and exogenous variables affecting the behavior of the social actors in those relationships" (p. 78).

One of the major contributions of his 1974 paper was his assault on the prior conceptualization of exchange that had failed to identify the causal relationships:

Unfortunately, the traditional notion of exchange says little about the theoretical cause-and-effect relations determining the exchange. To say that X will be exchanged for Y when both actors perceive their assortment to be improved is not sufficient for a theory. Marketers want to know why and when an individual will take a particular course of action. (p. 79)

In the 1975 article, Bagozzi continued his advocacy of the exchange concept by stating that "it is assumed that marketing theory is concerned with two questions: (1) Why do people and organizations engage in exchange relationships? and (2) How are exchanges created, resolved, or avoided?" (p. 32). In addition, he proposed that a general theory of marketing could be established on the exchange concept:

Although marketing seems to defy simple definition and circumscription, it is essential that marketers locate the distinctive focus (or foci) of the discipline. Failure to do so impedes both the growth of the discipline and the character of its performance. Exchange is a central concept in marketing, and it may well serve as the foundation for that elusive "general theory of marketing." (p. 39)

Bagozzi's 1978 article, which appeared in *American Behavioral Scientist*, presented several new thoughts that served to advance and realign the exchange concept. First, Bagozzi asserted that the exchange process should be viewed as a social activity rather than as insulated individuals making solitary decisions:

No longer are buyers and sellers treated solely as isolated actors emitting or responding to stimuli. Rather, marketing behavior is now regarded as an inherently social activity where the outcomes of exchange depend on bargaining, negotiation, power, conflict, and the shared meaning existing between buyer and seller. (p. 536)

Second, he suggested that exchange relationships are a function of three broad determinants:

1. Social actor variables: including attraction, similarity, expertise, prestige, etc.
2. Social influence variables: the specific actions, communications, and information transmitted between the parties.
3. Situational variables: including the availability of alternative sources of satisfaction, the physical and psychological setting, and the legal and normative setting.

Bagozzi's 1979 paper, entitled "Toward a Formal Theory of Marketing Exchanges," generally served to clarify and reiterate the current status of the exchange perspective. Perhaps the highlight of this paper is Bagozzi's presentation of a category system for evaluating exchanges:

> If the concept of exchanges is to be used in an explanatory — as opposed to a purely descriptive — sense, then it will have to be conceptualized as a phenomenon capable of variation in one or more ways. This author believes that exchanges might be fruitfully conceived as a three fold categorization of *outcomes, experiences,* and *actions,* each varying in degree and occurring to the actors as individuals, jointly or shared, or both. Outcomes in an exchange refer to physical, social or symbolic objects or events accruing to the actors as a consequence of their relationship ... Experiences are psychological states and consist of affective, cognitive, or moral dimensions. They typically are conveyed symbolically through the objects exchanged, the functions performed by the exchange, or the meanings attributed to the exchange ... The final variable with which to represent an exchange is the actions performed by the actors as a product of their interchange. Actions might represent individual choices and responses or joining commitments. (pp. 435-436)

Bagozzi's conceptualization of exchange was critiqued by Ferrell and Perrachione in 1980. They generally applauded Bagozzi for his efforts to advance the theory of marketing, but they strongly argued that his utilization of the exchange concept left much to be desired:

> Bagozzi has restated the exchange theories of other disciplines. He has also drawn many potentially useful and relevant concepts from other disciplines. Thus, what he has accomplished is not enough to qualify as a formal theory (or even the basis for a formal theory) of marketing exchanges.
>
> It is dangerous to borrow exchange theory concepts from economics and psychology and sociology, and apply them directly in marketing. It was their inadequacy that gave rise to the development of a distinct discipline of marketing in the first place. A return to these theories and concepts can at best

be only of limited utility in developing a formal theory of exchange for marketing, and reliance on them to the extent Bagozzi does may well be counter-productive. Many aspects of a marketing exchange theory will and must borrow from and/or be related to those areas; a good theory will have to be eclectic. We do not believe that what Bagozzi gives is sufficiently eclectic enough to provide the necessary bridge between marketing and related disciplines. (Ferrell and Perrachione 1980, p. 159)

Perhaps the most elegant statement related to exchange or transaction as the fundamental proposition on which to build marketing theory comes from Shelby Hunt (1976b, 1983a). After reviewing the debate about whether marketing is a science or an art, as well as different philosophies of science, Hunt (1983a) argued:

Consistent with the perspective of most marketing theorists (Alderson 1965; Bagozzi 1974, 1978, 1979; Kotler 1972) this writer has proposed that the basic subject matter of marketing is the exchange relationship or transaction. (p. 12)

He further suggested:

The preceding discussion implies that *marketing science is the behavioral science that seeks to explain exchange relationships.* Given this perspective of marketing science, and adopting the customary (albeit somewhat arbitrary) convention of designating one party to the exchange as the "buyer" and one party as the "seller" the fundamental explanada of marketing can be logically derived. The four interrelated sets of fundamental explanada of marketing science are:

The behaviors of buyers directed at consummating exchanges.

The behaviors of sellers directed at consummating exchanges.

The institutional framework directed at consummating and/or facilitating exchanges.

The consequences on society of the behaviors of buyers, the behaviors of sellers, and the institutional framework directed at consummating and/or facilitating exchanges. (p. 13)

A recent article by Houston and Gassenheimer (1987) has contributed a systematic examination of the literature on exchange, maintaining that exchange is the core concept of marketing and should have a role in distinguishing it from other disciplines. Based on their review of the literature, the authors discuss exchange as the result of goal-seeking behavior, occurring under specified conditions (as discussed by Alderson, Kotler, and Bagozzi), and consisting of the passing of value or utility. Further, they discuss the exchange relationship as a richer concept than exchange as an isolated act and identify social distance as an important characteristic associated with the variation seen in exchange relationships.

The social exchange school of thought seems to be one of the few in marketing that has a wide degree of consensus. At the same time, it must be recognized that despite Bagozzi's gallant efforts and Hunt's eloquent pleas, the social exchange school of thought has yet to provide propositions as to why exchange takes place between a buyer and a seller. McInnes (1964) and Houston and Gassenheimer (1987) seem to provide the best explanations of why an exchange takes place. According to McInnes (1964):

> Thus, the basic model of a market consists of a set of real but potential relationships in five dimensions: space, time, perception, evaluation, and ownership . . . Since market potentiality is measured by the extent of separation of the parties to an exchange in each of these five dimensions, the greater the separation, the greater the market potential . . . These dimensions form the basic pattern that makes a market; they are the five dimensions of market potential that confront every marketing agent and determine every marketing institution. (p. 59)

More recently, Houston and Gassenheimer (1987) have offered the following explanation:

> The driving force behind exchange is need satisfaction. We express it as the realization of utility where a utility function is a description of what "commodities" are used to satisfy needs . . . (p. 16)

Marketing is the study of potency variation resulting from exchange, and exchange is engaged in by an individual for the enhancement of the potency of his or her assortment. Several ways other than exchange can be used to enhance the potency of one's own assortment. They include, but are not limited to, self-production and certain forms of theft.

EVALUATION OF THE SOCIAL EXCHANGE SCHOOL

STRUCTURE: **Are the concepts properly defined and integrated to form a strong nomological network?**

Both the generic concept of marketing developed by Kotler (1972a) and the formal theory of marketing exchanges proposed by Bagozzi (1979) clearly meet the structural criterion of theory building. Unfortunately, the social exchange school of thought is a single construct theory that provides good normative rules for the marketing practitioner but does not provide any explanation as to why and how values are created and what motivates the buyer and the seller to engage in an exchange. Nonetheless, the concepts are well defined and properly structured, at least with more consistency than most other schools of thought.

Our score on structure = 8.

SPECIFICATION: **Are the relationships specified in a manner to delimit hypotheses or are they highly contingent?**

The older definitions of market transaction as the exchange of economic values provided a good demarcation of the domain of marketing. Unfortunately, the generic concept of marketing, which generalized market transaction as the exchange of any value, has created ambiguity as to the boundary of marketing. Indeed, Luck (1969) and others have vehemently argued that the broadening of the marketing concept to the exchange of any values results in the possibility of marketing losing its identity. To that extent, specification is weak.

Our score on specification = 4.

TESTABILITY: **Are the operational definitions provided to ensure testability and intersubjective consensus?**

The social exchange school has failed to provide operational definitions. Indeed, there seems to be no interest in empirical testing of the basic propositions. At the same time, it must be pointed out that, based on anecdotal case histories as well as personal experiences, it is possible to generate intersubjective consensus for the basic tenets of this school of thought. We believe, however, this type of face validity is not sufficient to score high on testability.

Our score on testability = 5.

EMPIRICAL SUPPORT: **What is the degree of confirmation in terms of empirical support?**

Because there has been virtually no interest in scientifically testing the basic propositions of the social exchange school, there exists little formal empirical support. However, this school of marketing thought is well supported by case histories and anecdotal evidence.

Our score on empirical support = 5.

RICHNESS: **How comprehensive and generalizable is the theory?**

The social exchange school is perhaps the most generalizable school among all we have studied in this book. It even surpasses the systems school, especially after Kotler's (1972a) brilliant attempt to develop a generic concept of marketing based on the exchange construct. Indeed, this school is so comprehensive that it begins to blur the boundaries of marketing and other behavioral sciences.

Our score on richness = 9.

SIMPLICITY: **How easy is it to communicate and implement the theory?**

The social exchange school is not only rich but also extremely simple. Perhaps this may be the reason why it has universal appeal. It is as easy to communicate because everyone has experiences to relate to its ideas and implications. Furthermore, it is easy to implement. For example, it is obvious to the marketing practitioner that he/she should channel his/her marketing efforts toward that aspect of exchange that has the highest separation between buyers and sellers. This results in enhancing the effectiveness of marketing. Also, he/she should use that element of the marketing mix that is best in bridging the gap. This results in improved efficiency and effectiveness of marketing.

Our score on simplicity = 9.

Table 5.3 summarizes our evaluation of the social exchange school of thought. It scores very well on the dimensions of structure, richness, and simplicity, but lower on the dimensions of specification, testability, and empirical support.

Table 5.3 Evaluation of the Social Exchange School*

Critierion	Rationale	Score
Structure	Limited construct results in good structure	8
Specification	Broadening the definition of exchange to any value has caused confusion between marketing and social exchange	4
Testability	Good face validity but no consensus or standard definitions of exchange	5
Empirical support	Ample case histories but no formal test of the exchange school	5
Richness	Perhaps the richest of all shcools of thought in terms of generalizability	9
Simplicity	Extremely simple to understand and implement	9
	TOTAL	40

* *Scores range from 1 (poor) to 10 (excellent).*

SUMMARY

The three schools of thought reviewed in this chapter are the organizational dynamics, the systems, and the social exchange schools of marketing. The organizational dynamics school is highly focused on the behavior of channel members in marketing. Furthermore, it has limited itself toward understanding psychological aspects as opposed to economic aspects of channel cooperation and conflict.

On the other hand, the systems school is more comprehensive and encompasses all functions and institutions of marketing as well as marketing as an institution within a society. Although the macroscopic systems have been more abstract and nontested, the microscopic systems, especially related to each element of the marketing mix (product, promotion, price, distribution) have received strong empirical support by marketing practitioners. At the same time, the systems school has also attempted to utilize quantitative tools and methods, including mathematical and simulation models. To that extent, it is closer to the buyer behavior school of marketing thought.

Finally, the social exchange school of marketing thought seems most promising in developing a general theory of marketing. This is because its constructs are simple but very comprehensive. Furthermore, they are actionable by both public policymakers and marketing practitioners. Unfortunately, there is very little formal testing of the propositions developed by the social exchange school even though there is considerable intuitive, experiential, and historical evidence to support its concepts.

6

WHAT WE HAVE LEARNED

Based on our historical review of marketing, we can reach several conclusions regarding the current health and welfare of the marketing discipline:

1. Marketing is now perceived as a legitimate scholarly discipline by our colleagues in related fields, such as economics, psychology, sociology, public administration, social work, political science, and mass communications. Although marketing scholars continue to adopt and apply theories from these other disciplines, marketing has begun to develop its own rather impressive library of internally generated theories. In fact, theories originated by marketing scholars are now being increasingly cited by researchers in these allied disciplines. In addition, the leading journals in marketing, such as the *Journal of Marketing*, the *Journal of Marketing Research*, and the *Journal of Consumer Research*, are widely respected and reviewed outside of the narrow confines of the marketing discipline.

2. Marketing is becoming increasingly disassociated from the negative stereotypes that once dominated the perceptions of most consumers. As consumers became more knowledgeable of the true purpose of marketing and as professional marketing organizations acted decisively to discipline unethical practitioners, many consumers gradually gained confidence in marketing's function in society. To be sure, some consumers continue to be victimized by unscrupulous marketers.

However, when compared to marketing's performance in earlier years, modern marketing is dramatically more socially responsible.

3. Marketing has demonstrated impressive versatility and vitality by moving beyond the narrow bounds of traditional business arenas and finding applications in nontraditional fields, such as health care, social services, telecommunications, and political science. This movement suggests that marketing has theories and principles that are applicable to a broader range of exchange relationships. Although marketing philosophers continue to debate the desirable boundaries of the marketing discipline, this controversy has become by default a moot point. While these philosophers debated, practitioners outside the traditional business boundaries decided that marketing could assist them in maximizing their exchange relationships.

4. Marketing has a rich heritage that too many marketing scholars and practitioners do not study or appreciate. In many instances marketing scholars attempt to publish "new" theoretical research that fails to incorporate the theoretical principles first spawned in earlier schools of marketing thought, such as the commodity, the functional, and the institutional schools. Unfortunately, too few doctoral programs in marketing explicitly stress coursework in marketing history. Furthermore, doctoral dissertations concerning marketing history are exceedingly rare. However, recent efforts by Ronald Savitt (1980), who has discussed the value of historical research in marketing and suggested a methodological framework for conducting it, and Stanley Hollander at Michigan State University, who has hosted regular (every other year) conferences on marketing history, may focus more attention on the history of marketing.

In this chapter, we will take stock of what we have learned from our review of the evolution of marketing thought, as well as begin to address the following issues raised in Chapter 1:

1. Is marketing a science or, at best, a standardized art?
2. What is, or should be, the proper domain of marketing theory?
3. What is, or should be, the dominant perspective in marketing?
4. What is, or should be, the relationship between marketing and society?
5. Is it really possible to create a general theory of marketing?

IS MARKETING A SCIENCE OR, AT BEST, A STANDARDIZED ART?

This question is still difficult to answer because a vigorous debate is currently raging in marketing regarding the metatheoretical criteria. While some notable scholars, led by Shelby Hunt (1983b), maintain that logical positivism is the proper foundation for theory development, another growing group, led by Paul Anderson (1983), has recently begun to argue that marketing theories should be judged with relativistic criteria. This controversy certainly bears directly on the distinction of science versus art.

In this book we utilized a metatheoretical evaluation system with six criteria that bridges the gap between the logical positivist perspective and the relativism perspective. The syntax criteria of structure and specification evaluate the consistency of the nomological network of constructs in a theory. Semantics criteria evaluate a theory's relationship to reality by analyzing its testability and empirical support. Finally, the pragmatics or relevance criteria of richness and simplicity scrutinize the applicability of a theory to those who are actively involved in marketing practice.

In short, the emphasis on syntax and semantics represents preference for logical positivism whereas the emphasis on pragmatics represents preference for relativism. In some sense, this is really a debate as to which is more important — rigor or relevance. It is argued that in our quest to become more scientific and, therefore, respected by traditional disciplines, we have emphasized too much rigor at the expense of relevance. Indeed, the same journals that have enhanced the respectability of marketing have come under some criticism with respect to relevance. Too many papers published in *the Journal of Consumer Research, the Journal of Marketing Research,* and even *the Journal of Marketing* are regarded as irrelevant to the advancement of marketing discipline and marketing practice. In fact, a backlash to this crisis in relevance has resulted in a proliferation of new journals with an emphasis toward balancing rigor and relevance (Luke and Doke 1987).

In addition to the dichotomy of logical postivism versus relativism as the appropriate foundation for theory development, there is a growing debate over appropriate methodology for empirical research and theory testing. This debate has largely focused on the dichotomy between the methods suggested by the tradition of logical positivism and the methods suggested by the philosophy of humanism. Most notably, Elizabeth Hirschman (1986) has argued that, because marketing is a socially constructed enterprise, research in marketing is in need of inputs from humanistic modes of inquiry. In contrast to the experimental and survey methodologies characterizing the logical positivist approach, the humanistic approach advocates more naturalistic forms of inquiry:

> . . . it advocates *in-dwelling* of the researcher with the phenonema under investigation. Rather than standing apart from the system being studied, the researcher immerses the self within it. Researcher understanding, therefore, is deemed within the humanistic perspective to arise from direct personal experience, rather than by the manipulation of experimental variables. (p. 238)

According to Hirschman, the different research methodologies advocated by the humanistic approach and the positivist approach result from differences in their basic philosophies, with the humanistic philosophy being virtually the converse of the logical positivist philosophy:

Humanistic Versus Positivistic Research Philosophies

The Humanistic Metaphysic	The Positivistic Metaphysic
1. Human beings construct multiple realities.	1. There is a single reality composed of discrete elements.
2. Researcher and phenomenon are mutually interactive.	2. The researcher and the phenomenon are independent.
3. Research inquiry is directed toward the development of idiographic knowledge.	3. It is possible and desirable to develop statements of truth . that are generalizable across time and context.
4. Phenomenal aspects cannot be segregated into "causes and effects."	4. Elements of reality can be segregated into causes and effects.
5. Inquiry is inherently value-laden.	5. It is possible and desirable to discover value-free objective knowledge.

Adapted from Hirschman (1986, p. 239).

Similarly, in a recent address as an Association for Consumer Research (ACR) Fellow, Everett Rogers has suggested the critical school paradigm as appropriate for guiding theory development and testing within marketing and consumer behavior. According to Rogers (1987), the critical school is more philosophical in its emphasis than is the traditional empirical school based on logical positivism; and it is based on a greater attention to context, an early Marxist orientation, and a concern with who controls a system. In contrast to the empirical school, which is strongest in the United States, the critical school tends to be concentrated in Europe. Advocating that consumer researchers can benefit from the insights of the critical school, Rogers (1987) listed four implications for consumer research:

1. "Consumer scholars should focus on the ownership and control of systems affecting individual consumer behavior." (p. 9)

2. "Consumer research should be cast in a wider scope, both in recognizing (1) that research questions of a global significance should be emphasized over culture-bound inquiries of national systems, and (2) that to understand consumer behavior is to understand society . . ." (p. 9)

3. "The critical school suggests to empirical scholars of consumer behavior that they should broaden the range of methodological tools they employ in their investigations." (p. 10)

4. "Ethical aspects of the consumer behavior they investigate should not be ignored by empirical scholars, even if these aspects cannot be studied with their usual research methods." (p. 10)

Table 6.1 provides a summary of the ratings we have given to the twelve schools of thought reviewed in this book. An analysis of the summary provides some interesting insights.

Borrowed Constructs Versus Our Own

The early schools of marketing thought, including the commodity and functional schools, were highly relevant and based on empirical observations. However, these schools failed to develop a rich syntax or conceptual base. But as marketing evolved over the past seventy-five years, the conceptual foundation has improved considerably. This movement is clearly a reflection of marketing theorists borrowing well-conceptualized constructs from other disciplines. For example, the managerial school borrowed economic concepts such as elasticity and marginal analysis, the regional school adopted concepts like spatial gravitation from geography, and, of course, the buyer behavior school borrowed heavily from psychology, sociology, and communications.

Although the adoption of well-defined theories from other disciplines is desirable, this activity may create a crisis of relevance. More precisely, most schools of marketing thought that relied extensively on borrowed concepts have generally scored low on the richness and the simplicity criteria. This weakness suggests that marketing theorists must place greater emphasis on developing *our own constructs and theories* that are fundamentally strong in all metatheoretical criteria. As we noted in the introduction to this chapter, marketing has begun to gain a measure of respect for some theories and concepts developed internally in recent years. Now we must continue this trend and not be content to merely borrow externally developed theories.

A few examples will illustrate this point. The functional school of thought was probably the earliest predecessor of the concept of value chain popularized by Porter (1985). Values added by different marketing functions such as place, time, and possession values are becoming increasingly important in market-driven industries. We hope that younger scholars in the discipline will add considerable rigor to these functional school concepts with proper codification, modeling, and empirical testing.

Similarly, the classification of products and services into three or four classes based on customer or market characteristics à la the commodity school has promise of becoming more meaningful than the traditional standard industrial classification of industries based on product characteristics. Additionally, the concepts of "wheel of retailing" and "laws of retail gravitation" from the regional school are our own and should be nurtured

Table 6.1 Summary of Evaluations*

Metatheory Critiera

Schools of Thought	Structure	Specification	Testability	Empirical Support	Richness	Simplicity	Total
Commodity	3	4	3	6	8	8	32
Functional	5	3	7	7	8	8	38
Regional	7	6	7	7	4	7	38
Institutional	7	7	4	5	5	8	36
Functionalist	7	7	2	3	8	2	29
Managerial	8	7	8	9	9	9	50
Buyer behavior	8	8	6	8	9	8	47
Activist	5	5	4	7	5	6	32
Macromarketing	4	4	6	6	7	4	31
Organizational dynamics	8	8	4	3	5	4	32
Systems	5	8	6	5	8	8	40
Social exchange	8	4	5	5	9	9	40

* *Scores range from 1 (poor) to 10 (excellent).*

and developed rather than abandoned for borrowed concepts from economics, psychology, or sociology.

Finally, the managerial school has generated several unique concepts of which we can be proud. These include the concepts of product life cycle, marketing myopia, marketing mix, and the marketing concept itself. Perhaps the single most unique contribution is the development of the concept of market segmentation and its corollaries of product differentiation and market differentiation. Indeed, it is a pleasant surprise to learn that the "hot" new concepts of business strategy and policy such as differentiation and focus are really based on concepts developed in marketing.

We strongly urge younger marketing scholars to enhance the rich concepts of marketing by developing better syntax (structure and specification). We believe this is preferable to borrowing concepts from other disciplines that may have better syntax but may be low in relevance or pragmatism (richness and simplicity).

Respectability Through the Buyer Behavior School

Not surprisingly, the buyer behavior school ranks very high on most of the metatheoretical criteria. Indeed, many scholars suggest that the respectability of the marketing discipline was enhanced significantly with the emergence of the buyer behavior school. First, by focusing on the consumer rather than the producer, the buyer behavior school gained a measure of independence and legitimacy by not appearing to serve the direct interests of profit-oriented marketing institutions. Second, this school utilized a broader variety of research methods than any previous school of marketing. These research methods ranged from such highly quantitative techniques as stochastic processes, multivariate statistics, and laboratory and field experiments, to such highly qualitative techniques as focus groups and motivation research. Finally, by using rigorous methods and producing research that advanced the theoretical boundaries of borrowed concepts, marketing researchers gained respect from colleagues in allied social sciences and quantitative disciplines. Researchers in these allied disciplines now have increasingly begun to use consumers as test subjects in field experiments to evaluate their theories.

However, even though the buyer behavior school added immeasurably to marketing's stature in the academic community, this school has lost sight, to some extent, of its marketing roots. As a result, many marketing practitioners and even some marketing academicians have suggested that buyer behavior researchers are contributing very little to the improvement of marketing practice (Engel, Blackwell, and Kollat 1978, Sheth 1979b). In response to this criticism, some scholars in this field have begun recently to emphasize the relevance of their research to marketing practitioners and scholars in other subareas of marketing, particularly marketing strategy, pricing, and advertising.

Dominance of the Managerial School

The robustness of the managerial school, in terms of its ratings on the metatheoretical criteria, is perhaps somewhat surprising. Indeed, our relatively high ranking of the managerial school may help to revive scholarly interest in this school. In the past the managerial school has been generally perceived as a hodgepodge of applied principles that are relevant for training marketing practitioners, but of little value to rigorous marketing theorists.

In our opinion, several factors indicate that the managerial school deserves more serious theoretical attention. First, as mentioned before, the managerial school of marketing has generated several constructs that legitimately can be declared as our own. These include the marketing mix, market segmentation, and possibly the product life cycle and strategic market planning. Except for the earliest schools of marketing thought (commodity, functional, and institutional), the managerial school is the only school that is likely to demarcate the boundaries of marketing.

Second, the managerial school has clearly demonstrated that it can accommodate the knowledge base from a broad blend of competing schools of thought, from the traditional commodity, functional, and institutional schools to the contemporary buyer behavior and organizational dynamics schools. As such, the managerial school may serve as an excellent foundation for the creation of the elusive "general theory" of marketing, or at least for the creation of several good "middle range" theories of marketing.

Finally, the managerial school has shown that, like the buyer behavior school, it can use a variety of research methods and techniques, including econometrics, psychometrics, biometrics, and computer simulation. In addition, this school has employed both field and laboratory experiments.

In summary, even though the question of marketing's status as an art or a science is contentious, we believe that the buyer behavior and managerial schools have clearly moved the marketing discipline away from a standardized art and toward the establishment of a science of marketing. While the identification of a set of "marketing laws" would presently be premature, we believe in the near future some marketing concepts will be accorded the stature of laws. To facilitate and legitimize this process, perhaps the marketing discipline should convene a special convention to nominate certain marketing concepts for designation as marketing laws. In our judgement, these would include the 20:80 ratio (20 percent of customers buying 80 percent of volume), the product life cycle, the psychology of complication and simplification, market segmentation, and balance of power.

WHAT IS, OR SHOULD BE, THE PROPER DOMAIN OF MARKETING THEORY?

The twelve schools of marketing thought have differing perspectives on this issue. The earlier schools tended to treat the marketing domain very narrowly so that primary attention was focused on basic commodity products, especially agricultural commodities (wheat, cotton, milk, cattle, etc.), manufacturing materials (steel, wire, cloth, etc.), and consumer necessities (housing, food, clothing, etc.). From this narrow concentration on basic commodity products, commodity theorists studied the products themselves, functional theorists evaluated the functions needed to market these commodity products, and institutional theorists analyzed the types of agents required to move these commodities from the producers to the consumers.

In contrast, within the past two decades many marketing scholars have accepted that marketing is applicable to a much broader range of exchange relationships. Nonetheless, like the earlier schools, the more modern schools have still usually concentrated on only one aspect of this broader domain of marketing. For instance, buyer behavior theorists have focused on the consumers, managerial theorists have analyzed the sellers, and organizational dynamics theorists have studied the institutions. Thus, even though the domain of marketing has broadened to include a variety of exchange relationships (services, industrial, social, international, nonprofit, etc.), individual schools of marketing thought have continued to study only one particular agent of these exchange relationships. In our opinion, several basic tenets of marketing can be used to define the proper domain of marketing:

Market Behavior as the Domain of Marketing

Marketing is the study of market behavior, just as psychology is the study of individual human behavior and sociology is the study of group or social behavior. Market behavior includes the behavior of buyers, sellers, intermediaries, and regulators in exchange relationships. To that extent, marketing is broader than any one school of marketing thought. Just as psychology has numerous subdivisions (social psychology, group dynamics, child psychology, clinical psychology, community psychology, organizational psychology, etc.), marketing also has many subdivisions, including services marketing, industrial marketing, international marketing, direct marketing, nonprofit marketing, and so on. Similarly, as psychology has several explanations or perspectives of human behavior (learning, conditioning, motivation, perception, information processing, etc.), marketing also has several explanations or perspectives of market behavior (commodity, functional, institutional, managerial, buyer behavior, etc.).

The principal point is that marketing is delimited as the study of market behavior. Market behavior as the central focus of marketing is more explicit in the earlier schools of thought and more implicit in more recent schools of marketing thought. Whether explicit or implicit, we agree with McInnes (1964), who pointed out that:

> Markets result from the social intercourse of men when the makers and users of economic goods and services seek to satisfy their needs and wants through exchange. (p. 53)

McInnes went on to suggest that:

> In an exchange economy, the relationship of producer and consumer — i.e., the market — is a universal fact. The mere fact of relationship, however, is insufficient to generate an exchange. The existence of a market relation is the foundation for exchange not a substitute for it . . . Producers and consumers are related by a market, but no exchange occurs until some force or agent brings them into actual contact. This force, making a potential market contact into a real market contact, is what is generally known as marketing. (pp. 56-57)

We believe that a market exists where there is potential for exchange. From this perspective, it makes little difference whether the market is viewed as a geographic area, a group of institutions, a process, or a classification of activities. From this perspective, a market exists when there are buyers and sellers in any combination of numbers, with or without face-to-face contact.

Marketing thought has usually assumed many sellers and many buyers, or at least a number of buyers and sellers. This is the more prevalent representation of marketing in which sellers are competing against one another for customers and customers are choosing between sellers and evaluating the trade-offs between making versus buying. The fundamental principles of market behavior in this situation are *competition and selection*, with a strong emphasis on promotion and differentiation.

Yet a single buyer and a single seller can constitute a market. Vertically integrated industries such as oil, steel, and telecommunications are examples. Marketing consists of internal marketing with an emphasis on transfer pricing and functional delineation between the internal or captive seller and the internal or dedicated buyer. In stark contrast to the competitive orientation, *cooperation and coordination* are the fundamental tenets of market behavior in this type of market.

A third market situation is where there are many customers but only a single supplier. This is often common in a market monopoly or a regulated monopoly. The supplier is primarily concerned with the allocation of products and service resources among customers, while the customers are primarily concerned with their dependence on the single supplier. The fundamental principles of *allocation and dependence* are necessary to understand market behavior in this situation. Therefore concepts of public interest (dependence) and universal service (allocation) become more relevant than competition, differentiation, and promotion.

Finally, it is possible that there is only one buyer and many suppliers. This is clearly true in the defense industry or when the government is the only buyer in the marketplace. In this situation, the market behavior is likely to be based on *strategic alliances and politics*. Planned selling and networking are much more important than other marketing activities.

The four combinations discussed above are summarized in the following:

		Buyers	
		One	Many
Sellers	One	Cooperation and coordination (Vertically integrated industry)	Allocation and dependence (Regulated industry)
	Many	Strategic alliance and politics (Defence industry)	Competition and selection (Competitive industry)

Our colleagues will notice that we are suggesting a level of richness in thinking that is not evident in present schools of marketing thought. By defining the domain of marketing as the study of market behavior, we are able to transcend aforementioned specific actors, processes, and functions prevalent in separate schools of marketing thought. At the same time, the new definition clearly allows the existing schools to continue to research and theorize in their areas of interest.

Market Transaction as Unit of Analysis

The fundamental unit of analysis in marketing is, or should be, the market interaction between two or more parties. Not all interactions are market transactions. For an interaction to become a market transaction as opposed to a social, psychic, or charitable interaction, we must limit the domain of marketing to those interactions that have clearly identified the roles of the parties to the transaction as providers (sellers) and customers (buyers). In other words, it is the *role definition of the parties* to an interaction that makes it a market transaction and not the object or the process of transaction.

While the great majority of market transactions will be characterized as exchange of value between two or more parties, we must include nonexchange-based transactions in our understanding of markets. Nonexchange-based mechanisms for market transactions include mandatory rules and regulations; transfer of products or services without exchange, such as in gift giving and charitable contributing; and many derived transactions, such as value-added services, parts, repairs, and maintenance created as a consequence of primary market behaviors.

In our opinion, the marketing discipline has unnecessarily emphasized voluntary exchange as the only mechanism to create markets. Indeed, Sheth (1985c) has enumerated numerous case histories in which markets have been created for products and services by mandatory laws, for example, lead-free gasoline and smoke detectors.

Need for Time Dynamics in Marketing

It is interesting to note that except for a few introduced by the managerial and the buyer behavior schools of marketing thought, the majority of marketing concepts are not specifically dynamic over time. The concepts of product life cycle and brand loyalty are probably the only concepts that have explicitly included time as a dimension.

It is obvious that marketing is a dynamic process and must be treated as such. Therefore, it is essential that dynamics of time be inherent in any conceptualization of marketing. Perhaps the popularity of the product life cycle is due to its inherent time-sensitive and time-shifting characteristics. Consequently, it is very likely that the domain of marketing will be defined around, not only the market, but also the concept of *repeated market transactions* or what is more popularly called "relationship marketing." This should strongly suggest that the focus is not on a single market transaction or on selling, but on a continued relationship between the buyer and the seller.

Constraints in Market Behavior

Market behavior is constrained by a number of forces. For example, the customer has resource constraints such as time, money, and expertise in creating market opportunities. The supplier has similar resource constraints (technology, people, and money) in providing market opportunities. Finally, there are likely to be social and legal normative constraints imposed on market behavior. Just as Freud had to develop the concept of the superego as the regulating mechanism between the ego and the id, we must formally conceptualize the normative mechanisms that regulate the market behavior of buyers and sellers.

This is really not as new a concept at it might at first appea
3 we found that the managerial school recognized the prese..
ogenous variables. However, that school of thought often treated them ..
uncontrollable factors within which marketing functions and practices
were carried out. In Chapter 4, we noted that the macromarketing school
was concerned with societal needs and concerns and their impact on
marketing as a social institution. In addition, this concept is inherently
included in the study of economics on both the buyer side (utility theory)
and the supplier side (theory of the firm).

However, the role of these exogenous variables, to date, has largely
gone unexplored. Consequently, the richness and inherent usefulness of
present schools of marketing thought are often limited. There are few
mechanisms that currently allow us to assess developments regarding these
exogenous variables (resource constraints of buyers and sellers and normative constraints from social and legal institutions), let alone incorporate
them into marketing thought.

While the foregoing discussion of the basic tenets of marketing is not
necessarily exhaustive, it does point out the often narrow approaches to
marketing thought contained in the existing schools of marketing. It logically follows that we need to expand our understanding of marketing to
incorporate the basic tenets of marketing, that is, market behavior, market
transactions as the unit of analysis, marketing as a dynamic process of
relationships between buyers and sellers, and the exogenous variables that
influence market behavior.

WHAT IS, OR SHOULD BE, THE DOMINANT PERSPECTIVE IN MARKETING?

As we presented in the last four chapters, each school of thought has its own
perspective. The commodity school focuses on the product, the functional
school on the activities, the institutional school on the actors, and the
regional school on the market arena. Similarly, the managerial school
focuses on the seller, the buyer behavior school on the consumer, and the
activist and macromarketing schools on the public interest. While marketing thought has been richly enhanced by these various perspectives, we
believe that this diversity resembles the proverbial seven blind men and the
elephant. Each perspective seems to define and structure marketing in a
manner that, at best, represents only a partial picture. What is needed is a
perspective that reflects the raison d'être of marketing, a perspective that is
the common cause that no stakeholder (consumer, seller, government, or
social critic) can question. Indeed, that perspective should really reflect
what marketing is all about.

Values as Marketing Perspective

In our opinion, the main purpose of marketing is to create and distribute values among the market parties through the process of market transactions and market relationships. This concept of creating and distributing value inherently implies that marketing objects, functions, and institutions must create "win-win" market behavior. In game theory language, marketing should be a *positive sum game* rather than a zero sum (or a negative sum) game. Even though this is a simple concept and most scholars are likely to agree to its importance, it is often not manifested in marketing practice. Indeed, if we agree that the role of marketing is to create and distribute values through market transactions and relationships, this concept immediately calls into question earlier concepts of selling and negotiating (win-lose), as well as the self-interest concept as the driving forces of marketing. We believe that the concept of win-win between market parties will go a long way in minimizing the negative stereotypes of marketing created by the concepts of selling and promoting.

It is our belief that we need a theory of marketing that identifies what values are or can be created by marketing, who creates them, and how they are distributed so that all parties benefit from market behavior. We have borrowed some concepts from economics and the behavioral sciences to address these issues. For example, several older schools of marketing thought have suggested form, possession, time, and place values as the domain of marketing. McInnes (1964) adds perception or information as one more value. We can also expand on the possession value by redefining it as possession and consumption value in order to include several psychological theories including conspicuous consumption, epistemic (novelty-curiosity) value, and emotional values inherent in products and services.

Government Versus Self-Regulation Perspective

It is obvious that if both customers and suppliers (including intermediaries) truly behave from the win-win perspective of marketing, it is very likely that the external regulation of marketing may become less relevant. In other words, market behavior becomes more and more self-regulated and the role of public policy, including legislation, regulation, and advocacy, becomes less and less meaningful. However, this is more an idealistic view rather than a realistic view of marketing for a number of reasons. First, human nature is documented to be driven by self-interest. Therefore, the win-win concept often requires behavior contrary to human instincts. Although this can be overcome by education and information, it is not likely to be manifested universally. Second, in order to create a win-win situation in a market transaction, it is critical that all parties concerned know what they want and communicate it freely to one another. This is also not likely to happen without conscious learning and education. Finally, even if the two parties know what they want and communicate it to each other, it may not be technologically or economically possible to create a market transaction that results in a surplus of value that then can be distributed among the parties. In short, the realistic constraints are too many for this utopian perspective of marketing.

However, it does not mean that we cannot set creation and distribution of values as the normative goal of marketing and measure performance of actors, functions, and institutions against this normative standard. We urge that this concept become the "test" of future marketing thought just as the results of "pure" or "perfect" competition are the test of economic market behavior, even though such market structures are largely nonexistent.

WHAT IS, OR SHOULD BE, THE RELATIONSHIP BETWEEN MARKETING AND SOCIETY?

The relationship between marketing and society has been an issue since the early days of merchant trades. Indeed, it predates industrialization. However, different schools of marketing thought have put different levels of emphasis on this issue. For example, the commodity, the functional, the institutional, and the regional schools of thought are practically silent on this issue. On the other hand, the activist and the macromarketing schools have emerged in order to focus almost exclusively on the relationship between marketing and society. In the middle are the buyer behavior and the managerial schools of marketing thought.

The most common understanding of the relationship between society and business in general and marketing in particular is that it is an advocacy or an adversary relationship. In other words, society through legislation and regulation acts as a watchdog to ensure that the marketing process will serve the public interest. Similarly, the marketer, through political action committees as well as public opinion, wants to ensure that the government does not abuse its authority.

The advocacy position is based on the assumption that the objectives, processes, and tools of the business institution are radically different from those of the society. For example, the profit motive of the business is considered incompatible with the public interest motive of the society. The process of market transactions, with its focus on creating and distributing economic values between buyers and sellers, is considered incompatible with the broader issues of resource utilization and noneconomic motives as well as present versus future generation perspectives inherent in society. Finally, the marketer utilizes tools and techniques of influence, competitive behavior, and managerial control through such practices as the Four Ps of marketing, which are often regarded as antisocial. There is even a deep-rooted concern that business, if it succeeds in creating values, may align the consumer on its side and in the process jeopardize the relationship of government by the people, of the people, and for the people.

National Marketing Policy

What should then be the relationship between marketing and society? We believe that the concept of advocacy must be displaced with the concept of partnership behavior between marketing and society. If both institutions behave as partners, it is very likely that we can generate an overall *national marketing policy* comparable to a national industrial or economic policy. The concept of partnership between business and government is not new. It was successfully practiced by the British during the colonial days; it is still practiced widely among many European nations, notably France; and more recently, it has been raised to a level of science in Japan.

What are the advantages of a national marketing policy based on the concept of partnership behavior between government and business? First, it will improve efficiency of market behavior by minimizing the watchdog process inherent in the advocacy philosophy. In short, costs associated with creation and distribution of values will be significantly reduced, which in turn will enhance the raison d'être of marketing.

Second, it will standardize and streamline the regulatory process in marketing. The conflicting laws and "Catch 22" phenomena currently inherent among different regulatory agencies (state versus federal, antitrust versus FTC, industry specific versus general regulation, as well as self-regulation) often act as inhibitors to creating and distributing values. Hopefully, a national marketing policy will become a facilitating process rather than an inhibitory process in marketing.

Third, a national marketing policy is likely to provide better continuity over time because it reflects what business and society believe they must do. This continuity over time will go a long way toward encouraging relationship marketing instead of marketing as selling and promotion. This, in turn, will disassociate marketing from its negative stereotypes.

While the discussion of specific content and structure of a national marketing policy are beyond the scope of this book, we do believe it must focus on the following issues: First, the role of the government should be to *provide incentives to both customers and suppliers* that will enhance creation and distribution of values. Second, the government must safeguard interests of both the consumers and suppliers. We strongly believe that just as there are marketing malpractices, there are also consumer malpractices that must be openly addressed and managed. These include such deviant behaviors as shoplifting, credit card fraud, vandalism, and emotional or physical abuse of marketing employees. Finally, the national marketing policy must address the issues of international marketing similar to what

GATT (General Agreements on Trade and Tariffs) does for international trade.

We believe that pieces of national marketing policy are already in place. For example, there are laws and regulations with respect to product safety, product packaging, trade practices, advertising, and physical distribution of products and services. However, what we do not have is the partnership attitude as well as an integrated relationship between marketing and society.

IS IT REALLY POSSIBLE TO CREATE A GENERAL THEORY OF MARKETING?

It is obvious from the preceding four chapters that we do not have "a," let alone "the" general theory of marketing. Rather, we have a collection of theories, each looking at marketing from a unique perspective. Copeland's trichotomy of goods is still well accepted by the commodity school; the wheel of retailing is firmly established in the institutional school; the Four Ps of marketing seems unshakable in the managerial school; and such theories as perceived risk and the Howard-Sheth theory of buyer behavior are still considered useful and relevant in the buyer behavior school.

But adding to the confusion is the semi-slippery understanding of what a general or master theory of marketing is or might be. Merton (1957) makes a distinction between isolated empirical findings, middle-range theories, and full-blown or master theories.

> I attempt to focus attention on what might be called theories of the middle range: theories intermediate to the minor working hypotheses evolved in abundance during the day-by-day routines of research, and the all-inclusive speculations comprising a master conceptual scheme from which it is hoped to derive a very large number of empirically observed uniformities of social behavior (pp. 5-6).

In marketing, we are able to identify several attempts at devising a master conceptual scheme or master theory. We also observe a number of theories of the middle range. In fact, several schools of marketing thought may be more adequately described as theories of the middle range. But what we really have in marketing theory are literally hundreds of minor working hypotheses.

Some General Theories of Marketing

Although he fell short of a general or master theory of marketing, Wroe Alderson (Alderson and Cox 1948, Alderson 1957, 1965) clearly intended to develop such a theory. Alderson's general theory as restated by Hunt, Muncy, and Ray (1981) is interesting and comprehensive. However, it is seemingly focused on and designed for packaged goods. Also, it seems to have largely ignored the international dimension as well as not fully incorporating the influence of exogenous systems and variables such as technology, government, cultural traditions, and even marketing infrastructures.

In a somewhat less ambitious work than that of Alderson, McInnes (1964) provides a beautiful view of the role of marketing and how marketing can realize its potential in creating perception (information), ownership, time, place, and functional values. However, he is also largely silent on exogenous systems and their impact on marketing. Furthermore, the role of resellers and intermediaries is very lightly treated. Perhaps the biggest weakness of both Alderson's and McInnes' theories of marketing is that they are highly descriptive. They provide very little normative value in terms of control of market behavior.

More recently, John Howard's (1983) marketing theory of the firm shows good promise. It is perhaps the only theory that explicitly brings together the managerial and the buyer behavior schools of marketing thought. Furthermore, it is based on the concept of the product life cycle, and therefore it is time-sensitive and dynamic. Finally, it incorporates both the normative aspect as well as exogenous forces, and marketing within and outside of the organization of a firm.

Although Howard's theory has the potential to become a general theory of marketing, the potential has yet to be realized. First of all, it is based on secondary evidence. It needs to be tested as a general theory of marketing comparable to the testing of the Howard-Sheth theory of buyer behavior. Second, it is much more a theory of the firm rather than a true theory of marketing. It is more managerial in that sense. Finally, it needs considerable integration between the buyer side and the supplier side of the equation, especially with a focus on competitive behavior and competitive strategies.

Ingredients for a General Theory of Marketing

Do we believe that a general theory of marketing is possible? Our answer is a definite "yes," especially as measured by Hunt's criteria of a general theory: lawlike generalizations, unification of middle-range theories, and explanation of large numbers of working hypotheses. We believe that some of the ideas expressed in this chapter may become the building blocks for the development of a general theory of marketing. These include:

1. Marketing is a study of market behavior rather than marketer behavior or buyer behavior.
2. Market behavior is measured by a fundamental unit of analysis called the market transaction. It is a more specified type of interaction between

two or more parties in which they take the roles of customers and suppliers.

3.   We must focus on the dynamic nature of marketing. This can be achieved by understanding and explaining how *repeated* market transactions take place between two or more parties. The emphasis on repeated transactions will shift the focus of marketing away from marketing equals selling and toward the concept of relationship marketing.

4.   Marketing as a study of market behavior must include constraints on that behavior. These constraints can reside with the buyers, with the suppliers, or with such external institutions as the government and other societal stakeholders.

5.   The raison d'être of marketing is to create and distribute values. This can be achieved by ensuring that the process of marketing results in a positive sum or a win-win situation between two or more parties to a market transaction. Although it is difficult to enumerate the precise nature of values, it is safe to include function, perception, possession, time, and place values that bridge the gap between supplier resources and consumer needs.

6.   In order to ensure that the general theory of marketing gains the respect of the scientific community, it must be strong on the syntax, the semantics, and the pragmatics metatheory criteria. In other words, it must score high on structure and specification, on testability and empirical support, and finally on richness and simplicity.

The Role of the Managerial and Systems Approach in a General Theory of Marketing

Merton (1957, p. 9) argued that the major task of sociology was to develop theories of the middle range. One can only speculate what he would recommend to his colleagues in sociology thirty years later. Our guess is that he would still urge a focus on middle-range theories.

We do not share in the belief that marketing needs to focus primarily on theories of the middle range in the next few years. We have many concepts in marketing, some borrowed, some unique to marketing. We have different schools of thought that approach marketing from different perspectives and motives. Consequently, it seems appropriate to work toward integration and consolidation so that a general theory will have more solid blocks on which to build. The fact that we observe so little work on a general theory of marketing is less a criticism of marketing theorists than it is a criticism of the unsystematic and unintegrated body of knowledge that our metatheory evaluation revealed.

Will one approach to general theory development be more likely to emerge than others? To date, we have seen the systems approach of

Alderson (1957, 1965) and the more managerial approaches of McInnes (1964) and Howard (1983) as the most likely approaches. There is a logical reason why a general theory of marketing will most likely come out of these two approaches. These are the only approaches that take, or have the capacity to take, a truly comprehensive view of marketing that includes the environment, and all relevant actors, as well as nontraditional elements like global competitors. Also, both approaches are able to incorporate the critical ingredients summarized in the previous section.

It is our hope that we will eventually have several general theories of marketing. But that seems a long distance into the future. We must not lose sight, however, of the fact that there is real value in working *toward* general theories of marketing. It is only by exploring the assumptions and linkages necessary to build such theories that we truly move toward marketing as a science.

We hope our colleagues and future scholars of marketing will take up this challenge. We also hope that the voyage through the history of marketing thought presented in this book will whet their appetites for development of a general theory of marketing.

REFERENCES

AAKER, DAVID A. and DONALD E. BRUZZONE (1985), "Causes of Irritation in Advertising," *Journal of Marketing*, 49 (Spring), pp. 47-57.

ACHROL, RAVI SINGH, TORGER REVE, and LOUIS W. STERN (1983), "The Environment of Marketing Channels: A Framework for Comparative Analysis," *Journal of Marketing*, 47 (Fall), pp. 55-67.

ALBA, JOSEPH W. and J. WESLEY HUTCHINSON (1987), "Dimensions of Consumer Expertise," *Journal of Consumer Research*, 13 (March), pp. 411-454.

ALDERSON, WROE (1945), "Factors Governing the Development of Marketing Channels," in *Marketing Channels*, R. M. Clewett, ed., Homewood, Illinois: Richard D. Irwin, Inc.

ALDERSON, WROE (1948), "A Formula for Measuring Productivity in Distribution," *Journal of Marketing*, 12 (April), pp. 442-448.

ALDERSON, WROE (1949), "Scope and Place of Wholesaling in the United States," *Journal of Marketing*, 14 (September), pp. 144-155.

ALDERSON, WROE (1954a), "A Functionalist Approach to Competition," in *The Role and Nature of Competition in Our Marketing Economy*, Harvey W. Huegy, ed., Urbana: Bureau of Economic and Business Research, University of Illinois, pp. 40-49.

ALDERSON, WROE (1954b), "Factors Governing the Development of Marketing Channels," in *Marketing Channels for Manufactured Products*, Richard Clewett, ed., Homewood, Illinois: Richard D. Irwin, Inc., pp. 5-34.

ALDERSON, WROE (1956), "A Functionalist Approach to Consumer Motivation," in *Consumer Behavior and Motivation*, Robert H. Cole, ed., Urbana: Bureau of Economic and Business Research, University of Illinois, pp. 7-24.

ALDERSON, WROE (1957), *Marketing Behavior and Executive Action: A Functionalist Approach to Marketing Theory*, Homewood, Illinois: Richard D. Irwin, Inc.

ALDERSON, WROE (1958), "The Analytical Framework for Marketing," in *Conference of Marketing Teachers from Far Western States*, Proceedings, D. J. Duncan, ed., Berkeley: University of California Press.

ALDERSON, WROE (1965), *Dynamic Marketing Behavior: A Functionalist Theory of Marketing*, Homewood, Illinois: Richard D. Irwin, Inc.

ALDERSON, WROE and REAVIS COX (1948), "Towards a Theory of Marketing," *Journal of Marketing*, 13 (October), pp. 137-152.

ALDERSON, WROE and MILES W. MARTIN (1965), "Toward a Formal Theory of Transactions and Transvections," *Journal of Marketing Research*, 2 (May), pp. 117-127.

ALDRICH, HOWARD E., (1979), *Organizations and Environments*, Englewood Cliffs, New Jersey: Prentice-Hall, Inc.

ALLPORT, GORDON W. (1961), *Pattern and Growth in Personality*, New York: Holt, Rinehart and Winston, Inc.

AMSTUTZ, ARNOLD E. (1967), *Computer Simulation of Competitive Market Response*, Cambridge: Massachusetts Institute of Technology, The M.I.T. Press.

AMSTUTZ, ARNOLD E. (1968), "Systems Analysis for Marketing Management," in *Changing Marketing Systems . . . : Consumer, Corporate and Government Interfaces*, Reed Moyer, ed., Chicago: American Marketing Association, pp. 300-306.

ANAND, PUNAM (1987), "Inducing Franchisees to Relinquish Control: An Attribution Analysis," *Journal of Marketing Research*, 24 (May), pp. 215-221.

ANAND, PUNAM and LOUIS W. STERN (1985), "A Sociopsychological Explanation for Why Marketing Channel Members Relinquish Control," *Journal of Marketing Research*, 22 (November), pp. 365-376.

ANDERSON, ERIN, WUJIN CHU, and BARTON A. WEITZ (1987), "Industrial Purchasing: An Empirical Exploration of the Buyclass Framework," *Journal of Marketing*, 51 (July), pp. 71-86.

ANDERSON, ERIN, LEONARD M. LODISH, and BARTON A. WEITZ (1987), "Resource Allocation Behavior in Conventional Channels," *Journal of Marketing Research*, 24 (February), pp. 85-97.

ANDERSON, JAMES C. and JAMES A. NARUS (1984), "A Model of the Distributor's Perspective of Distributor-Manufacturer Working Relationships," *Journal of Marketing*, 48 (Fall), pp. 62-74.

ANDERSON, PAUL F., (1982), "Marketing, Strategic Planning, and the Theory of the Firm," *Journal of Marketing*, 46 (Spring), pp. 15-26.

ANDERSON, PAUL F., (1983), "Marketing, Scientific Progress, and Scientific Method," *Journal of Marketing*, 47 (Fall), pp. 18-31.

ANDERSON, PAUL F. (1986), "On Method in Consumer Research: A Critical Relativist Perspective," *Journal of Consumer Research*, 13 (September), pp. 155-173.

ANDERSON, PAUL F. and TERRY M. CHAMBERS (1985), "A Reward/Measurement Model of Organizational Buying Behavior," *Journal of Marketing*, 49 (Spring), pp. 7-23.

ANDREASEN, ALAN R. (1965), "Attitudes and Customer Behavior: A Decision Model," in *New Research in Marketing*, Lee E. Preston, ed., Berkeley: Institute of Business and Economic Research, University of California, pp. 1-16.

ANDREASEN, ALAN R. (1975), *The Disadvantaged Consumer*, New York: The Free Press.

ANDREASEN, ALAN R. (1977), "A Taxonomy of Consumer Satisfaction/ Dissatisfaction Measures," in *Conceptualization and Measurement of Consumer Satisfaction and Dissatisfaction*, H. Keith Hunt, ed., Cambridge, Massachusetts: Marketing Science Institute, pp. 11-35.

ANDREASEN, ALAN R. (1982), "Disadvantaged Hispanic Consumers: A Research Perspective and Agenda," *The Journal of Consumer Affairs*, 16 (Summer), pp. 46-61.

ARMSTRONG, GARY M., C. L. KENDALL, and FREDERICK A. RUSS (1975), "Applications of Consumer Information Processing Research to Public Policy Issues," *Communications Research*, 2, pp. 232-245.

ARMSTRONG, GARY M., METIN N. GUROL, and FREDERICK A. RUSS (1979), "Detecting and Correcting Deceptive Advertising," *Journal of Consumer Research*, 6 (December), pp. 237-246.

ARNDT, JOHAN (1967), *Word of Mouth Advertising: A Review of the Literature*, New York: Advertising Research Foundation, Inc.

ARNDT, JOHAN (1978), "How Broad Should the Marketing Concept Be?", *Journal of Marketing*, 42 (January), pp. 101-103.

ARNDT, JOHAN (1979), "Toward a Concept of Domesticated Markets," *Journal of Marketing*, 43 (Fall), pp. 69-75.

ARNDT, JOHAN (1985), "On Making Marketing Science More Scientific: Role of Orientations, Paradigms, Metaphors, and Puzzle Solving," *Journal of Marketing*, 49 (Summer), pp. 11-23.

ASHBY, HAROLD J., JR. (1973), "The Black Consumer," in *New Consumerism: Selected Readings*, William T. Kelley, ed., Columbus, Ohio: Grid, Inc., pp. 149-176.

ASPINWALL, L., (1958), "The Characteristics of Goods and Parallel Systems Theories," in *Managerial Marketing*, Eugene J. Kelley and William Lazer, eds., Homewood, Illinois: Richard D. Irwin, Inc., pp. 434-450.

BAGOZZI, RICHARD P. (1974), "Marketing as an Organized Behavioral System of Exchange," *Journal of Marketing*, 38 (October) 4, pp. 77-81.

BAGOZZI, RICHARD P. (1975), "Marketing as Exchange," *Journal of Marketing*, 39 (October) 4, pp. 32-39.

BAGOZZI, RICHARD P. (1977), "Marketing at the Societal Level: Theoretical Issues and Problems," in *Macro-Marketing: Distributive Processes from a Societal Perspective*, Charles C. Slater, ed., Boulder: Business Research Division, Graduate School of Business Administration, University of Colorado, pp. 6-51.

BAGOZZI, RICHARD P. (1978), "Marketing as Exchange: A Theory of Transactions in the Marketplace," *American Behavioral Scientist*, 21 (March/April) 4, pp. 535-556.

BAGOZZI, RICHARD P. (1979), "Toward a Formal Theory of Marketing Exchanges," in *Conceptual and Theoretical Developments in Marketing*, O. C. Ferrell, Stephen W. Brown, and Charles W. Lamb, Jr., eds., Chicago: American Marketing Association, pp. 431-447.

BAGOZZI, RICHARD P. (1984), "A Prospectus for Theory Construction in Marketing," *Journal of Marketing*, 48 (Winter), pp. 11-29.

BAGOZZI, RICHARD P. (1986), *Principles of Marketing Management*, Chicago: Science Research Associates.

BALDERSTON, F. (1964), "Design of Marketing Channels" in *Theory in Marketing*, Reavis Cox, Wroe Alderson, and Stanley J. Shapiro, eds., Homewood, Illinois: Richard D. Irwin, Inc., pp. 163-175.

BALIGH, HELMY H. and LEON E. RICHARTZ (1967), *Verticle Market Structures*, Boston: Allyn and Bacon, Inc.

BANKS, SEYMOUR (1968), "A Non-Systematic Look at Systems: A Triumph of Optimism over Experience," in Robert L. King, ed., *Marketing and the New Science of Planning*, Chicago: American Marketing Association, pp. 24-28.

BARKSDALE, H. C. (1980), "Wroe Alderson's Contributions to Marketing Theory," *Theoretical Developments in Marketing*, Charles W. Lamb, Jr., and Patrick M. Dunne, eds., Chicago: American Marketing Association, pp. 1-4.

BARTELS, ROBERT (1951), "Can Marketing Be a Science?", *Journal of Marketing*, 15 (January), pp. 319-328.

BARTELS, ROBERT (1962), *The Development of Marketing Thought*, Homewood, Illinois: Richard D. Irwin, Inc.

BARTELS, ROBERT (1965), "Development of Marketing Thought: A Brief History," in *Science in Marketing*, George Schwartz, ed., New York: John Wiley & Sons, Inc., pp. 47-69.

BARTELS, ROBERT (1968a), "Are Domestic and International Marketing Dissimilar?", *Journal of Marketing*, 32 (July), pp. 56-61.

BARTELS, ROBERT (1968b), "The General Theory of Marketing," *Journal of Marketing*, 32 (January), pp. 29-33.

BARTELS, ROBERT (1970), *Marketing Theory and Metatheory*, Homewood, Illinois: Richard D. Irwin, Inc.

BARTELS, ROBERT (1974), "The Identity Crisis in Marketing," *Journal of Marketing*, 38 (October), pp. 73-76.

BASS, FRANK M. (1969), "A New Product Growth Model for Consumer Durables," *Management Science*, 15 (January), pp. 215-227.

BASS, FRANK M., ROBERT D. BUZZELL, MARK R. GREENE, WILLIAM LAZER, EDGAR A. PESSEMIER, DONALD L. SHAWVER, ABRAHAM SHUCHMAN, CHRIS A. THEODORE, GEORGE W. WILSON, EDS. (1961), *Mathematical Models and Methods in Marketing*, Homewood, Illinois: Richard D. Irwin, Inc.

BAUER, RAYMOND A. (1960), "Consumer Behavior as Risk Taking," in *Dynamic Marketing for a Changing World*, Robert S. Hancock, ed., Chicago: American Marketing Association, pp. 389-398.

BAUER, RAYMOND A. and STEPHEN A. GREYSER (1967), "The Dialogue That Never Happens," *Harvard Business Review*, 45 (November-December), pp. 2-12, 186-190.

BAUER, RAYMOND A. and SCOTT M. CUNNINGHAM (1970), *Studies in the Negro Market*, Cambridge, Massachusetts: Marketing Science Institute.

BEEM, EUGENE R. (1973), "The Beginnings of the Consumer Movement," in *New Consumerism: Selected Readings*, William T. Kelley, ed., Columbus, Ohio: Grid, Inc., pp. 13-25.

BEIER, FREDERICK J. and LOUIS W. STERN (1969), "Power in the Channel of Distribution," in *Distribution Channels: Behavioral Dimensions*, Louis W. Stern, ed., Boston: Houghton Mifflin Company, pp. 92-116.

BELK, RUSSELL W. (1974), "An Exploratory Assessment of Situational Effects in Buyer Behavior," *Journal of Marketing*, 38, pp. 156-163.

BELL, MARTIN L. (1966), *Marketing: Concepts and Strategy*, Boston: Houghton Mifflin Company.

BENNETT, PETER D. (1965), *Marketing and Economic Development*, Chicago: American Marketing Association.

BERTALANFFY, LUDVIG VON (1968), *General System Theory*, New York: George Braziller, Inc.

BETTMAN, JAMES R. (1979), *An Information Processing Theory of Consumer Choice*, Reading, Massachusetts: Addison-Wesley Publishing Company, Inc.

BIEHAL, GABRIEL and DIPANKAR CHAKRAVARTI (1986), "Consumers' Use of Memory and External Information in Choice: Macro and Micro Perspectives," *Journal of Consumer Research*, 12 (March), pp. 382-405.

BLACK, WILLIAM C., LYMAN E. OSTLUND, and ROBERT A. WESTBROOK (1985), "Spatial Demand Models in an Intrabrand Context," *Journal of Marketing*, 49 (Summer), pp. 106-113.

BLAIR, EDWARD and KENNETH P. UHL (1977), "Wroe Alderson and Modern Marketing Theory," in *Macro-Marketing: Distributive Processes From a Societal Perspective*, Charles C. Slater, ed., Boulder: Business Research Division, Graduate School of Business Administration, University of Colorado.

BLATTBERG, ROBERT C. and SUBRATA K. SEN (1976), "Market Segments and Stochastic Brand Choice Models," *Journal of Marketing Research*, 13 (February), pp. 34-45.

BLOCH, PETER H., DANIEL L. SHERRELL, and NANCY M. RIDGWAY (1986), "Consumer Search: An Extended Framework," *Journal of Consumer Research*, 13 (June), pp. 119-126.

BLOZAN, WILLIAM and PAUL PRABHAKER (1984), "Notes on Aggregation Criteria in Market Segmentation," *Journal of Marketing Research*, 21 (August), pp. 332-335.

BONOMA, THOMAS V. and GERALD ZALTMAN, EDS. (1978), *Organizational Buying Behavior*, Chicago: American Marketing Association.

BONOMA, THOMAS V., RICHARD BAGOZZI, and GERALD ZALTMAN (1978), "The Dyadic Paradigm with Specific Application Toward Industrial Marketing," in *Organizational Buying Behavior*, Thomas V. Bonoma and Gerald Zaltman, eds, Chicago: American Marketing Association, pp. 49-66.

BORDEN, NEIL H. (1964), "The Concept of the Marketing Mix," *Journal of Advertising Research*, 4 (June), pp. 2-7.

BOULDING, KENNETH (1956), "General Systems Theory — The Skeleton of Science," *Management Science*, 2 (April), pp. 197-208.

BOURNE, FRANCIS S. (1957), "Group Influence in Marketing and Public Relations," in *Some Applications of Behavioral Research*, Rensis Likert and Samuel P. Hayes, Jr., eds., Paris: United Nations Educational, Scientific and Cultural Organization, pp. 207-257.

BOURNE, FRANCIS S. (1965), "Group Influence in Marketing and Public Relations," in *Dimensions of Consumer Behavior*, J. V. McNeal, ed., New York: Appleton-Century-Crofts, pp. 137-146.

BREYER, RALPH F. (1934), *The Marketing Institution*, New York: McGraw-Hill Book Co.

BRIEN, RICHARD H. (1968), "Marketing Information Systems in Practice: The User's View," in *Marketing and the New Science of Planning*, Robert L. King, ed., Chicago: American Marketing Association, pp. 172-175.

BRIEN, RICHARD H. and JAMES E. STAFFORD (1968), "Marketing Information Systems: A New Dimension for Marketing Research," *Journal of Marketing*, 32 (July), pp. 19-23.

BRITT, STEWART HENDERSON (1974), "Standardizing Marketing for the International Market," *Columbia Journal of World Business*, (Winter), pp. 39-45.

BROWN, GEORGE H. (1952-1953), "Brand Loyalty — Fact or Fiction?" *Advertising Age*, 23 (June 9), pp. 53-55; (June 30), pp. 45-47; (July 14), pp. 54-56; (July 28), pp. 46-48; (August 11), pp. 56-58; (September 1), pp. 44-48; (September 22), pp.80-82; (October 6), pp. 82-86; (December 1), pp. 76-79; 24 (January 26), pp. 75-76.

BROWN, JAMES R. and RALPH L. DAY (1981), "Measures of Manifest Conflict in Distribution Channels," *Journal of Marketing Research*, 18 (August) 3, pp. 263-274.

BROWN, STEPHEN W. and RAYMOND FISK (1984), *Marketing Theory: Distinguished Contributions*, New York: John Wiley & Sons, Inc.

BUCKLIN, LOUIS P. (1962), "Retail Strategy and the Classification of Consumer Goods," *Journal of Marketing*, 27 (October), pp. 50-55.

BUCKLIN, LOUIS P. (1965), "Postponement, Speculation and the Structure of Distribution Channels," *Journal of Marketing Research*, 2 (February), pp. 26-31.

BUCKLIN, LOUIS P. (1966), *A Theory of Distribution Channel Structure*, Berkeley: Institute of Business and Economic Research, University of California.

BUCKLIN, LOUIS P. and JAMES M. CARMAN (1974), "Vertical Market Structure Theory and the Health Care Delivery System," in *Marketing Analysis for Societal Problems*, Jagdish N. Sheth and Peter L. Wright, eds., Urbana-Champaign: Bureau of Economic and Business Research, College of Commerce and Business Administration, University of Illinois, pp. 7-41.

BULLOCK, HENRY A. (1961), "Consumer Motivations in Black and White," *Harvard Business Review*, 39 (May-June), pp. 89-104; (July-August), pp.110-124.

BUTLER, RALPH STARR (1923), *Marketing and Merchandising*, New York: Alexander Hamilton Institute.

BUZZELL, ROBERT D. (1963), "Is Marketing a Science," *Harvard Business Review*, 41 (January/February), pp. 32-40, 166-170.

BUZZELL, ROBERT D. (1968), "Can You Standardize Multinational Marketing?", *Harvard Business Review*, 46 (November/December), pp. 102-113.

CADOTTE, ERNEST R. and LOUIS W. STERN (1979), "A Process Model of Interorganization Relations in Marketing Channels," in *Research in Marketing*, Jagdish N. Sheth, ed., Volume 2, Greenwich, Connecticut: JAI Press, Inc., pp. 127-158.

CADOTTE, ERNEST R., ROBERT B. WOODRUFF, and ROGER L. JENKINS (1987), "Expectations and Norms in Models of Consumer Satisfaction," *Journal of Marketing Research*, 24 (August), pp. 305-314.

CADY, JOHN (1982), "Reasonable Rules and Rules of Reason: Vertical Restrictions on Distributors," *Journal of Marketing*, 46 (Summer), pp. 27-37.

CAPLOVITZ, DAVID (1963), *The Poor Pay More: Consumer Practices of Low-Income Families*, New York: The Free Press of Glencoe.

CARMAN, JAMES (1973), "On the Universality of Marketing," *Journal of Contemporary Business*, 2 (Autumn), pp. 1-16.

CARSON, RACHEL L. (1962), *Silent Spring,* Boston: Houghton Mifflin Company.

CASH, HAROLD C. and W. J. E. CRISSY (1958), *A Point of View for Salesmen, The Psychology of Selling,* Volume 1, New York: Personnel Development Associates.

CHASE, STUART and F. J. SCHLINK (1927), *Your Money's Worth: A Study in the Waste of the Consumer's Dollar,* New York: The Macmillan Company.

CHILDERS, TERRY L. and ROBERT W. RUEKERT (1982), "The Meaning and Determinants of Cooperation Within an Interorganizational Marketing Network," in *Marketing Theory: Philosophy of Science Perspectives,* Ronald F. Bush and Shelby D. Hunt, eds., Chicago: American Marketing Association, pp. 116-119.

CLARK, FRED E. (1922), *Principles of Marketing,* New York: The Macmillan Company.

CLARK, LINCOLN H., ED. (1954), *Consumer Behavior (Volume 1): The Dynamics of Consumer Reaction,* New York: New York University Press.

CLARK, LINCOLN H., ED. (1955), *Consumer Behavior (Volume 2): The Life Cycle and Consumer Behavior,* New York: New York University Press.

CLARK, LINCOLN H., ED. (1958), *Consumer Behavior (Volume 3): Research on Consumer Reactions,* New York: Harper and Brothers, Publishers.

CONVERSE, PAUL D. (1943), *A Study of Retail Trade Areas in East Central Illinois,* Urbana: University of Illinois Press.

CONVERSE, PAUL D. (1949), "New Laws of Retail Gravitation," *Journal of Marketing,* 14 (October), pp. 379-84.

CONVERSE, PAUL D. (1959), *The Beginning of Marketing Thought in the United States,* University of Texas: Bureau of Business Research.

CONVERSE, PAUL D. and HARVEY HUEGY (1940), *The Elements of Marketing,* New York: Prentice-Hall, Inc.

COOPER, LEE G. (1987), "Do We Need Critical Relativism?" *Journal of Consumer Research,* 14 (June), pp. 126-127.

COPELAND, MELVIN T. (1923), "The Relation of Consumers' Buying Habits to Marketing Methods," *Harvard Business Review,* 1 (April), pp. 282-289.

COPELAND, MELVIN T. (1925), *Principles of Merchandising,* Chicago: A. W. Shaw Co.

COX, DONALD F., ED. (1967), *Risk Taking and Information Handling in Consumer Behavior,* Boston: Division of Research, Graduate School of Business Administration, Harvard University.

COX, REAVIS, CHARLES S. GOODMAN, and THOMAS C. FICHANDLER (1965), *Distribution in a High-Level Economy,* Englewood Cliffs, New Jersey: Prentice-Hall, Inc.

CRON, WILLIAM L. and JOHN W. SLOCUM, Jr. (1986), "The Influence of Career Stages on Salespeople's Job Attitudes, Work Perceptions, and Job Performance," *Journal of Marketing Research,* 23 (May), pp. 119-129.

CROSBY, LAWRENCE A. and JAMES R. TAYLOR (1982), "Consumer Satisfaction With Michigan's Container Deposit Law - An Ecological Perspective," *Journal of Marketing,* 46 (Winter), pp. 47-60.

CUNNINGHAM, ROSS M. (1956), "Brand Loyalty — What, Where, How Much?" *Harvard Business Review,* 34 (January/February), pp. 116-128.

CYERT, RICHARD M. and JAMES G. MARCH (1963), *A Behavioral Theory of the Firm,* Englewood Cliffs, New Jersey: Prentice-Hall, Inc.

CZEPIEL, JOHN A., LARRY J. ROSENBERG, and CAROL SUPRENANT (1980), "The Development of Thought, Theory and Research in Consumer Satisfaction," in *Theoretical Developments in Marketing*, CHARLES W. LAMB, JR., and PATRICK M. DUNNE, EDS., Chicago: American Marketing Association, pp. 216-219.

DAVIDSON, WILLIAM R. (1961), "Channels of Distribution - One Aspect of Marketing Strategy," *Business Horizons* (February), pp. 84-90.

DAVIS, HARRY L. and BENNY P. RIGAUX (1974), "Perception of Marital Roles in Decision Processes," *Journal of Consumer Research*, 1 (June), pp. 51-62.

DAWSON, LESLIE (1979), "Resolving the Crisis in Marketing Thought," *Management International Review*, 19 (3), pp.74-84.

DAY, GEORGE S. (1981), "The Product Life Cycle: Analysis and Applications Issues," *Journal of Marketing*, 45 (Fall), pp. 60-67.

DAY, GEORGE S. (1984), *Strategic Market Planning: The Pursuit of Competitive Advantage*, St. Paul, Minnesota: West Publishing Company.

DAY, GEORGE S. and DAVID A. AAKER (1970), "A Guide to Consumerism," *Journal of Marketing*, 34 (July), pp. 12-19.

DAY, GEORGE S. and ROBIN WENSLEY (1983), "Marketing Theory with a Strategic Orientation," *Journal of Marketing*, 47 (Fall), pp. 79-89.

DAY, RALPH L., ED. (1977), *Consumer Satisfaction, Dissatisfaction and Complaining Behavior*, Bloomington/Indianapolis: Department of Marketing, School of Business, Indiana University.

DAY, RALPH L. and H. KEITH HUNT, EDS. (1983), *International Fare in Consumer Satisfaction and Complaining Behavior*, Bloomington: School of Business, Indiana University.

DAY, RALPH L. and E. LAIRD LANDON, JR. (1977), "Toward a Theory of Consumer Complaining Behavior," in *Consumer and Industrial Buying Behavior*, Arch G. Woodside, Jagdish N. Sheth, and Peter D. Bennett, eds., New York: Elsevier North-Holland, Inc., pp. 425-437.

DEAN, JOEL (1950), "Pricing Policies for New Products," *Harvard Business Review*, 28 (November), pp. 45-53.

DEAN, JOEL (1951), *Managerial Economics*, Englewood Cliffs, New Jersey: Prentice-Hall, Inc.

DHOLAKIA, NIKHILESH, A. FUAT FIRAT, and RICHARD P. BAGOZZI (1980), "The De-Americanization of Marketing Thought," in *Theoretical Developments in Marketing*, Charles W. Lamb, Jr. and Patrick M. Dunne, eds., Chicago: American Marketing Association, pp. 25-29.

DICHTER, ERNEST (1947), "Psychology in Market Research," *Harvard Business Review*, 25 (Summer), 432-443.

DICHTER, ERNEST (1962), "The World Consumer," *Harvard Business Review*, 40 (July-August), 113-122.

DICHTER, ERNEST (1964), *Handbook of Consumer Motivation: The Psychology of the World of Objects*, New York: McGraw-Hill Book Company, Inc.

DICKSON, PETER R. and JAMES L. GINTER (1987), "Market Segmentation, Product Differentiation, and Marketing Strategy," *Journal of Marketing*, 51 (April), pp. 1-10.

DOWLING, GRAHAME R. (1983), "The Application of General Systems Theory to an Analysis of Marketing Systems," *Journal of Macromarketing*, 3 (Fall), pp. 22-32.

DOYLE, PETER and JOHN SAUNDERS (1985), "Market Segmentation and Positioning in Specialized Industrial Markets," *Journal of Marketing*, 49 (Spring), pp. 24-32.

DRUCKER, PETER (1969), "The Shame of Marketing," *Marketing/Communications*, 297 (August), pp. 60-64.

DUBINSKY, ALAN J., ROY D. HOWELL, THOMAS N. INGRAM, and DANNY N. BELLENGER (1986), "Salesforce Socialization," *Journal of Marketing*, 50 (October), pp. 192-207.

DUDDY, EDWARD A. and DAVID A. REVZAN (1947), *Marketing: An Institutional Approach*, New York: McGraw-Hill Book Company, Inc.

DUNCAN, C. S. (1921), *Marketing: Its Problems and Methods*, New York: D. Appleton and Co.

DUNN, S. WATSON (1981), "Regulation in Advertising" in *Research in Marketing*, Jagdish N. Sheth, ed., Volume 4, Greenwich, Connecticut: JAI Press, Inc., pp. 117-141.

DWYER, F. ROBERT and ORVILLE C. WALKER, JR. (1981), "Bargaining in an Asymmetrical Power Structure," *Journal of Marketing*, 45 (Winter), pp. 104-115.

DWYER, F. ROBERT and M. ANN WELSH (1985), "Environmental Relationships of the Internal Political Economy of Marketing Channels," *Journal of Marketing Research*, 22 (November), pp. 397-414.

DWYER, F. ROBERT, PAUL H. SCHURR, and SEJO OH (1987), "Developing Buyer-Seller Relationships," *Journal of Marketing*, 51 (April), pp. 11-27.

EDWARDS, WARD (1961), "Behavioral Decision Theory," *Annual Review of Psychology*, 12, pp. 473-498.

EL-ANSARY, ADEL I. (1979), "The General Theory of Marketing Revisited," in *Conceptual and Theoretical Developments in Marketing*, O. C. Ferrell, Stephen W. Brown, and Charles W. Lamb, Jr., Chicago: American Marketing Association, pp. 399-407.

ELIASHBERG, JEHOSHUA, STEPHEN A. LATOUR, ARVIND RANGASWAMY, and LOUIS W. STERN (1986), "Assessing the Predictive Accuracy of Two Utility-Based Theories in a Marketing Channel Negotiation Context," *Journal of Marketing Research*, 23 (May), pp. 101-110.

EMERSON, RICHARD M. (1962), "Power-Dependence Relations," *American Sociological Review*, 27 (February), pp. 31-41.

EMERY, F. E. and E. L. TRIST (1965), "The Causal Texture of Organizational Environments," *Human Relations*, 18 (February), pp. 21-32.

ENGEL, JAMES F., ROGER D. BLACKWELL, and DAVID T. KOLLAT (1978), "The Current Status of Consumer Behavior Research: Problems and Prospects (Chapter 21)," in *Consumer Behavior*, 3rd Edition, Hinsdale, Illinois: The Dryden Press, pp. 564-584.

ENGEL, JAMES F., ROGER D. BLACKWELL, and PAUL W. MINIARD (1986), *Consumer Behavior*, 5th Edition, Chicago: The Dryden Press.

ENGEL, JAMES F., DAVID T. KOLLAT, and ROGER D. BLACKWELL (1968), *Consumer Behavior*, New York: Holt, Rinehart and Winston, Inc.

ENIS, BEN M. (1974), *Marketing Principles: The Management Process*, Pacific Palisades, California: Goodyear Publishing Company, Inc.

ENIS, BEN M. (1979), "Countering the Goods/Services Taxonomy: An Alternative Taxonomy for Stategy Formulation," *Proceedings of the Sixth International Research Seminar in Marketing*, Gordes, France.

ENIS, BEN M. and KENNETH J. ROERING (1980), "Product Classification Taxonomies: Synthesis and Consumer Implications," in *Theoretical Developments in Marketing*, Chicago: American Marketing Association, pp. 186-189.

ENIS, BEN M. and KENNETH J. ROERING (1981), "The Marketing of Services: Different Product Properties, Similar Marketing Strategies," *Proceedings, Services Conference*, Chicago: American Marketing Association.

ENIS, BEN M. and E. THOMAS SULLIVAN (1985), "The AT&T Settlement: Legal Summary, Economic Analysis, and Marketing Implications," *Journal of Marketing*, 49 (Winter), pp. 127-136.

ERICKSON, GARY M. (1985), "A Model of Advertising Competition," *Journal of Marketing Research*, 22 (August), pp. 297-304.

ETGAR, MICHAEL (1978), "Intrachannel Conflict and Use of Power," *Journal of Marketing Research*, 15 (May), pp. 273-274.

EVANS, KENNETH R. and RICHARD F. BELTRAMINI (1987), "A Theoretical Model of Consumer Negotiated Pricing: An Orientation Perspective," *Journal of Marketing*, 51 (April), pp. 58-73.

EXECUTIVE OFFICE OF THE PRESIDENT (1963), *Consumer Advisory Council, First Report*, Washington, D.C.: United States Government Printing Office (October).

FARLEY, JOHN U. (1967), "Estimating Structural Parameters of Marketing Systems: Theory and Application," in *Changing Marketing Systems . . . : Consumer Corporate and Government Interfaces*, Reed Moyer, ed., Chicago: American Marketing Association, pp. 316-321.

FARLEY, JOHN U., JOHN A. HOWARD, and L. WINSTON RING (1974), *Consumer Behavior: Theory and Applications*, Boston, Massachusetts: Allyn and Bacon, Inc.

FATT, ARTHUR C. (1967), "The Danger of 'Local' International Advertising," *Journal of Marketing*, (January), pp. 60-62.

FERBER, ROBERT, ED. (1974), *Handbook of Marketing Research*, New York: McGraw-Hill Book Company.

FERN, EDWARD F. and JAMES R. BROWN (1984), "The Industrial/Consumer Marketing Dichotomy: A Case of Insufficient Justification," *Journal of Marketing*, 48 (Spring), pp. 68-77.

FERRELL, O. C. and LARRY G. GRESHAM (1985), "A Contingency Framework for Understanding Ethical Decision Making in Marketing," *Journal of Marketing*, 49 (Summer), pp. 87-96.

FERRELL, O. C. and J. R. PERRACHIONE (1980), "An Inquiry into Bagozzi's Formal Theory of Marketing Exchanges," in *Theoretical Developments in Marketing*, Charles W. Lamb, Jr., and Patrick M. Dunne, eds., Chicago: American Marketing Association, pp. 158-161.

FESTINGER, LEON (1957), *A Theory of Cognitive Dissonance*, New York: Row, Peterson and Company.

FISHBEIN, MARTIN (1963), "An Investigation of the Relationships Between Beliefs About an Object and the Attitude Toward That Object," *Human Relations*, 16 (August), pp. 233-239.

FISHBEIN, MARTIN, ED. (1967), *Readings in Attitude Theory and Measurement*, New York: John Wiley & Sons, Inc.

FISHBEIN, MARTIN and ICEK AJZEN (1975), *Belief, Attitude, Intention, and Behavior: An Introduction to Theory and Research*, Reading, Massachusetts: Addison-Wesley Publishing Company.

FISK, GEORGE (1967), *Marketing Systems: An Introductory Analysis*, New York: Harper and Row.

FISK, GEORGE, ED. (1974) *Marketing and Social Priorities*, Chicago: American Marketing Association.

FISK, GEORGE (1981), "An Invitation to Participate in Affairs of the Journal of Macromarketing," *Journal of Macromarketing*, 1 (Spring), pp. 3-6.

FISK, GEORGE, JOHAN ARNDT, and KJELL GRONHAUG, EDS. (1978), *Future Directions for Marketing*, Cambridge, Massachusetts: Marketing Science Institute.

FISK, GEORGE and ROBERT W. NASON, EDS. (1979), *Macro-Marketing: New Steps on the Learning Curve*, Boulder: Business Research Division, Graduate School of Business Administration, University of Colorado.

FISK, GEORGE, ROBERT W. NASON, and PHILLIP D. WHITE, EDS. (1980), *Macromarketing: Evolution of Thought*, Boulder: University of Colorado, Business Research Division.

FOOTE, NELSON N., ED. (1961), *Consumer Behavior (Volume 4): Household Decision-Making*, New York: New York University Press.

FORD, GARY T. and JOHN E. CALFEE (1986), "Recent Developments in FTC Policy on Deception," *Journal of Marketing*, 50 (July), pp. 82-103.

FORRESTER, JAY W. (1958), "Industrial Dynamics: A Major Breakthrough for Decision Makers," *Harvard Business Review*, 36 (July-August), pp. 37-66.

FORRESTER, JAY W. (1959), "Advertising: A Problem in Industrial Dynamics," *Harvard Business Review*, 59 (March/April), pp. 100-110.

FRANK, RONALD E. (1962), "Brand Choice as a Probability Process," *Journal of Business*, 35 (January), pp. 43-56.

FRANK, RONALD E. (1974), "The *Journal of Consumer Research*: An Introduction," *Journal of Consumer Research*, 1 (June), iv-v.

FRAZIER, GARY L. (1983a), "Interorganizational Exchange Behavior in Marketing Channels: A Broadened Perspective," *Journal of Marketing*, 47 (Fall), pp. 68-78.

FRAZIER, GARY L. (1983b), "On the Measurement of Interim Power in Channels of Distribution," *Journal of Marketing Research*, 20 (May), pp. 158-166.

FRAZIER, GARY L. and JAGDISH N. SHETH (1985), "An Attitude-Behavior Framework for Distribution Channel Management," *Journal of Marketing*, 49 (Summer), pp. 38-48.

FRAZIER, GARY L. and JOHN O. SUMMERS (1984), "Interfirm Influence Strategies and Their Application Within Distribution Channels," *Journal of Marketing*, 48 (Summer), pp. 43-55.

FRAZIER, GARY L. and JOHN O. SUMMERS (1986), "Perceptions of Interfirm Power and Its Use Within a Franchise Channel of Distribution," *Journal of Marketing Research*, 23 (May), pp. 169-176.

FRENCH, JOHN R. P., JR. and BERTRAM RAVEN (1959), "The Bases of Social Power," in *Studies in Social Power*, Dorwin Cartwright, ed., Ann Arbor: Research Center for Group Dynamics, Institute for Social Research, University of Michigan, pp. 150-167.

FRENCH, WARREN A., HIRAM C. BARKSDALE, WILLIAM D. PERRAULT, JR., JOHAN ARNDT, and JEHIEL ZIF (1983), "The Problems of Older Consumers: A Comparison of England, Israel, Norway and the United States," in *1983 AMA Educators' Proceedings,* Chicago: American Marketing Association, pp. 390-395.

FREUD, SIGMUND (1953), *The Standard Edition of the Complete Psychological Works of Sigmund Freud,* J. Strachey, ed. (24 Volumes), London: Hogarth Press.

FTC STAFF REPORT ON TELEVISION ADVERTISING TO CHILDREN (1978), Washington, D.C.: Federal Trade Commission.

FULLBROOK, EARL S. (1940), "The Functional Concept in Marketing," *Journal of Marketing,* 4 (January), pp. 229-237.

GALBRAITH, JOHN KENNETH (1958), *The Affluent Society,* Boston: Houghton Mifflin Company.

GARDNER, DAVID M., ED. (1971), *Proceedings 2nd Annual Conference of the Association for Consumer Research,* College Park, Maryland: Association for Consumer Research, p. i.

GARDNER, DAVID M. (1973), "Dynamic Homeostasis: Behavioral Research and the FTC," in *Advances in Consumer Research,* Scott Ward and Peter L. Wright, eds., Urbana, Illinois: Association for Consumer Research, 1, pp. 108-113.

GARDNER, DAVID M. (1976), "Deception in Advertising: A Receiver Oriented Approach to Understanding," *Journal of Advertising,* 5 (Fall), pp. 5-11, 19.

GARDNER, DAVID M. (1987), "The Product Life Cycle: A Critical Look at the Literature," in *Review of Marketing,* Michael J. Houston, ed., Chicago: American Marketing Association.

GARDNER, DAVID M. and RUSSELL W. BELK, EDS. (1980), *A Basic Bibliography on Experimental Design in Marketing,* Chicago: American Marketing Association.

GARDNER, EDWARD H. (1945), "Consumer Goods Classification," *Journal of Marketing,* 9 (January), pp. 275-276.

GARDNER, MERYL PAULA (1985), "Mood States and Consumer Behavior: A Critical Review," *Journal of Consumer Research,* 12 (December), pp. 281-300.

GARRETT, DENNIS E. (1986), "Consumer Boycotts: Are Targets Always the Bad Guys?" *Business and Society Review,* No. 58 (Summer), pp. 17-21.

GARRETT, DENNIS E. (1987), "The Effectiveness of Marketing Policy Boycotts: Environmental Opposition to Marketing," *Journal of Marketing,* 51 (April), pp. 46-57.

GASKI, JOHN F. (1984), "The Theory of Power and Conflict in Channels of Distribution," *Journal of Marketing,* 48 (Summer), pp. 9-29.

GASKI, JOHN F. (1986), "Interrelations Among A Channel Entity's Power Sources: Impact of the Exercise of Reward and Coercion on Expert, Referent, and Legitimate Power Sources," *Journal of Marketing Research,* 23 (February), pp. 62-77.

GASKI, JOHN F. (1987), "The Inverse Power Source-Power Relationship: An Empirical Note on a Marketing Anomaly," in *Research in Marketing,* Jagdish N. Sheth, ed., Volume 9, Greenwich, Connecticut: JAI Press, Inc., pp. 145-161.

GASKI, JOHN F. and MICHAEL J. ETZEL (1986), "The Index of Consumer Sentiment Toward Marketing," *Journal of Marketing,* 50 (July), pp. 71-81.

GASKI, JOHN F. and JOHN R. NEVIN (1985), "The Differential Effects of Exercised and Unexercised Power Sources in a Marketing Channel," *Journal of Marketing Research,* 22 (May), pp. 130-142.

GATIGNON, HUBERT (1984), "Competition as a Moderator of the Effect of Advertising on Sales," *Journal of Marketing Research*, 21 (November), pp. 387-398.

GATIGNON, HUBERT and THOMAS S. ROBERTSON (1985), "A Propositional Inventory for New Diffusion Research," *Journal of Consumer Research*, 11 (March), pp. 849-867.

GELB, BETSY D. and MARY C. GILLY (1979), "The Effect of Promotional Techniques on Purchase of Preventative Dental Care," 6 (December), pp. 305-308.

GOBLE, ROSS and ROY SHAW (1975), *Controversy and Dialogue in Marketing*, Englewood Cliffs, New Jersey: Prentice-Hall, Inc.

GOLDSTUCKER, JAC L. (1965), "Trading Areas," in *Science in Marketing*, George Schwartz, ed., New York: John Wiley & Sons, Inc., pp. 281-320.

GOLDSTUCKER, JAC L. (1966), "A Systems Framework for Retail Location," in *Science, Technology, and Marketing*, Raymond M. Hass, ed., Chicago: American Marketing Association, pp. 412-429.

GRAHAM, JOHN L. (1987), "A Theory of Interorganizational Negotiations," in *Research in Marketing*, Jagdish N. Sheth, ed., Volume 9, Greenwich, Connecticut: JAI Press, Inc., pp. 163-183.

GREENE, C. SCOTT and PAUL MIESING (1984), "Public Policy, Technology, and Ethics: Marketing Decisions for NASA's Space Shuttle," *Journal of Marketing*, 48 (Summer), pp. 56-67.

GRETHER, E. T. (1950), "A Theoretical Approach to the Study of Marketing," in *Theory in Marketing*, Reavis Cox and Wroe. Alderson, eds., Homewood, Illinois: Richard D. Irwin, Inc. pp. 113-123.

GRETHER, E. T. (1983), "Regional-Spatial Analysis in Marketing," *Journal of Marketing*, 47 (Fall), pp. 36-43.

GROVER, RAJIV and V. SRINIVASAN (1987), "A Simultaneous Approach to Market Segmentation and Market Structuring," *Journal of Marketing Research*, 24 (May), pp. 139-153.

HAAS, RAYMOND M., ED. (1966), *Science, Technology, and Marketing*, Chicago: American Marketing Association.

HAAS, ROBERT W. (1986), *Industrial Marketing Management*, 3rd Edition, Boston: Kent Publishing Company.

HALBERT, MICHAEL (1964), "The Requirements for Theory in Marketing," in *Theory in Marketing*, Reavis Cox, Wroe Alderson, and Stanley J. Shapiro, eds., Richard D. Irwin, Inc., pp. 17-36.

HALL, A. D. and R. Z. FAGEN (1968), "Definition of a System," in *Modern Systems Research for the Behavioral Scientist: A Sourcebook*, Walter Buckley, ed., Chicago: Aldine Publishing Company, pp. 81-92.

HALL, EDWARD T. (1960), "The Silent Language in Overseas Business," *Harvard Business Review*, 38 (May-June), pp. 87-96.

HANSEN, FLEMMING (1972), *Consumer Choice Behavior: A Cognitive Theory*, New York: The Free Press.

HAUSER, JOHN R. (1986), "Agendas and Consumer Choice," *Journal of Marketing Research*, 23 (August), pp. 199-212.

HAVLENA, WILLIAM J. and MORRIS B. HOLBROOK (1986), "The Varieties of Consumption Experience: Comparing Two Typologies of Emotion in Consumer Behavior," *Journal of Consumer Research*, 13 (December), pp. 394-404.

HEATH, ROBERT L. and RICHARD ALAN NELSON (1985), "Image and Issue Advertising: A Corporate and Public Policy Perspective," *Journal of Marketing*, 49 (Spring), pp. 58-68.

HEIDER, FRITZ (1958), *The Psychology of Interpersonal Relations*, New York: John Wiley & Sons, Inc.

HILL, R. M., R. S. ALEXANDER, and J. S. CROSS (1975), *Industrial Marketing*, 4th Edition, Homewood, Illinois: Richard D. Irwin, Inc.

HIRSCHMAN, ELIZABETH C. (1980), "Innovativeness, Novelty Seeking, and Consumer Creativity," *Journal of Consumer Research*, 7 (December), pp. 283-295.

HIRSCHMAN, ELIZABETH C. (1983), "Religious Affiliation and Consumption Processes: An Initial Pardaigm," in *Research in Marketing*, Jagdish N. Sheth, ed., Volume 6, Greenwich, Connecticut: JAI Press, Inc., pp. 131-170.

HIRSCHMAN, ELIZABETH C. (1986), "Humanistic Inquiry in Marketing Research: Philosophy, Method, and Criteria," *Journal of Marketing Research*, 23 (August), pp. 237-249.

HOFER, CHARLES W. and DAN SCHENDEL (1978), *Strategy Formulation: Analytical Concepts*, St. Paul, Minnesota: West Publishing Co.

HOLBROOK, MORRIS B. (1985), "Why Business is Bad for Consumer Research: The Three Bears Revisited," in *Advances in Consumer Research*, Elizabeth C. Hirschman and Morris B. Holbrook, eds., Volume 12, Provo, Utah: Association for Consumer Research, pp. 145-156.

HOLBROOK, MORRIS B. and ELIZABETH C. HIRSCHMAN (1982), "The Experiential Aspects of Consumption: Consumer Fantasies, Feelings, and Fun," *Journal of Consumer Research*, 9 (September), pp. 132-140.

HOLBROOK, MORRIS B. and JOHN A. HOWARD (1977), "Frequently Purchased Nondurable Goods and Services," in *Selected Aspects of Consumer Behavior: A Summary from the Perspective of Different Disciplines*, Robert Ferber, ed., Washington, D.C.: National Science Foundation, Directorate for Research Applications, Research Applied to National Needs, pp. 189-222.

HOLLOWAY, ROBERT J., ED. (1967a), *A Basic Bibliography on Experiments in Marketing*, Chicago: American Marketing Association.

HOLLOWAY, ROBERT J. (1967b), "An Experiment on Consumer Dissonance," *Journal of Marketing*, 31 (January), pp. 39-43.

HOLLOWAY, ROBERT J. and ROBERT S. HANCOCK, EDS. (1964), *The Environment of Marketing Behavior: Selections from the Literature*, New York: John Wiley & Sons, Inc.

HOLLOWAY, ROBERT J. and ROBERT S. HANCOCK, EDS. (1974), *The Environment of Marketing Management: Selections from the Literature*, 3rd Edition, New York: John Wiley & Sons, Inc.

HOLTON, RICHARD H. (1958), "The Distinction Between Convenience Goods, Shopping Goods, and Specialty Goods," *Journal of Marketing*, 23 (July), pp. 53-56.

HOMANS, GEORGE C. (1961), *Social Behavior: Its Elementary Forms*, New York: Harcourt, Brace, and World, Inc.

HOUSTON, FRANKLIN S. (1986), "The Marketing Concept: What It Is and What It Is Not," *Journal of Marketing*, 50 (April), pp. 81-87.

HOUSTON, FRANKLIN S. and JULE B. GASSENHEIMER (1987), "Marketing and Exchange," *Journal of Marketing*, 51 (October), pp. 3-18.

HOVLAND, CARL I. (1954), "Effects of the Mass Media of Communication," in *Handbook of Social Psychology*, Volume 2, Gardner Lindzey, ed., Cambridge, Massachusetts: Addison-Wesley Publishing Company, Inc., pp. 1062-1103.

HOWARD, JOHN A. (1957), *Marketing Management: Analysis and Decision*, Homewood, Illinois: Richard D. Irwin, Inc.

HOWARD, JOHN A. (1963a), *Marketing: Executive and Buyer Behavior*, New York: Columbia University Press.

HOWARD, JOHN A. (1963b), *Marketing Management: Analysis and Planning*, Revised Edition, Homewood, Illinois: Richard D. Irwin, Inc.

HOWARD, JOHN A. (1977), *Consumer Behavior: Application of Theory*, New York: McGraw-Hill Book Company, Inc.

HOWARD, JOHN A. (1983), "Marketing Theory of the Firm," *Journal of Marketing*, 47 (Fall), pp. 90-100.

HOWARD, JOHN A. (1988), *Consumer Behavior in Marketing Strategy*, Englewood Cliffs, New Jersey: Prentice-Hall, Inc.

HOWARD, JOHN A. and JAMES HULBERT (1973), *Advertising and the Public Interest: A Staff Report to the Federal Trade Commission*, Chicago: Crain Communications, Inc.

HOWARD, JOHN A. and JAGDISH N. SHETH (1969), *The Theory of Buyer Behavior*, New York: John Wiley & Sons, Inc.

HOWARD, RONALD A. (1963), "Stochastic Process Models of Consumer Behavior," *Journal of Advertising Research*, 3 (September), pp. 35-42.

HUBER, JOEL, MORRIS B. HOLBROOK, and BARBARA E. KAHN (1986), "Effects of Competitive Context and of Additional Information on Price Sensitivity," *Journal of Marketing Research*, 23 (August), pp. 250-260.

HUFF, DAVID L. (1964), "Defining and Estimating a Trading Area," *Journal of Marketing*, 28 (July), pp. 34-38.

HUFF, DAVID L. and ROLAND T. RUST (1984), "Measuring the Congruence of Market Areas," *Journal of Marketing*, 48 (Winter), pp. 68-74.

HULL, CLARK L. (1952), *A Behavior System: An Introduction to Behavior Theory Concerning the Individual Organism*, New Haven, Connecticut: Yale University Press.

HUNT, H. KEITH, ED. (1977), *Conceptualization and Measurement of Consumer Satisfaction and Dissatisfaction*, Cambridge, Massachusetts: Marketing Science Institute.

HUNT, H. KEITH and RALPH L. DAY, EDS. (1979), *Refining Concepts and Measures of Consumer Satisfaction and Complaining Behavior*, Bloomington/Indianapolis: Department of Marketing, School of Business, Division of Research, Indiana University.

HUNT, SHELBY D. (1971), "The Morphology of Theory and the General Theory of Marketing," *Journal of Marketing*, 35, April, pp. 65-68.

HUNT, SHELBY D. (1976a), *Marketing Theory: Conceptualizations of Research in Marketing*, Columbus, Ohio: Grid Publishing.

HUNT, SHELBY D. (1976b), "The Nature and Scope of Marketing," *Journal of Marketing*, 40 (July), pp. 17-28.

HUNT, SHELBY D. (1977), "The Three Dichotomies Model of Marketing: An Elaboration of Issues," in *Macro-Marketing: Distributive Processes from a Societal Perspective*, Charles C. Slater, ed., Boulder: Business Research Division, Graduate School of Business Administration, University of Colorado, pp. 52-56.

HUNT, SHELBY D. (1983a), "General Theories and the Fundamental Explananda of Marketing," *Journal of Marketing,* 47 (Fall), pp. 9-17.

HUNT, SHELBY D. (1983b), *Marketing Theory: The Philosophy of Marketing Science,* Homewood, Illinois: Richard D. Irwin, Inc.

HUNT, SHELBY D. and JOHN J. BURNETT (1982), "The Macromarketing/Micromarketing Dichotomy: A Taxonomical Model," *Journal of Marketing,* 46 (Summer), pp. 11-26.

HUNT, SHELBY D. and LAWRENCE B. CHONKO (1984), "Marketing and Machiavellianism," *Journal of Marketing,* 48 (Summer), pp. 30-42.

HUNT, SHELBY D. and JOHN R. NEVIN (1974), "Power in a Channel of Distribution: Sources and Consequences," *Journal of Marketing Research,* 11 (May), pp. 186-193.

HUNT, SHELBY D. and SCOTT VITELL (1986), "A General Theory of Marketing Ethics," *Journal of Macromarketing,* 6 (Spring), pp. 5-16.

HUNT, SHELBY D., LAWRENCE B. CHONKO, and JAMES B. WILCOX (1984), "Ethical Problems of Marketing Researchers," *Journal of Marketing Research,* 21 (August), pp. 309-324.

HUNT, SHELBY D., JAMES A. MUNCY, and NINA M. RAY (1981), "Alderson's General Theory of Marketing: A Formalization," in *Review of Marketing 1981,* Ben M. Enis and Kenneth J. Roering, eds., Chicago: American Marketing Association, pp. 267-272.

HUTCHINSON, KENNETH D. (1952), "Marketing as a Science: An Appraisal," *Journal of Marketing,* 16 (January), pp. 286-293.

HUTT, MICHAEL D., MICHAEL P. MOKWA, and STANLEY J. SHAPIRO (1986), "The Politics of Marketing: Analyzing the Parallel Political Marketplace," *Journal of Marketing,* 50 (January), pp. 40-51.

INDUSTRIAL MARKETING COMMITTEE REVIEW BOARD (1954), "Fundamental Differences Between Industrial and Consumer Marketing," *Journal of Marketing,* 19 (October), pp. 152-158.

JACKSON, DONALD W., JR., JANET E. KEITH, and RICHARD K. BURDICK (1984), "Purchasing Agents' Perceptions of Industrial Buying Center Influence: A Situational Approach," *Journal of Marketing,* 48 (Fall), pp. 75-83.

JACOBY, JACOB (1978), "Consumer Research: A State of the Art Review," *Journal of Marketing,* 40 (April), pp. 87-96.

JACOBY, JACOB and CONSTANCE SMALL (1975), "The FDA Approach to Defining Misleading Advertising," *Journal of Marketing,* 39 (October), pp. 65-68.

JACOBY, JACOB, DONALD E. SPELLER, and CAROL A. KOHN (1974), "Brand Choice Behavior as a Function of Information Load," *Journal of Marketing Research,* 11 (February), pp. 63-69.

JOHNSTON, WESLEY J. and THOMAS V. BONOMA (1981), "Purchase Process for Capital Equipment and Services" *Industrial Marketing Management,* 10 (October), pp. 253-264.

JUDD, ROBERT C. (1964), "The Case for Redefining Services," *Journal of Marketing,* 28 (January), pp. 58-59.

KAHLE, LYNN R. (1986), "The Nine Nations of North America and the Value Basis of Geographic Segmentation," *Journal of Marketing,* 50 (April), pp. 37-47.

KAISH, STANLEY (1967), "Cognitive Dissonance and the Classification of Consumer Goods," *Journal of Marketing,* 31 (October), pp. 28-31.

KALLET, ARTHUR (1935), *Counterfeit — Not Your Money Buy What It Buys*, New York: The Vanguard Press.

KALLET, ARTHUR and F. J. SCHLINK (1933), *100,000,000 Guinea Pigs: Dangers in Everyday Food, Drugs, and Cosmetics*, New York: The Vanguard Press.

KANGUN, NORMAN, ED. (1972), *Society and Marketing*, New York: Harper and Row, Inc.

KANGUN, NORMAN (1974), "Environmental Problems and Marketing: Saint or Sinner?" in *Marketing Analysis for Societal Problems*, Jagdish N. Sheth and Peter L. Wright, eds., Urbana-Champaign: Bureau of Economic and Business Research, College of Commerce and Business Administration, University of Illinois.

KASSARJIAN, HAROLD H. (1969), "The Negro and American Advertising, 1946-1965," *Journal of Marketing Research*, 6 (February), pp. 29-39.

KASSARJIAN, HAROLD H. (1971), "Personality and Consumer Behavior: A Review," *Journal of Marketing Research*, 8 (November), pp. 409-418.

KASSARJIAN, HAROLD H. and THOMAS S. ROBERTSON, EDS. (1981), *Perspectives in Consumer Behavior*, 3rd Edition, Glenview, Illinois: Scott, Foresman and Company.

KASULIS, JACK J. and ROBERT E. SPEKMAN (1980), "A Framework for the Use of Power," *European Journal of Marketing*, 14 (Number 4), pp. 180-191.

KATONA, GEORGE C. (1953), "Rational Behavior and Economic Behavior," *Psychological Review*, 60 (September), pp. 307-318.

KATONA, GEORGE C. (1960), *The Powerful Consumer: Psychological Studies of the American Economy*, New York: McGraw-Hill Book Company, Inc.

KATONA, GEORGE C. (1964), *The Mass Consumption Society*, New York: McGraw-Hill Book Company, Inc.

KATONA, GEORGE C. and EVA MUELLER (1953), *Consumer Attitudes and Demand: 1950-1952*, Ann Arbor: Survey Research Center, Institute for Social Research, University of Michigan.

KATONA, GEORGE C. and EVA MUELLER (1956), *Consumer Expectations: 1953-1956*, Ann Arbor: Survey Research Center, Institute for Social Research, University of Michigan.

KATZ, DANIEL (1960), "The Functional Approach to the Study of Attitudes," *Public Opinion Quarterly*, 24 (Summer), pp. 163-204.

KATZ, DANIEL and EZRA STOTLAND (1959), "A Preliminary Statement to a Theory of Attitude Structure and Change," in *Psychology: A Study of Science*, Volume 3, Sigmund Koch, ed., New York: McGraw-Hill Book Company, Inc., pp. 423-475.

KATZ, DANIEL and ROBERT L. KAHN (1966), *The Social Psychology of Organizations*, New York: John Wiley & Sons, Inc.

KATZ, ELIHU and PAUL F. LAZARSFELD (1955), *Personal Influence: The Part Played by People in the Flow of Mass Communications*, New York: The Free Press.

KEITH, ROBERT J. (1960), "The Marketing Revolution," *Journal of Marketing*, 24 (January), pp. 35-38.

KELLEY, WILLIAM T., ED. (1973), *New Consumerism: Selected Readings*, Columbus, Ohio: Grid, Inc.

KELLY, EUGENE and WILLIAM LAZER, EDS. (1958), *Managerial Marketing: Perspectives and Viewpoints*, Homewood, Illinois: Richard D. Irwin, Inc.

KERIN, ROGER A. and ROBERT A. PETERSON (1983), *Perspectives on Strategic Marketing Management*, 2nd Edition, Boston: Allyn and Bacon, Inc.

KOHLI, AJAY K. (1985), "Some Unexplored Supervisory Behaviors and Their Influence on Salespeople's Role Clarity, Specific Self-Esteem, Job Satisfaction, and Motivation," *Journal of Marketing Research*, 22 (November), pp. 424-433.

KOTLER, PHILIP (1967), *Marketing Management: Analysis, Planning and Control*, Englewood Cliffs, New Jersey: Prentice-Hall, Inc.

KOTLER, PHILIP (1972a), "A Generic Concept of Marketing," *Journal of Marketing*, 36 (April), pp. 46-54.

KOTLER, PHILIP (1972b), "What Consumerism Means for Marketers," *Harvard Business Review*, 50 (May-June), pp. 48-57.

KOTLER, PHILIP (1975), *Marketing for Nonprofit Organizations*, Englewood Cliffs, New Jersey: Prentice-Hall, Inc.

KOTLER, PHILIP (1986a), "Global Standardization — Courting Danger," *The Journal of Consumer Marketing*, 3 (Spring), pp. 13-15.

KOTLER, PHILIP (1986b), "Megamarketing," *Harvard Business Review*, 64 (March-April), pp. 117-124.

KOTLER, PHILIP and GARY ARMSTRONG (1987), *Marketing: An Introduction*, Englewood Cliffs, New Jersey: Prentice-Hall, Inc.

KOTLER, PHILIP and GERALD ZALTMAN (1971), "Social Marketing: An Approach to Planned Social Change," *Journal of Marketing*, 35 (July), pp. 3-12.

KOTLER, PHILIP and SIDNEY J. LEVY (1969), "Broadening the Concept of Marketing," *Journal of Marketing*, 33 (January), pp. 10-15.

KRAPFEL, ROBERT E., JR. (1985), "An Advocacy Behavior Model of Organizational Buyers' Vendor Choice," *Journal of Marketing*, 49 (Fall), pp. 51-59.

KRUGMAN, HERBERT E. (1965), "The Impact of Television Advertising: Learning Without Involvement," *Public Opinion Quarterly*, 29 (Fall), pp. 349-356.

KUEHN, ALFRED A. (1962), "Consumer Brand Choice as a Learning Process," *Journal of Advertising Research*, 2 (December), pp. 10-17.

KUHN, ALFRED (1963), *The Study of Society: A Unified Approach*, Homewood, Illinois: Dorsey Press.

KUHN, THOMAS S. (1962), *The Structure of Scientific Revolutions*, Chicago: University of Chicago Press.

LACZNIAK, GENE R. (1983), "Framework for Analyzing Marketing Ethics," *Journal of Macromarketing*, 5 (Spring), pp. 7-17.

LACZNIAK, GENE R. and PATRICK E. MURPHY, EDS. (1985), *Marketing Ethics: Guidelines for Managers*, Lexington, Massachusetts: Lexington Books.

LAMB, RUTH DEFOREST (1936), *American Chamber of Horrors: The Truth About Food and Drugs*, New York: Farrar & Rinehart, Inc.

LAVIDGE, ROBERT J. and GARY A. STEINER (1961), "A Model for Predictive Measurements of Advertising Effectiveness," *Journal of Marketing*, 25 (October), pp. 59-62.

LAURENT, GILLES and JEAN-NOEL KAPFERER (1985), "Measuring Consumer Involvement Profiles," *Journal of Marketing Research*, 22 (February), pp. 41-53.

LAZER, WILLIAM (1966), "Education for Marketing in the 1970s," *Journal of Marketing*, 30 (July), pp. 33-37.

LAZER, WILLIAM (1971), *Marketing Management: A Systems Perspective,* New York: John Wiley & Sons, Inc.

LAZER, WILLIAM and EUGENE J. KELLEY (1962), "The Systems Approach to Marketing," in *Managerial Marketing: Perspectives and Viewpoints,* William Lazer and Eugene J. Kelley, eds., Homewood, Illinois: Richard D. Irwin, Inc.

LEIGH, THOMAS W. and ARNO J. RETHANS (1984), "A Script-Theoretic Analysis of Industrial Purchasing Behavior," *Journal of Marketing,* 48 (Fall), pp. 22-32.

LELE, MILIND M. and JAGDISH N. SHETH (1987), *The Customer is Key: Gaining an Unbeaten Advantage Through Customer Satisfaction,* New York: John Wiley & Sons, Inc.

LEONG, SIEW MENG (1985), "Metatheory and Metamethodology in Marketing: A Lakatosian Reconstruction," *Journal of Marketing,* 49 (Fall), pp. 23-40.

LEVITT, THEODORE (1958), "The Dangers of Social Responsibility," *Harvard Business Review,* 36 (September/October), pp. 41-50.

LEVITT, THEODORE (1960), "Marketing Myopia," *Harvard Business Review,* 38 (July/August), pp. 45-56.

LEVITT, THEODORE (1965), "Exploit the Product Life Cycle," *Harvard Business Review,* 43 (November/December), pp. 81-94.

LEVITT, THEODORE (1981), "Marketing Intangible Products and Product Intangibles," *Harvard Business Review,* 59 (May/June), pp. 94-102.

LEVITT, THEODORE (1983), "The Globalization of Markets," *Harvard Business Review,* 61 (May/June), pp. 92-102.

LEWIS, RICHARD J. and LEO G. ERICKSON (1969), "Marketing Functions and Marketing Systems: A Synthesis," *Journal of Marketing,* 33 (July), pp. 10-14.

LOVELOCK, CHRISTOPHER H. (1983), "Classifying Services to Gain Strategic Marketing Insights," *Journal of Marketing,* 47 (Summer), pp. 9-20.

LUCAS, GEORGE H., JR., A. PARASURAMAN, ROBERT A. DAVIS, and BEN M. ENIS (1987), "An Empirical Study of Salesforce Turnover," *Journal of Marketing,* 51 (July), pp. 34-59.

LUCK, DAVID J. (1959), "On the Nature of Specialty Goods," *Journal of Marketing,* 24 (July), pp. 61-64.

LUCK, DAVID J. (1969), "Broadening the Concept of Marketing — Too Far," *Journal of Marketing,* 33 (July), pp. 53-55.

LUKE, ROBERT H. and E. REED DOKE (1987), "Marketing Journal Hierarchies: Faculty Perceptions, 1986-87," *Journal of the Academy of Marketing Science,* 15 (Spring), pp. 74-78.

LUSCH, ROBERT F. (1976), "Sources of Power: Their Impact on Intrachannel Conflict," *Journal of Marketing Research,* 13 (November), pp. 382-390.

LUSCH, ROBERT F. and JAMES R. BROWN (1982), "A Modified Model of Power in the Marketing Channel," *Journal of Marketing Research,* 19 (August), pp. 312-323.

MACKENZIE, KENNETH D. and FRANCESCO M. NICOSIA (1968), "Marketing Systems: Toward Formal Descriptions and Structural Properties," in *Marketing and the New Science of Planning,* Robert L. King, ed., Chicago: American Marketing Association, pp. 14-23.

MACKENZIE, SCOTT B., RICHARD J. LUTZ, and GEORGE E. BELCH (1986), "The Role of Attitude Toward the Ad as a Mediator of Advertising Effectiveness: A Test of Competing Explanations," *Journal of Marketing Research,* 23 (May), pp. 130-143.

MAGEE, JOHN (1960), "The Logistics of Distribution," *Harvard Business Review*, 38 (July/August), pp. 89-101.

MAGNUSON, WARREN G. and JEAN CARPER (1968), *The Dark Side of the Marketplace: The Plight of the American Consumer*, Englewood Cliffs, New Jersey: Prentice-Hall, Inc.

MALLEN, BRUCE E. (1963), "A Theory of Retailer-Supplier Conflict, Control, and Cooperation," *Journal of Retailing*, 39 (Summer) pp. 24-32, 51.

MALLEN, BRUCE E., ED. (1967), *The Marketing Channel: A Conceptual Viewpoint*, New York: John Wiley & Sons, Inc.

MALLEN, BRUCE E. (1973), "Functional Spin-Off: A Key to Anticipating Change in Distribution Structure," *Journal of Marketing*, 37 (July), pp. 18-25.

MARCH, JAMES G. and HERBERT A. SIMON (1958), *Organizations*, New York: John Wiley & Sons, Inc.

MARKIN, ROM J. (1969), *The Psychology of Consumer Behavior*, Englewood Cliffs, New Jersey: Prentice-Hall, Inc.

MARTINEAU, PIERRE (1958), "Social Classes and Spending Behavior," *Journal of Marketing*, 23 (October), pp. 121-129.

MASLOW, ABRAHAM H. (1954), *Motivation and Personality*, New York: Harper and Row, Inc.

MASSY, WILLIAM F. (1969), "Forecasting the Demand for New Convenience Products," *Journal of Marketing Research*, 6 (November), pp. 405-412.

MASSY, WILLIAM F., DAVID B. MONTGOMERY, and DONALD G. MORRISON (1970), *Stochastic Models of Buying Behavior*, Cambridge: Massachusetts Institute of Technology, The M.I.T. Press.

MATTHEWS, J. B. and R. E. SHALLCROSS (1935), *Partners in Plunder: The Cost of Business Dictatorship*, New York: Covici, Friede, Publishers.

MCALISTER, LEIGH, MAX H. BAZERMAN, and PETER FADER (1986), "Power and Goal Setting Channel Negotiations," *Journal of Marketing Research*, 23 (August), pp. 228-236.

MCCAMMON, BERT (1963), "Alternative Explanations of Institutional Change and Channel Evolution," in *Toward Scientific Marketing*, Stephen A. Greyser, ed., Chicago: American Marketing Association, pp. 477-490.

MCCAMMON, BERT (1965), "The Emergence and Growth of Contractually Integrated Channels in the American Economy," in *Economic Growth, Competition, and World Markets*, Peter D. Bennett, ed., Chicago: American Marketing Association, pp. 496-515.

MCCARTHY, E. JEROME (1960), *Basic Marketing: A Managerial Approach*, Homewood, Illinois: Richard D. Irwin, Inc.

MCCLELLAND, DAVID C. (1961), *The Achieving Society*, Princeton, New Jersey: D. Van Nostrand Company, Inc.

MCCRACKEN, GRANT (1986), "Culture and Consumption: A Theoretical Account of the Structure and Movement of the Cultural Meaning of Consumer Goods," *Journal of Consumer Research*, 13 (June), pp. 71-84.

MCGARRY, EDMUND D. (1950), "Some Functions of Marketing Reconsidered," in *Theory in Marketing*, Reavis Cox and Wroe Alderson, eds., Chicago: Richard D. Irwin, Inc., pp. 263-279.

McGregor, Douglas (1960), *The Human Side of Enterprise*, New York: McGraw-Hill Book Company, Inc.

McKitterick, John B. (1957), "What is the Marketing Management Concept," in *The Frontiers of Marketing Thought and Action*, Frank Bass, ed., Chicago: American Marketing Association, pp. 71-82.

McInnes, William (1964), "A Conceptual Approach to Marketing," in *Theory in Marketing*, Reavis Cox, Wroe Alderson, and Stanley J. Shapiro, eds., Homewood, Illinois: Richard D. Irwin, Inc., pp. 51-67.

McNeal, James U. (1987), *Children as Consumers: Insights and Implications*, Lexington, Massachusetts: Lexington Books.

McNiven, Malcolm A. (1968), "Marketing Research and Marketing Information Systems," in *Marketing and the New Science of Planning*, Robert L. King, ed., Chicago: American Marketing Association, pp. 169-171.

Merton, Robert K. (1957), *Social Theory and Social Structure*, New York: The Free Press.

Mick, David Glen (1986), "Consumer Research and Semiotics: Exploring the Morphology of Signs, Symbols, and Significance," *Journal of Consumer Research*, 13 (September), pp. 196-213.

Miller, Neal E. (1959), "Liberalization of Basic SR Concepts: Extensions to Conflict Behavior, Motivation, and Social Learning," in *Psychology: A Study of Science*, Volume 2, Sigmund Koch, ed., New York: McGraw-Hill Book Company, Inc., pp. 196-292.

Miracle, Gordon E. (1965), "Product Characteristics and Marketing Strategy," *Journal of Marketing*, 29 (January), pp. 18-24.

Monieson, David D. and Stanley J. Shapiro (1980), "Biological and Evolutionary Dimensions of Aldersonian Thought: What He Borrowed Then and What He Might Have Borrowed Now," in *Theoretical Developments in Marketing*, Charles W. Lamb, Jr. and Patrick M. Dunne, eds., Chicago: American Marketing Association, pp. 7-12.

Montgomery, David B. and Charles B. Weinberg (1979), "Toward Strategic Intelligence Systems," *Journal of Marketing*, 43 (Fall), pp. 41-52.

Morgan, Fred W. (1982), "Marketing and Product Liability: A Review and Update," *Journal of Marketing*, 46 (Summer), pp. 69-78.

Moyer, Reed (1968), *Changing Marketing Systems . . . : Corporate and Government Interfaces*, Chicago, Illinois: American Marketing Association.

Moyer, Reed, ed. (1972), *Macro Marketing: A Social Perspective*, New York: John Wiley & Sons, Inc.

Muncy, James A. and Raymond P. Fisk (1987), "Cognitive Relativism and the Practice of Marketing Science," *Journal of Marketing*, 51 (January), pp. 20-33.

Murphy, Patrick E. and Ben M. Enis (1986), "Classifying Products Strategically," *Journal of Marketing*, 50 (July), pp. 24-42.

Myers, John G., William F. Massy, and Stephen A. Greyser (1980), *Marketing Research and Knowledge Development: An Assessment of Marketing Management*, Englewood Cliffs, New Jersey: Prentice-Hall, Inc.

Nader, Ralph (1965), *Unsafe at Any Speed*, New York: Grossman.

Nagle, Thomas (1984), "Economic Foundations for Pricing," *Journal of Business*, 57 (January), pp. S3-S26.

NEWMAN, JOSEPH W. (1977), "Consumer External Search: Amount and Determinants," in *Consumer and Industrial Buying Behavior*, Arch G. Woodside, Jagdish N. Sheth, and Peter D. Bennett, eds., New York: Elsevier North-Holland, Inc., pp. 79-94.

NICKELS, WILLIAM (1974), "Conceptual Conflicts in Marketing," *Journal of Economics and Business*, 26 (Winter), pp. 140-143.

NICOSIA, FRANCESCO M. (1962), "Marketing and Alderson's Functionalism," *Journal of Business*, 35 (October), pp. 403-413.

NICOSIA, FRANCESCO M. (1966), *Consumer Decision Processes: Marketing and Advertising Implications*, Englewood Cliffs, New Jersey: Prentice-Hall, Inc.

OHLIN, BERTIL (1931), *Interregional and International Trade*, Boston: Harvard University Press.

O'SHAUGHNESSY, JOHN and MICHAEL J. RYAN (1979), "Marketing, Science and Technology," in *Conceptual and Theoretical Developments in Marketing*, O. C. Ferrell, Stephen W. Brown, and Charles W. Lamb, Jr., eds., Chicago: American Marketing Association, pp. 577-589.

OSGOOD, CHARLES E. (1957a), "A Behavioristic Analysis of Perception and Language as Cognitive Phenomena," in *Contemporary Approaches to Cognition: A Symposium Held at the University of Colorado*, Cambridge, Massachusetts: Harvard University Press, pp. 75-118.

OSGOOD, CHARLES E. (1957b), "Motivational Dynamics of Language Behavior," in *Nebraska Symposium on Motivation*, Marshall R. Jones, ed., Volume 5, Lincoln: University of Nebraska Press, pp. 348-424.

OXENFELDT, A. R. (1960), "A Multi-State Approach to Pricing," *Harvard Business Review*, 38 (July/August), pp. 125-133.

PACKARD, VANCE O. (1960), *The Waste Makers*, New York: The David McKay Company, Inc.

PESSEMIER, EDGAR and MOSHE HANDELSMAN (1984), "Temporal Variety in Consumer Behavior," *Journal of Marketing Research*, 21 (November), pp. 435-444.

PETER, J. PAUL and JERRY C. OLSON (1983), "Is Science Marketing?", *Journal of Marketing*, 47 (Fall), pp. 111-125.

PETERS, THOMAS J. and ROBERT H. WATERMAN, JR. (1982), *In Search of Excellence: Lessons from America's Best-Run Companies*, New York: Harper and Row, Publishers, Inc.

PETERSON, ROBERT A. and VIJAY MAHAJAN (1978), "Multi-Product Growth Models," in *Research in Marketing*, Jagdish N. Sheth, ed., Volume 1, Greenwich, Connecticut: JAI Press, Inc., pp. 201-231.

PETROSHIUS, SUSAN M. and KENT B. MONROE (1987), "Effect of Product-Line Pricing Characteristics on Product Evaluations," *Journal of Consumer Research*, 13 (March), pp. 511-519.

PFEFFER, J. and G. R. SALANCIK (1978), *The External Control of Organizations*, New York: Harper & Row.

PHILLIPS, LYNN W. and BRIAN STERNTHAL (1977), "Age Differences in Information Processing: A Perspective on the Aged Consumer," *Journal of Marketing Research*, 14 (November), pp. 444-457.

PHILLIPS, MARY C. (1934), *Skin Deep: The Truth About Beauty Aids — Safe and Harmful*, New York: The Vanguard Press.

POLLAY, RICHARD W. (1986), "The Distorted Mirror: Reflections on the Unintended Consequences of Advertising," *Journal of Marketing*, 50 (April), pp. 18-36.

POPPER, EDWARD and SCOTT WARD (1980), *Children's Purchasing Requests and Parental Responses*, Boston: Marketing Science Institute.

PORTER, MICHAEL E. (1980), *Competitive Strategy: Techniques for Analyzing Industries and Competitors*, New York: The Free Press.

PORTER, MICHAEL E. (1985), *Competitive Advantage: Creating and Sustaining Superior Performance*, New York: The Free Press.

POST, JAMES E. (1985), "Assessing the Nestlé Boycott: Corporate Accountability and Human Rights," *California Management Review*, 27 (Winter), pp. 113-131.

PRESTON, IVAN L. (1976), "A Comment on 'Defining Misleading Advertising' and 'Deception in Advertising'," *Journal of Marketing*, 40 (July), pp. 54-57.

PRESTON, IVAN L. (1982), "The Association Model of the Advertising Communication Process," *Journal of Advertising*, 11 (Number 2), pp. 3-15.

PUNJ, GIRISH and RICHARD STAELIN (1983), "A Model of Consumer Information Search Behavior for New Automobiles," *Journal of Consumer Research*, 10 (March), pp. 366-380.

PUTO, CHRISTOPHER P., WESLEY E. PATTON III, and RONALD H. KING (1985), "Risk Handling Strategies in Industrial Vendor Selection Decisions," *Journal of Marketing*, 49 (Winter), pp. 89-98.

RAMOND, C. K. and HENRY ASSAEL (1974), "An Empirical Framework for Product Classification," in *Models of Buyer Behavior: Conceptual, Quantitative, and Empirical*, Jagdish N. Sheth, ed., New York: Harper & Row, Publishers, Inc., pp. 347-362.

RAO, VITHALA R. (1984), "Pricing Research in Marketing: The State of the Art," *Journal of Business*, 57 (January), pp. S39-S60.

REIBSTEIN, DAVID J. and HUBERT GATIGNON (1984), "Optimal Product Line Pricing: The Influence of Elasticities and Cross-Elasticities," *Journal of Marketing Research*, 21 (August), pp. 259-267.

REIDENBACH, R. ERIC and TERENCE A. OLIVA (1981), "General Living Systems Theory and Marketing: A Framework for Analysis," *Journal of Marketing*, 45 (Fall), pp. 30-37.

REIDENBACH, R. ERIC and TERENCE A. OLIVA (1983), "Toward a Theory of the Macro Systemic Effects of the Marketing Function," *Journal of Macromarketing*, 3 (Fall), pp. 33-40.

REILLY, WILLIAM J. (1931), *The Law of Retail Gravitation*, Austin, Texas: The University of Texas.

RESNIK, ALAN J. and ROBERT R. HARMON (1983), "Consumer Complaints and Managerial Response: A Holistic Approach," *Journal of Marketing*, 47 (Winter), pp. 86-97.

RETHANS, ARNO J. (1979), "The Aldersonian Paradigm: A Perspective for Theory Development and Synthesis," in *Conceptual and Theoretical Developments in Marketing*, O. C. Ferrell, Stephen W. Brown, and Charles W. Lamb, Jr., eds., Chicago: American Marketing Association.

REVZAN, DAVID A. (1961), *Wholesaling in Marketing Organization*, New York: John Wiley & Sons, Inc.

REVZAN, DAVID A. (1965), *The Marketing Significance of Geographical Variations in Wholesale/Retail Sales Ratios*, Berkeley: University of California, Institute of Business and Economic Research.

REVZAN, DAVID A. (1967), *The Marketing Significance of Geographical Variations in Wholesale/Retail Sales Ratios, Part II: New and Supplementary Analysis and Revisions,* Berkeley: University of California, Institute of Business and Economic Research.

RHOADES, E. L. (1927), *Introductory Readings in Marketing,* Chicago: A. W. Shaw Company.

RICHINS, MARSHA (1983), "Negative Word-of-Mouth by Dissatisfied Consumers: A Pilot Study," *Journal of Marketing,* 47 (Winter), pp. 68-78.

RICKS, DAVID A., JEFFREY S. ARPAN, and MARILYN Y. FU (1974), "Pitfalls in Advertising Overseas," *Journal of Advertising Research,* (December), pp. 47-51.

RIDGEWAY, VALENTINE F. (1957), "Administration of Manufacturer-Dealer Systems," *Administrative Science Quarterly,* 1 (March), pp. 464-483.

ROBERTSON, THOMAS S. (1971), *Innovative Behavior and Communication,* New York: Holt, Rinehart and Winston, Inc.

ROBICHEAUX, ROBERT A. and ADEL I. EL-ANSARY (1975-76), "A General Model for Understanding Channel Member Behavior," *Journal of Retailing,* 52 (Winter), pp. 13-30, 93-94.

ROBIN, DONALD P. (1978), "A Useful Scope for Marketing," *Journal of the Academy of Marketing Science,* 6 (Summer), pp. 228-238.

ROBIN, DONALD P. and R. ERIC REIDENBACH (1987), "Social Responsibility, Ethics, and Marketing Strategy: Closing the Gap Between Concept and Application," *Journal of Marketing,* 51 (January), pp. 44-58.

ROBINSON, PATRICK J., CHARLES W. FARIS, and YORAM WIND (1967), *Industrial Buying and Creative Marketing,* Boston: Allyn and Bacon, Inc.

ROGERS, EVERETT M. (1962), *Diffusion of Innovations,* New York: The Free Press of Glencoe.

ROGERS, EVERETT M. (1983), *Diffusion of Innovations,* 3rd Edition, New York: The Free Press.

ROGERS, EVERETT M. (1987), "The Critical School and Consumer Research," in *Advances in Consumer Research,* Melanie Wallendorf and Paul F. Anderson, eds., Volume 14, Provo, Utah: Association for Consumer Research, pp. 7-11.

ROOK, DENNIS W. (1985), "The Ritual Dimension of Consumer Behavior," *Journal of Consumer Research,* 12 (December), pp. 251-264.

ROOK, DENNIS W. and SIDNEY J. LEVY (1983), "Psychosocial Themes in Consumer Grooming Rituals," in *Advances in Consumer Research,* Richard P. Bagozzi and Alice M. Tybout, eds., Volume 10, Ann Arbor, Michigan: Association for Consumer Research, pp. 329-333.

RUEKERT, ROBERT W. and ORVILLE C. WALKER, JR. (1987), "Marketing's Interaction With Other Functional Units: A Conceptual Framework and Empirical Evidence," *Journal of Marketing,* 51 (January), pp. 1-19.

RUSSO, J. EDWARD (1976), "When Do Advertisements Mislead the Consumer: An Answer from Experimental Psychology," in *Advances in Consumer Research,* Beverlee B. Anderson, ed., Volume 3, Ann Arbor, Michigan: Association for Consumer Research, pp. 273-275.

RYAN, FRANKLIN W. (1935), "Functional Concepts in Market Distribution," *Harvard Business Review,* 13 (January), pp. 205-224.

SAVITT, RONALD (1980), "Historical Research in Marketing," *Journal of Marketing*, 44 (Fall), pp. 52-58.

SAVITT, RONALD (1981), "The Theory of Interregional Marketing," in *Regulation of Marketing and the Public Interest*, F. Balderston, James Carman, and Francesco M. Nicosia, eds., New York: Pergamon, pp. 229-238.

SCHEWE, CHARLES D., ED. (1985), *The Elderly Market: Selected Readings*, Chicago: American Marketing Association.

SCHLINK, F. J. (1935), *Eat, Drink and Be Wary*, New York: Covici, Friede, Publishers.

SETHI, S. PRAKASH (1971), *Up Against the Corporate Wall: Modern Corporations and Social Issues in the Seventies*, Englewood Cliffs, New Jersey: Prentice-Hall, Inc.

SETHI, S. PRAKASH (1979), *Promises of the Good Life*, Homewood, Illinois: Richard D. Irwin, Inc.

SEXTON, DONALD E., JR. (1971), "Comparing the Cost of Food to Blacks and to Whites — A Survey," *Journal of Marketing*, 35 (July), pp. 40-46.

SHAW, ARCH (1912), "Some Problems in Market Distribution," *Quarterly Journal of Economics*, 26 (August), pp. 706-765.

SHAWVER, DONALD L. and WILLIAM O. NICKELS (1979), "A Rationalization for Macro-Marketing Concepts and Definitions," in *Macro-Marketing: New Steps on the Learning Curve*, George Fisk and Robert W. Nason, eds., Boulder: Business Research Division, Graduate School of Business Administration, University of Colorado.

SHETH, JAGDISH N. (1967), "A Review of Buyer Behavior," *Management Science*, 13 (August), pp. B718-B756.

SHETH, JAGDISH N. (1973), "A Model of Industrial Buyer Behavior," *Journal of Marketing*, 37 (October), pp. 50-56.

SHETH, JAGDISH N. (1974a), "A Field Study of Attitude Structure and the Attitude-Behavior Relationship," in *Models of Buyer Behavior: Conceptual, Quantitative, and Empirical*, Jagdish N. Sheth, ed., New York: Harper & Row Publishers, Inc., pp. 242-268.

SHETH, JAGDISH N. (1974b), "A Theory of Family Buying Decisions," in *Models of Buyer Behavior: Conceptual, Quantitative, and Empirical*, Jagdish N. Sheth, ed., New York: Harper & Row, Publishers, Inc., pp. 17-33.

SHETH, JAGDISH N. (1979a), "The Specificity of Industrial Marketing," P. U. *Management Review*, 2 (December/January), pp. 53-56.

SHETH, JAGDISH N. (1979b), "The Surpluses and Shortages in Consumer Behavior Theory and Research," *Journal of the Academy of Marketing Science*, 7 (Fall), pp. 414-427.

SHETH, JAGDISH N. (1985a), "History of Consumer Behavior: A Marketing Perspective," in *Historical Perspective in Consumer Research: National and International Perspectives, Proceedings of the Association for Consumer Research International Meeting in Singapore*, Chin Tiong Tan and Jagdish N. Sheth, eds., Singapore: School of Management, National University of Singapore, pp. 5-7.

SHETH, JAGDISH N. (1985b), "Presidential Address: Broadening the Horizons of ACR and Consumer Behavior," in *Advances in Consumer Research*, Elizabeth C. Hirschman and Morris B. Holbrook, eds., Volume 12, Provo, Utah: Association for Consumer Research, pp. 1-2.

SHETH, JAGDISH N. (1985c), *Winning Back Your Market: The Inside Stories of the Companies That Did It*, New York: John Wiley & Sons, Inc.

SHETH, JAGDISH N. (1986), "Global Markets or Global Competition?", *The Journal of Consumer Marketing*, 3 (Spring), pp. 9-11.

SHETH, JAGDISH N. and GARY L. FRAZIER (1982), "A Model of Strategy Mix Choice for Planned Social Change," *Journal of Marketing*, 46 (Winter), pp. 15-26.

SHETH, JAGDISH N. and DAVID M. GARDNER (1982), "History of Marketing Thought: An Update" in *Marketing Theory: Philosophy of Science Perspectives*, Ronald Bush and Shelby Hunt, eds., American Marketing Association, pp. 52-58.

SHETH, JAGDISH N. and DENNIS E. GARRETT (1986a), *Marketing Management: A Comprehensive Reader*, Cincinnati, Ohio: South-Western Publishing Company.

SHETH, JAGDISH N. and DENNIS E. GARRETT (1986b), *Marketing Theory: Classic and Contemporary Readings*, Cincinnati, Ohio: South-Western Publishing Company.

SHETH, JAGDISH N. and BARBARA L. GROSS (1988), "Parallel Development of Marketing and Consumer Behavior: A Historical Perspective," in *Historical Perspectives in Marketing*, Ronald A. Fullerton and Terence Nevitt, eds., Lexington, Massachusetts: Lexington Books.

SHETH, JAGDISH N. and S. PRAKASH SETHI (1977), "A Theory of Cross-Cultural Buyer Behavior," in *Consumer and Industrial Buying Behavior*, Arch G. Woodside, Jagdish N. Sheth, and Peter D. Bennett, eds., New York: Elsevier North-Holland, Inc., pp. 369-386.

SHETH, JAGDISH N. and PETER L. WRIGHT, EDS. (1974), *Marketing Analysis for Societal Problems*, Urbana-Champaign: Bureau of Economic and Business Research, College of Commerce and Business Administration, University of Illinois.

SHUGAN, STEVEN M. (1987), "Estimating Brand Positioning Maps Using Supermarket Scanning Data," *Journal of Marketing Research*, 24 (February), pp. 1-18.

SINCLAIR, UPTON B. (1906), *The Jungle*, New York: The Jungle Publishing Company.

SLATER, CHARLES C., ED. (1977), *Macro-Marketing: Distributive Processes from a Societal Perspective*, Boulder: Business Research Division, Graduate School of Business Administration, University of Colorado.

SMITH, WENDELL R. (1956), "Product Differentiation and Market Segmentation as Alternative Marketing Strategies," *Journal of Marketing*, 21 (July), pp. 3-8.

SORENSON, RALPH Z. and ULRICH E. WIECHMANN (1975), "How Multinationals View Marketing Standardization," *Harvard Business Review*, 53 (May/June), pp. 38-54, 166-167.

STAUDT, THOMAS A. (1958), "Business Management as a Total System of Action and the Role of Marketing," in *Managerial Marketing: Perspectives and Viewpoints*, Eugene J. Kelley and William Lazer, eds., Homewood, Illinois: Richard D. Irwin, Inc.

STEINER, ROBERT L. (1976), "The Prejudice Against Marketing," *Journal of Marketing*, 40 (July), pp. 2-9.

STERN, LOUIS W., ED. (1969), *Distribution Channels: Behavioral Dimensions*, Boston: Houghton Mifflin Company.

STERN, LOUIS W. and RONALD H. GORMAN (1969), "Conflict in Distribution Channels: An Exploration," in *Distribution Channels: Behavioral Dimensions*, Boston: Houghton Mifflin Company, pp. 156-175.

STERN, LOUIS W. and TORGER REVE (1980), "Distribution Channels as Political Economies: A Framework for Comparative Analysis," *Journal of Marketing,* 44 (Summer) 3, pp. 52-64.

STERNTHAL, BRIAN, ALICE M. TYBOUT, and BOBBY J. CALDER (1987), "Confirmatory Versus Comparative Approaches to Judging Theory Tests," *Journal of Consumer Research,* 14 (June), pp. 114-125.

STEWART, PAUL W. and J. FREDERIC DEWHURST (1939), *Does Distribution Cost Too Much? A Review of the Costs Involved in Current Marketing Methods and a Program for Improvement,* New York: The Twentieth Century Fund, Inc.

STIGLER, GEORGE J. (1951), "The Division of Labor is Limited by the Extent of the Market," *Journal of Political Economy,* 54 (June), pp. 185-193.

STURDIVANT, FREDERICK D. (1968), "Better Deal for Ghetto Shoppers," *Harvard Business Review,* 46 (March/April), pp. 130-139.

SUJAN, HARISH (1986), "Smarter Versus Harder: An Exploratory Attributional Analysis of Salespeople's Motivation," *Journal of Marketing Research,* 23 (February), pp. 41-49.

TELLIS, GERARD J. (1986), "Beyond the Many Faces of Price: An Integration of Pricing Strategies," *Journal of Marketing,* 50 (October), pp. 146-160.

TUCKER, W. T. (1974), "Future Directions in Marketing Theory," *Journal of Marketing,* 38 (April), pp. 30-35.

TULL, DONALD S., VAN R. WOOD, DALE DUHAN, TOM GILLPATRICK, KIM R. ROBERTSON, and JAMES G. HELGESON (1986), "'Leveraged' Decision Making in Advertising: The Flat Maximum Principle and Its Implications," *Journal of Marketing Research,* 23 (February), pp. 25-32.

UHL, KENNETH P. (1968), "Marketing Information Systems and Subsystems," in *Marketing and the New Science of Planning,* Robert L. King, ed., Chicago: American Marketing Association, pp. 163-168.

UHL, KENNETH P. and GREGORY D. UPAH (1983), "The Marketing of Services: Why and How is it Different?", in *Research in Marketing,* Jagdish N. Sheth, ed., Volume 6, Greenwich, Connecticut: JAI Press, Inc., pp. 231-257.

VAILE, ROLAND S., E. T. GRETHER, and REAVIS COX (1952), *Marketing in the American Economy,* New York: The Ronald Press Company.

VANDERBLUE, HOMER B. (1921), "The Functional Approach to the Study of Marketing," *Journal of Political Economy,* 29, (October), pp. 676-683.

VENKATESH, ALLADI and NIKHILESH DHOLAKIA (1986), "Methodological Issues in Macromarketing," *Journal of Macromarketing,* 6 (Fall), pp. 36-52.

WALES, HUGH and LYNDON E. DAWSON, JR. (1979), "The Anomalous Qualities Between Present-Day Conferences and Alderson's Marketing Theory Seminars," in *Conceptual and Theoretical Developments in Marketing,* O. C. Ferrell, Stephen W. Brown, and Charles W. Lamb, eds., Chicago: American Marketing Association, pp. 222-227.

WARNER, W. LLOYD, MARCHIA MEEKER, and KENNETH EELLS (1949), *Social Class in America,* Chicago: Science Research Associates.

WEBSTER, FREDERICK E., JR. and YORAM WIND (1972), "A General Model for Understanding Organizational Buying Behavior," *Journal of Marketing,* 36 (April), pp. 12-19.

WEITZ, BARTON A. (1981), "Effectiveness in Sales Interactions: A Contingency Framework," *Journal of Marketing,* 45 (Winter), pp. 85-103.

WEITZ, BARTON A., HARISH SUJAN, and Mita Sujan (1986), "Knowledge, Motivation, and Adaptive Behavior: A Framework for Improving Selling Effectiveness," *Journal of Marketing*, 50 (October), pp. 174-191.

WELD, L. D. H. (1916), *The Marketing of Farm Products*, New York: The Macmillan Company.

WELD, L. D. H. (1917), "Marketing Functions and Mercantile Organization," *American Economic Review*, 7 (June), pp. 306-318.

WELLS, WILLIAM D. (1975), "Psychographics: A Critical Review," *Journal of Marketing Research*, 12 (May), pp. 196-213.

WESTBROOK, ROBERT A. (1987), "Product/Consumption-Based Affective Responses and Postpurchase Processes," *Journal of Marketing Research*, 24 (August), pp. 258-270.

WHITE, PHILIP D. and CHARLES C. SLATER, EDS. (1978), *Macromarketing: Distributive Processes from a Societal Perspective, An Elaboration of Issues*, Boulder: Business Research Division, University of Colorado.

WHYTE, WILLIAM H., JR. (1955), "The Web of Word of Mouth," in *Consumer Behavior (Volume 2): The Life Cycle and Consumer Behavior*, Lincoln H. Clark, ed., New York: New York University Press, pp. 113-122.

WILKIE, WILLIAM L. and EDGAR A. PESSEMIER (1973), "Issues in Marketing's Use of Multi-Attribute Attitude Models," *Journal of Marketing Research*, 10 (November), pp. 428-441.

WILLIAMS, KAYLENE C. and ROSANN L. SPIRO (1985), "Communication Style in the Salesperson-Customer Dyad," *Journal of Marketing Research*, 22 (November), pp. 434-442.

WIND, YORAM (1986), "The Myth of Globalization," *The Journal of Consumer Marketing*, 3 (Spring), pp. 23-26.

WIND, YORAM and R. THOMAS (1980), "Conceptual and Methodological Issues in Organizational Buying Behavior," *European Journal of Marketing*, 14, (5/6), pp. 239-263.

WIND, YORAM and THOMAS S. ROBERTSON (1983), "Marketing Strategy: New Directions for Theory and Research," *Journal of Marketing*, 47 (Spring), pp. 12-25.

WINTER, FREDERICK (1984), "Market Segmentation: A Tactical Approach," *Business Horizons*, 27 (January/February), pp. 57-63.

WOODSIDE, ARCH G., JAGDISH N. SHETH, and PETER D. BENNETT, EDS. (1977), *Consumer and Industrial Buying Behavior*, New York: Elsevier North-Holland, Inc.

WRIGHT, PETER L. (1973), "Use of Consumer Judgment Models in Promotion Planning," *Journal of Marketing*, 37 (October), pp. 27-33.

ZAKIA, RICHARD D. and MIHAI NADIN (1987), "Semiotics, Advertising and Marketing," *The Journal of Consumer Marketing*, 4 (Spring), pp. 5-12.

ZALTMAN, GERALD, CHRISTIAN R. A. PINSON, and REINHARD ANGELMAR (1973), *Metatheory in Consumer Research*, New York: Holt, Rinehart and Winston, Inc.

ZALTMAN, GERALD and ROBERT DUNCAN (1977), *Strategies for Planned Change*, New York: John Wiley & Sons, Inc.

ZALTMAN, GERALD, KAREN LEMASTERS, and MICHAEL HEFFRING (1982), *Theory Construction in Marketing*, New York: John Wiley & Sons, Inc.

ZEITHAML, CARL P. and VALARIE A. ZEITHAML (1984), "Environmental Management: Revising the Marketing Perspective," *Journal of Marketing*, 48 (Spring), pp. 46-53.

ZEITHAML, VALARIE A., A. PARASURAMAN, and LEONARD L. BERRY (1985), "Problems and Strategies in Services Marketing," *Journal of Marketing*, 49 (Spring), pp. 33-46.

ZIELINSKI, JOAN and THOMAS S. ROBERTSON (1982), "Consumer Behavior Theory: Excesses and Limitations," in *Advances in Consumer Research*, Andrew A. Mitchell, ed., Volume 9, Ann Arbor, Michigan: Association for Consumer Research, pp. 8-12.

ZIF, JEHIEL (1980), "A Managerial Approach to Macromarketing," *Journal of Marketing*, 44 (Winter), pp. 36-45.

ZIKMUND, WILLIAM G. and WILLIAM J. STANTON (1971), "Recycling Solid Wastes: A Channels of Distribution Problem," *Journal of Marketing*, 35 (July), pp. 34-39.